PHILADELPHIA
AND THE
CIVIL WAR

PHILADELPHIA
AND THE
CIVIL WAR

Arsenal of the Union

ANTHONY WASKIE, PhD
foreword by EDWIN C. BEARSS

Charleston   London

THE
History
PRESS

Published by The History Press
Charleston, SC 29403
www.historypress.net

Cover image: Parade of the Philadelphia Zouaves Corps in front of Independence Hall—
1862. *Courtesy of the Historical Society of Pennsylvania.*

First published 2011

Manufactured in the United States

ISBN 978.1.60949.011.9

Library of Congress Cataloging-in-Publication Data

Waskie, Anthony J. (Anthony Joseph), 1946-
Philadelphia and the Civil War : arsenal of the Union / Anthony Waskie.
p. cm.
ISBN 978-1-60949-011-9
1. Philadelphia (Pa.)--History--Civil War, 1861-1865. I. Title.
F158.44.W37 2011
974.8'03--dc22
2011004527

Notice: The information in this book is true and complete to the best of our knowledge. It is
offered without guarantee on the part of the author or The History Press. The author and
The History Press disclaim all liability in connection with the use of this book.

Dedicated to the memory of my parents,
Anthony Sr. and Eileen Slusser-Waskie, with love and devotion.

Contents

Foreword, by Edwin C. Bearss   9
Acknowledgements   11
Introduction   13

Philadelphia at the Outbreak of Rebellion   17
Ethnic Make-up of Philadelphia, Immigration
   and Military Participation   28
First Philadelphia Volunteers to the Warfront
   and the Baltimore Riot   32
Political Opposition to the War   39
Abraham Lincoln in Philadelphia   45
Philadelphia Civil War Military Hospitals   52
Benevolent and Volunteer Service Organizations of Philadelphia 62
Southwark Refreshment Saloon Movement   69
Benevolence of Volunteer Firemen   78
The Union League of Philadelphia   80
Civil War Philadelphia Railroad Transportation   84
War Industries and Manufacturing   89
Financing the War   93
Training Camps   96
Philadelphia during the Gettysburg Campaign   100
Philadelphia-Based Military Units   107
Philadelphia Commanders   147

CONTENTS

Philadelphia and the Navy   154
U.S. Marine Corps   158
Principal Civil War–Era Cemeteries   163
Prominent Civil War–Era Philadelphians   167
Notable Women of Philadelphia   174
"Three Sundays in April"—Triumph to Tragedy   187
"Johnny Comes Marching Home" and Welcome Back   190
Independence Hall during the Civil War   194
Civil War–Era Veterans' Organizations   198
Medal of Honor Recipients   206
Philadelphia's Civil War Memorials, Monuments and Parks   208

Appendix. Philadelphia-Based Civil War Museums,
      Institutions and Organizations   213
Notes   215
Bibliography   237
Index   249
About the Author   255

Foreword

I visited Washington, D.C., and other cities before and after serving in the U.S. Marine Corps in World War II, and later I undertook college studies in history. I entered the National Park Service as a historian and was later named chief historian.

Since my retirement in 1995 from the NPS, I have continued to hone my skills as a research historian, lecturer and tour guide to familiarize myself with the battlefields of the nation and their stories. It is only by walking in the footsteps of history that you can really understand and appreciate the events described in books. To expand my repertoire, I have developed and organized tours of the two Civil War capital cities—Richmond and Washington—focusing on the related political, social, business, industrial and military sites.

April 10, 2010, found me in Philadelphia to speak at the annual Preservation Luncheon of the Grand Army of the Republic Museum and Library, where I received the annual Samuel P. Town "Grand Army" award. As a historian at Laurel Hill Cemetery, Dr. Waskie gave me a tour and also led me to other historic sites. Before returning to Washington, Waskie told me he was working on a guidebook, *Philadelphia and the Civil War*, and invited me to read and comment on his manuscript. If warranted, he wished to know if I would write an endorsement. My answer was yes. My visit to Philadelphia satisfied me that like Washington and Richmond, Philadelphia was worthy of an outstanding guidebook as the nation approached the sesquicentennial of the Civil War. After a careful review of Andy's manuscript, I found it to be a tour de force equal or better than Civil War guidebooks for other cities.

FOREWORD

Because of the publications relating to Civil War cities, I have been leading tours for many years. I cannot say this for Philadelphia. My familiarity with Philadelphia was more with sites associated with the Revolutionary War and the founding of our nation, particularly those administered by the National Park Service. I have led tours of these sites for the Smithsonian Institution's study programs.

Speaking engagements had introduced me to a number of local Civil War sites and their significance, as well as historians at these locations. Among these is Andy Waskie. He received his doctorate in Germanic philology at New York University and is currently on the faculty of Temple University, where he is a professor of German. While that is his vocation, his avocation is what sparked our mutual interest: history, interpretation and preservation.

We first met at a Civil War seminar at Princeton University in the mid-1990s. Since then, we have participated as resource specialists in numerous Civil War seminars and workshops. On several occasions, he asked me to speak to Philadelphia groups. He wears numerous hats, serving on the executive board of the Civil War History Consortium of Philadelphia, as president of the General Meade Society and as co-director of the Civil War & Emancipation Studies at Temple.

Among Dr. Waskie's many talents are his communicative skills in a "first-person" historical presentation. I was at the Harrisburg Community College's annual seminar when I first saw Andy morph into "General Meade." It was a masterful performance, and I and others in the audience were mesmerized. On several of my speaking expeditions to Philadelphia, Dr. Waskie, in his own unique style, sparked my interest in Civil War Philadelphia. I believe he will inform, educate and spark the interest of anyone who reads this book.

Edwin C. Bearss
Arlington, Virginia
January 6, 2011

Acknowledgements

O n such a broad subject as the Civil War history of Philadelphia, I was able to draw on a rich source of information, documents, references, photos, images and much benevolent assistance in preparing the present work in the very best traditions of the Quaker City and its long tradition of civic goodwill.

I must thank a number of individuals and institutions without whose help I could not have completed this work. It can often be invidious to single out individuals in a limited space, so I wish to thank all of the many people who rendered me such invaluable service. To all of them, I express my sincere thanks and heartfelt gratitude. I must, however, mention a few who went over and above the call to assist.

First and foremost, my beautiful and accomplished wife, Carol, was instrumental in her help from start to finish. Thanks also go to premier national historian Edwin C. Bearss of the National Park Service; Jon Sirlin for expert legal advice; Gene Stackhouse; Mr. Germantown History; Dr. Sanford Sher for his important work on behalf of Mower Hospital; Ed Colimore at the *Philadelphia Inquirer* for his insights into the press in Civil War Philadelphia; the staff at the Instructional Support Center at Temple University, especially Joanna Inman and Mike Dubinski; Dr. Dan Rolph at the Historical Society of Pennsylvania; Dr. Robert Hicks at the Library of the College of Physicians; Dr. Phil Lapsansky at the Library Company of Philadelphia; David Cassedy and Jim Mundy, curators at the Union League of Philadelphia, the archives of the Union League, soon to become the Templeton Center for Civil War Studies; Joyce Werkman of Camp William Penn Museum; Laurel Hill Cemetery, including Carol Yaster, Gwen Kaminski, Bill Doran and Russ Dodge; Tom and Jeanne O'Toole and Arlene and Steve Harris of the General Meade Society; and my student, Thomas Golanoski, who provided vital support.

The following institutions opened their collections to me and were most helpful: the Grand Army of the Republic Museum and Library; the Paley Library and Urban Archives at Temple University; the Army Heritage and Education Center in Carlisle, Pennsylvania; the Pennsylvania State Archives in Harrisburg; University of Pennsylvania Archives, Philadelphia; the Abraham Lincoln Foundation of the Union League; and Laurel Hill Cemetery.

Introduction

Philadelphia is the birthplace of the nation and is often noted as a shrine of the Revolutionary War, the first long-term capital of the republic and the colonial city of William Penn. Few realize, however, that the city played a very significant and even vital role in the American Civil War, earning it the title of "Arsenal of the Union." The might of the city's manufacturing base and heavy industries fired by anthracite coal created the iron and steel that produced weapons, ordnance, locomotives and rails that served the war effort. Uniforms, blankets and woolens, leather products, ambulances and other military supplies that brought ultimate victory were also manufactured here. Some would even say that the locomotives alone produced by Matthias Baldwin were indispensable to victory.

At the outbreak of hostilities in 1861, Philadelphia was the second largest city in the country and the closest urban center to the warfront—indeed, in proximity to the seceded state of Virginia, the expected scene of conflict. This made Philadelphia a border city with close ties to both North and South. As a major transportation hub, manufacturing center and location of the finest civilian hospitals and medical schools in the nation, the city was destined to become crucial to the war effort. Civic associations such as the Union League, Christian Commission, Sanitary Commission and its Great Central Fair made heroic efforts to support the soldiery at the front and the loved ones at home. The war was financed in Philadelphia. It was home to the largest free black community in the North and was a center of abolitionism, a safe haven and support for the Underground Railroad and a destination for fugitive slaves. After War Department authorization, large numbers of "colored" troops (as African Americans were then known) were recruited from Philadelphia and vicinity and trained at nearby Camp William Penn. By war's end, over twelve thousand African American soldiers had been sent to the warfront from the Philadelphia region, proving their valor and courage in battle, contributing greatly to winning the war and helping to emancipate their Southern brethren in bondage.

Philadelphia had one of the largest and oldest navy yards in the country, as well as many private shipyards. In addition to building many fine warships for naval service, the city was also home to several major military facilities, including armories and arsenals.

Nearly 100,000 Philadelphians entered the military service, of whom close to 20,000 died in service. This was an enviable record of service and sacrifice that few other cities could equal. Philadelphia could also claim some of the most notable commanders of both North and South, including the redoubtable victor of Gettysburg, General George G. Meade, and Confederate commander General John C. Pemberton, as well as Union generals and naval commanders McClellan, Humphreys, Gibbon and Crawford; Admirals Porter and Dahlgren; and fallen heroes such as Koltes, Greble, the Ellets, Bohlen and Birney, to name just a few.

Any visit to Philadelphia should retrace a journey through time to the large number of sites to be found there that are closely identified with the Civil War era, including forts, training camps, recruiting stations, hospitals, arsenals and depots. Also of importance will be a visit to the fortifications that were hastily erected to guard against the Confederate invasion of June 1863, which was fortuitously halted at Gettysburg. Other sites include the homes of war heroes, cultural institutions and locales associated with the homefront, such as the Southwark Refreshment Saloon movement.

In the postwar period, Philadelphia became a center for veterans' organizations, such as the Loyal Legion and the Grand Army of the Republic. These veterans' groups played a significant role in the postwar period with many patriotic projects, activities and initiatives for the widows and orphans, remembrance of the fallen and pensions for their wounded and debilitated comrades. The veterans were eager to memorialize their honorable service through ceremonies, parades, reunions and monumentation. Most of these shrines to the "mystic cords of memory" still dot the landscape of the city, including one of the earliest Lincoln Memorials in the nation (1871). Homage must also be paid to many of the era's illustrious greats, civil and military, by visiting their final resting places in Laurel Hill and Woodlands Cemeteries and other Victorian-era burial grounds.

Although the city has previously been better known for its early American past, much is being done to highlight, interpret and preserve the rich Civil War–era history of Philadelphia. Another famous Pennsylvania site, Gettysburg, attracts millions of visitors to wonder at the heroic sacrifice of a generation. Although this battlefield has earned its place in the pantheon of American history, the battle itself lasted for only a few days of bloody conflict. Philadelphia's role continued for four years. Clearly, without Philadelphia's many and varied contributions, the North could not have prevailed at Gettysburg, nor could the nation have remained united and a people in bondage been freed.

This book is an attempt to highlight Philadelphia's distinguished role of commitment to total war to preserve the Union and exemplary sacrifices suffered thereby. This is done in order to draw attention to the city's record as "Arsenal of the Union" and the extraordinary contributions of its citizens in the crisis that marked a turning point in our nation's history. With the onset of the anniversary of the sesquicentennial of the Civil War now upon us, I felt compelled to try and tell the story of Philadelphia in the victorious prosecution of the Civil War to ultimate victory.

In a sense, this work could serve as a tour guide to Civil War Philadelphia. If the reader is inspired by the details to seek further information, then I have been successful in my task. If it leads the reader to a personal visit and journey into that period, then I have surpassed my modest goals. Although I could not include all the information and details I felt necessary to a more complete picture of Philadelphia and its Civil War history, I have attempted within the restraints of the publication to tell the most salient details of that history. I beg the indulgence of the reader and pledge to provide more specifics in future efforts.

I have drawn largely on a number of classic sources for the information contained in this treatment. I have attempted to revise, update and expand the contents to reflect much additional research and recent scholarship. The works cited provided valuable information and a starting point upon which to expand. Some of the sources were written years after the conflict, when memory of the events had begun to fade; others were contemporary and had the advantage of eyewitness accounts as they occurred and drew largely on the participants and veterans themselves for background. I acknowledge the vital contents drawn from these sources but have added much new and fresh assessments and detail. I cite especially *Philadelphia in the Civil War 1861–1865*, by Frank Taylor (1913), published for the fiftieth anniversary of the Battle of Gettysburg by the city as a tribute to the veterans and citizens of Philadelphia. Taylor was himself a veteran.

Philadelphia at the
Outbreak of Rebellion

Philadelphia in 1860 was a metropolis of nearly 600,000 inhabitants, booming with industry and commerce, a transportation hub of enormous proportions and a destination for many new immigrants from Europe, primarily Ireland and Germany. The city had been consolidated with the county by act of the Pennsylvania legislature in 1854, thereby creating the second largest city in the nation after New York. Although it stretched over 130 square miles, its hub was the bustling central district huddled along the Delaware and Schuylkill Rivers. There were, however, also older towns and communities—Frankford, Germantown, Kensington, Southwark and Manayunk—within its borders dating back to William Penn and the colonial period with their own unique identities. These areas were also heavily populated and boasted of their own industries, products and cultures.[1]

The ethnic populations of the city were concentrated among the Irish, constituting approximately 14 percent of the population; the Germans, approximately 10 percent; and the free black population, 4 percent. Each community tended to cluster together in enclaves, although the Irish were found living in the most diverse areas and districts. They often worked as unskilled labor or as domestics and lived where they worked, often in and among the more privileged classes. The Germans were found mostly in the Northern Liberties, Kensington and Fishtown neighborhoods. The black community was concentrated along the Lombard Street corridor and extended outward many blocks in each direction from the Delaware to the Schuylkill River.[2]

Philadelphia was at that time the fourth largest city of the western world, with only London, Paris and New York being larger. Consolidation had created the impetus for prolific growth, fruitful commerce, a leading role in finance, innovations in technology and manufacturing, some of the finest institutions of higher learning in the country and a center of medicine unrivaled anywhere.[3]

The advances in transportation and connections through the city by railroad, steamer, turnpike and canals made Philadelphia a hub for travel and commerce, linking the city in all directions with the nation. Philadelphia now had fast and efficient contacts not only with the North and South but also with the West, which was growing in importance. Nevertheless, Philadelphia remained a "border city," lying almost on the Mason-Dixon line, or the demarcation between North and South. The city lay closest to Southern cities such as Baltimore, Washington and Richmond, which would ensure a pivotal yet grim importance as a center of any Northern war effort and destination for troop transportation.[4]

The consolidation act of 1854 vested much executive power in a mayor who was elected every two years. Appropriately, the clearest and strongest of the mayor's powers under the new city charter pertained to the police. The mayor's police powers were really the only clear rules that made his office strong in municipal affairs. City councils had developed autonomous departments such as gas production, street-lighting, the waterworks and public buildings to operate independent of the mayor. The new charter gave the mayor the power to appoint police officers with the advice and consent of the Select Council, dismiss them, prescribe their duties and rules and regulations and command them when necessary.[5]

Despite this rosy picture in 1860, many problems lurked under the surface. The growth of the heavily populated working-class districts created some of the city's worst slums. The rampant poverty resulted in hazards to health and safety, created filthy streets and neighborhoods and often resulted in a higher crime rate, youth gangs and a dissolute lifestyle.

Bad streets and the lack of transportation obligated workingmen to live close to the place of their labor. The houses tended to cluster around mills and factories, creating spheres within the city. Domestics and menial workers gathered in alleys and side streets close behind the town houses of their employers. This created a jumbled, indiscriminate clutter within the city.

Philadelphia was an industrial city with large factories that dominated a few enterprises, such as heavy industry and the manufacture of locomotives, textiles, gas fixtures, bricks, iron products and machinery, shipbuilding and the production of wagons, carts and carriages. Smaller manufactures operated in smaller shops making hats, clothes, suits and shoes; binding books; printing documents and papers; and creating all the other household items needed on a daily basis. The large factories tended to be located on the outskirts of the city, but the small shops were located in the neighborhoods where the workers lived.[6]

The political make-up of the city was decidedly in favor of the Democratic Party. Due to the many commercial connections to the South and the presence of many Southern families in the city, as well as rich and privileged Philadelphians with large Southern holdings, there was much sympathy for the South's position, and there were concerted attempts by the leaders of the "Democracy" (contemporary name of the party) to avoid antagonizing the Southern position. Charles Godfrey Leland, a respected Philadelphia author, remarked that "in Philadelphia all things Southern were exalted and worshipped" in the mid-nineteenth century.[7]

Though most Philadelphians abhorred slavery, they were also not friendly to free blacks, seeking to confine them to a menial role in society. Free blacks aggregated close to twenty-four thousand inhabitants of the population clustered around the Lombard Street corridor.[8]

Philadelphians were slow to support the newly founded Republican Party. In fact, the very first national presidential nominating convention of the party was held in the city in June 1856 in Musical Fund Hall (Eighth and Locust Streets), where the first presidential candidate, John C. Fremont, was nominated to run in the 1856 election. The Republican mayoral candidate was William B. Thomas, a wealthy grain dealer and devoted abolitionist. Thomas received less than 1 percent of the vote in a losing cause. In fact, it would only be in 1866 that the first mayor could be elected under the Republican name. He was Morton McMichael.[9]

Philadelphia politics had followed a consistent course, favoring acquiescence to the South's policies throughout the mid-nineteenth century. Antislavery Republicanism made little headway in the city. The ticket that carried the city in November 1860 against a divided Democratic opposition did not even call itself Republican but rather the "People's Party," a fusion ticket whose rallying cry was tariff protection, which appealed to many voters.[10]

The Democrats in the presidential election of 1860 had two factions: a Southern one favoring John C. Breckinridge and a Northern one favoring Stephen A. Douglas. The city's Democratic Party tried to unite to agree on a slate of electors who would vote for either Democratic candidate, depending on which of them could defeat Lincoln and throw the election into the

House of Representatives. This plot was sabotaged by a city politician and newspaper editor, John Forney, who led a separatist Douglas movement that undermined any agreement and split the Democratic ticket in the city, leading to a Lincoln majority. Forney's motives were suspect, because behind the scenes he was already engaged in consultations with the People's Party leaders and the Republicans to support them, for which he was given a clerkship in the House of Representatives.[11]

On November 6, 1860, the long political struggle between the North and the South on the slavery question ended with the election to the presidency of Abraham Lincoln and the triumph of the Republican Party. The accession of an antislavery party to political power filled the South with anger and created great excitement and anxiety throughout the country. Hardly had the result been announced before some of the Southern extremists began military preparations and set in motion an oft-repeated threat of Secession and resistance to alleged Northern aggression. Meetings were held in every city, town and village of the South, and those in attendance were addressed in vehement language by radicals, politicians and prominent speakers. On December 20, the state convention of South Carolina, after a brief debate, passed the first ordinance of Secession by a unanimous vote. The dire consequences of the election of Lincoln, and the expected antislavery policies of his administration, seemed to have inaugurated a crisis in the Union and a potential catastrophe for the nation.[12]

The election of Abraham Lincoln to the presidency in 1860 excited comparatively little interest in Philadelphia. The result had been accepted beforehand as a foregone conclusion. "We never saw a Selection," said a Philadelphia paper on November 7, "for even ward officers, it excited so little interest. After nightfall persons began to assemble about the newspaper and telegraph offices to get some news. But there was even here nothing like the interest usually evinced in a Presidential election."

About nine o'clock at night a procession made its appearance on Chestnut Street with a transparency at its head bearing the inscription, "Lincoln on his way to the White House." The style and illumination of this text were, however, so equivocal as to make it uncertain what party the men belonged to. Finally, when the procession reached Fifth and Chestnut Streets, a disturbance occurred that caused the intervention of the police and the arrest of the more active participants. During the evening, processions were formed by the Lincoln Marching Clubs, or "Wide Awakes," belonging to the different wards, each having transparencies with most given out in the respective ward.[13]

In reaction to the election, many Democrats and their organizations adopted resolutions regretting the result of the election but declaring it to be the duty of all Democrats to acquiesce in the will of the majority constitutionally expressed. At the same time it was resolved "to extend to that portion of their fellow-countrymen of the South, who think differently, the assurance of a cordial and respectful fellow-feeling, under the invasion of their constitutional rights and domestic peace and dignity to which they have been so long subjected by the controlling voice of the party which has now prevailed in the choice of a Chief Magistrate."[14] The South was also urged to reflect well before proceeding to extreme measures and was appealed to not desert "the weaker Democracy in the North, struck down in their defense." The sentiments expressed by Mr. Lincoln in his speeches were denounced as being "subversive of our mixed federal and national system," and it was declared that they (members of the party) were "not yet able to spare a single star or a single stripe from the glorious flag of the Union."[15]

A series of resolutions was adopted by the city councils of Philadelphia to invite all fellow citizens who loved the Union to assemble at the old State House (Independence Hall), at twelve noon of a day to be appointed for the purpose, there to express their attachment to the Constitution of the United States and their love for the Union that it creates and protects and for conciliation.

In accordance with the resolutions of the city councils, Mayor Henry issued a proclamation calling a meeting of citizens to Independence Square "to counsel together to avert the danger which threatens our country." At the request of members of the bar who desired to participate, the courts adjourned on the day of the meeting, and the navy yard was closed by order of Commodore Charles Stewart. The meeting was held on Thursday, December 13, 1860, in the presence of an immense concourse of spectators, estimated to number over fifty thousand.

A series of resolutions was read at the demonstration proclaiming the attachment of the people of Philadelphia to the Union; pledging that every statute in force in Pennsylvania, if there were any such, invading the constitutional rights of a sister state should be repealed; recognizing the obligations of the act of Congress of 1850, commonly known as the Fugitive Slave Law; pointing "with pride and satisfaction" to the recent punishment and conviction in Philadelphia of those who had broken the provisions of the Fugitive Slave Law by aiding in the attempted rescue of a slave as proof that Philadelphia was faithful in obedience to the law; recommending to the legislature of Pennsylvania the passage of a law giving compensation in case of the rescue of a slave by the county in which such rescue occurred; acknowledging and submitting "obediently and cheerfully" to the decisions of the Supreme Court of the United States as to the recognition of slaves as property and the rights of slave owners in the territories; declaring that "all denunciations of slavery as existing in the United States, and of our fellow-citizens who maintain that institution and who hold slaves under it, are inconsistent with that spirit of brotherhood and kindness which ought to animate all who live under and profess to support the Constitution of the Union"; cordially approving the suggestion that a convention of delegates from the states be held for the purpose of suggesting remedies for the dangers that menaced the Union; and appealing to those Southern states that were considering the question of seceding from the Union to forbear and not destroy "so great and so fair an inheritance."[16]

Many of the elite members of some of the oldest families of Philadelphia endorsed the effort at compromise, including Charles and Edward Ingersoll, Judge George Woodward, Charles E. Lex, Theodore Cuyler, Isaac Hazlehurst and other Democrats and those hoping for compromise.[17]

The demonstrations on behalf of union and peace were not confined to this mass meeting. Nearly all the stores on Second, Third, Market, Chestnut and Eighth Streets were closed and decorated with flags. The Continental Hotel (Ninth and Chestnut Streets) displayed three large American flags. The balcony was draped with the national colors, and along the front of the building was exhibited the motto "Concession before Secession." A number of private dwellings were decorated with bunting, and attached to the horses and cars of the street railway lines were small streamers of red, white and blue. On December 15, it was announced that Mayor Henry had been authorized to transmit the resolutions adopted by the meeting and reports of the speeches to the authorities of South Carolina.[18]

On the other side of the issue, many Republicans abhorred the measures being taken in the Deep South and held their own meetings to consider resolutions of support for Major Robert Anderson and the garrison of Fort Sumter in Charleston Harbor, then under a siege by rebellious forces.

In the Board of Trade Room, many prominent members of the party of Lincoln resolved "to meet for the purpose of taking into consideration the situation of that patriot soldier of Charleston, Maj. Robert Anderson." At a resolution, William D. Lewis Sr. was chosen to preside. In taking the chair, Mr. Lewis said that the meeting was one of the most important that had been held in Philadelphia since the Declaration of Independence and that it had been called "for the purpose of declaring our determination to support the Federal authorities in any measures they may take to support Maj. Anderson, that gallant man who at present represents our government in the harbor of Charleston, and all other measures calculated to prevent the entire overthrow of all law and order."[19]

The progress of these events caused intense excitement in Philadelphia, where the people were decided in their support of the Union. The geographical position of the state of Pennsylvania, added to its overshadowing political importance, made the duties of the governor peculiarly responsible and perplexing. Separated from the slaveholding states by an imaginary borderline, and looked to from both the North and the South to exhaust its great moral and political power to avert the threatened conflict, every expression from its government was awaited with profound interest.[20]

When news of the firing upon Fort Sumter on April 12, 1861, reached Philadelphia by telegraph on the same day, it did not become generally known until published in the newspapers of the following day. On Saturday, April 13, a feverish interest in the dispatches from the seat of hostilities followed the announcement in the morning papers that war had actually commenced. The streets in the center of the city were thronged until a late hour at night, and "anyone who hinted any sympathy with the Secessionists was made to take an unequivocal stand." At an early hour on Sunday, groups of men gathered around the newspaper and telegraph offices and eagerly discussed the news of the surrender of Fort Sumter, as published in the extras. The feeling in opposition to Secession was very strong.[21]

A handbill was circulated during the day calling upon "young men desirous of rallying around the standard of the Union" to enroll themselves immediately in the new volunteer Light Artillery Regiment, "now rapidly filling up, and ready to march upon the receipt of orders from the Governor."[22] This circular was issued by Captain J. Brady, acting major. At most of the city armories the volunteers gathered during the day, discussing the probable effect of the news from a military point of view. The Union feeling was strongly voiced, and it was agreed on all hands that the government should be sustained at all hazards and independent of party affiliation. During the evening, the throngs on the street increased, and the newspaper extras, announcing that a proclamation would be issued by the president calling for seventy-five thousand volunteers, were quickly sold out.[23]

The excitement built during the day, and indignation increased with the arrival of each new dispatch. Many denounced the officials of the United States military for permitting Fort Sumter to be reduced. Soon after the first reports of the outbreak of war arrived, many volunteers

Call to Arms, a lithograph from *Harper's Weekly*, July 18, 1863, depicting a scene during the panic at the Confederate invasion of Pennsylvania. It shows a recruiting station at city hall next to Independence Hall. *GAR Museum Collection.*

wishing to enlist for the defense of the Union rushed to meetings held throughout the city by various military groups and organizations such as the First and Second Regiments of the Washington Brigade then forming under General William F. Small.[24]

Excitement was aroused in the city by the reports from the South, and this excitement rose to a fever pitch. Business stopped. Nothing was done at the Stock Exchange. The news from the warfront brought the markets to a standstill, and prices tumbled downward. Similarly, in the outdoor markets the war dispatches, combined with the early April rainy weather, limited operations, and sales remained quiet.[25]

The weather, however, proved to be no deterrent to the crowds that gathered around the newspaper offices far into the night. On Sunday the crowds remained unabated, and many assembled about ten o'clock in the morning learned that the momentous events of the previous day had been confirmed: Fort Sumter had been taken, and Major Robert Anderson and his command were surrendered into the hands of General Beauregard and his Rebel forces. Sunday newspapers were devoured by many Philadelphians who never read them before. Everywhere people uttered expressions of indignation and hatred as the realization of the events that had transpired became clearer. Woe to anyone who dared express any sympathy toward the Secessionists. One Southern sympathizer was chased from Third and Chestnut Streets to Doctor Jayne's drugstore (Chestnut Street below Third), from which he was eventually rescued by the police.[26] Another man standing within a crowd ventured to justify the actions of the Charleston Rebels and for this had his hat smashed down over his eyes while a dozen or so boots left their imprints on his body as he was hurried out of the group.[27]

In the evening, one intoxicated man, whose overindulgence had dangerously distorted his sense of humor, announced himself as being in favor of the South. Immediately, bystanders made a rush for the supposed reckless supporter of Secession, who was compelled to quickly apologize and declare that he really was a true Union man. Before he was released, however, the prankster was forced to take off his hat and give three cheers for the Union, much to the amusement of the onlookers.[28]

By such means as these, some of the people gave vent to the emotions that enveloped the entire city. By Monday, the demand for national flags was unprecedented. From private houses, business offices, hotels, factories and government buildings the national colors were seen waving as a sign of loyalty. Indeed, not to have them invited a possible attack from the crowds who still roamed the streets, now in search of premises that lacked the appropriate patriotic display. A group gathered at 337 Chestnut Street outside the office of the *Palmetto Flag*, a newspaper recently founded that was known to have Southern sympathies. Only the arrival of Mayor Henry and a squad of police, with the mayor waving a small flag from one of the upper windows in the building, prevented the place from being stormed and the editors from being attacked. Having been assured by the mayor, the mob then went to the office of the *Daily Argus*—a paper aligned with the Democratic Party and later to be called "Copperhead" as a derisive nickname—which was the only news office in the vicinity that failed to display the flag. The editors here were given an ultimatum—show the flag in fifteen minutes or suffer the consequences. Although the order was abhorrent to the owners of the newspaper, within the stated time a flag was hastily hung out, and the crowd, again appeased, moved on.[29]

The crowds on the following Monday, April 15, 1861, however, had no sympathy for noncompliance. They next visited the offices of a Sunday newspaper that was forced to show the national colors and then moved on to the post office on Dock Street. Here the mob remained standing in front of the building, hooting and shouting, until a flag was finally produced. No violence was done anywhere by the patriotic-minded; the crowds cheered the flags and then moved on until finally satisfied with the displays.[30]

The schoolchildren quickly followed the example set by the adults, for the next day the Northwest Grammar School raised a large United States flag in the presence of a number of citizens of the Tenth Ward,[31] and later, the pupils of Central High School presented a flag to the school during an impressive assembly program that was attended by a number of visitors.[32]

While some citizens marched through the streets demanding to see their country's emblem, others signed a circular addressed to President

Lincoln, pledging him their faith and continued support. Pledge lists were placed at various newspaper offices, hotels and reading rooms throughout Philadelphia, and as soon as one was filled it was sent to Washington; many thousands signed the circular. The Board of Trade quickly published resolutions declaring the support of its members, and the community as well, for the Union, the Constitution and the flag of the United States.[33]

The next day, Tuesday, April 16, in view of the crowds that had marched through the city on Monday and to prevent any serious public outbreak, Mayor Henry issued a proclamation stating that all treasonable activity or violence to persons or to property of the inhabitants of Philadelphia would not be tolerated. He requested all good citizens to report the names of persons giving aid to the enemy by enlisting, or by procuring enlistments for the South, or by furnishing the enemy with arms, ammunition, provisions or other assistance. He commanded all persons to refrain from assembling unlawfully, riotously or tumultuously on the streets of the city so that the peace and credit of Philadelphia might be preserved.[34]

Meeting on Friday, the select and common councils of the city quickly passed various resolutions and ordinances relating to the state of war in the country and military preparations in Philadelphia. City councils met to take swift action, passing a number of ordinances. The first was a request made by citizens to form companies composed of one hundred men each for home defense in the Home Guard. The Committee on Finance was then asked to report on an ordinance for a loan of $1 million to meet the many demands arising from the present unsettled conditions, one of which was to provide a fund for the relief of families of volunteers who had enlisted in the defense of their country. Following this, the commissioner of city property was asked to place any unoccupied halls at the disposal of drilling parties. An appropriation of $50,000 was granted for the purchase of arms for the Home Guard and for other defense purposes, and a committee of five was appointed to help the mayor carry out this ordinance. Resolutions were approved that expressed the satisfaction of the councils at the measures taken by the national government in putting down the rebellion and on the conduct of Major Anderson in the defense of Fort Sumter. Finally, an ordinance was passed appropriating $5,000 to be used by the mayor in such ways as he thought necessary for the preservation of the peace of the city, for the detection of all persons engaged in treasonable designs and for the apprehension of persons molesting the property of citizens of Philadelphia.[35]

On the Sunday after the outbreak of the war, in one of the large churches in Germantown, at the request of the parishioners and with the permission of the rector, the organist played "The Star-Spangled Banner" and "Hail Columbia," the unofficial national airs. The effect was described as "electric."[36]

In fact, during the entire four years of the war, the Philadelphia churches and clergy supported the Union and the war efforts of both the local and national governments, being one of the most ardent and effective groups to do so. Not only the ministers but the churches themselves responded to the national crisis with support, donations and prayerful entreaties and comfort at the emergency. Some denominations, after much debate, reported that it was their obligation to uphold the federal government in the exercise of all its powers under the Constitution to quell the rebellion. This included almost all the faiths found in the city. They likewise expressed their determination to stand by the Union and to aid the national government in its war measures.[37]

Ethnic Make-up of Philadelphia, Immigration and Military Participation

L arge-scale European immigration to Philadelphia after the great influx that arrived prior to the Revolution did not begin again until the end of the Napoleonic Wars in 1815. There were many Philadelphia merchants active in overseas trade, and many ships were bringing immigrants to the city. In the 1820s alone, nearly twenty thousand immigrants, almost 10 percent of the national total, came to the city as two lines of Philadelphia-based sailing ships ran regularly to Liverpool, the main center for Irish as well as English emigration.[38]

Immigration continued steadily in the 1830s and early 1840s. Between 1830 and the great Irish famine migration of 1847, about 60,000 immigrants landed in Philadelphia. But many more people were by this time coming to the city via New York, for Philadelphia's share of all immigrant arrivals had fallen to about 5 percent, where it would remain until the Civil War era. A reason for declining immigration was the distance involved in reaching the city and the presence of ice in the river during winter. The city bought an iceboat in 1838, but many were not confident it could do the job. The city faced the massive Irish and German migrations of the late 1840s with only one line of sailing ships to and from Europe.[39] Increased demand brought forth an increased supply, however. Two new lines of sailing ships were established between Liverpool and Philadelphia; another line plied between Philadelphia and Londonderry; and individual ships sailed from other ports. All told in the eight years from 1847 through 1854, over 120,000 immigrants arrived in Philadelphia, now the nation's fourth largest immigrant port. The total for 1853 alone (19,211) exceeded the total for the entire decade of the 1820s.[40]

The season for immigration to Philadelphia lasted from April to October, and the trip took about a month. The passenger lines continued to service Philadelphia all during the conflict. Between 1855 and 1864, more than fifty thousand immigrants came to the city.[41]

As a result of the immigrant wave of previous decades, by 1850 approximately 30 percent of Philadelphians were foreign-born, the highest proportion ever recorded. The Germans (twenty thousand) and Irish (seventy thousand) accounted for more than three-quarters of the total. This made the population of Philadelphia approximately 14 percent Irish and 10 percent German, and the remainder a combined 5 percent, were primarily immigrants from England, Scotland, Wales, France and other European backgrounds.[42]

In the absence of good public transportation, most Philadelphians of all origins and classes lived near their jobs, and the immigrants were thus spread around the city. The Kensington mill district also had a significant population of British and Irish immigrants.[43]

The free blacks made up 4 percent of the population, making Philadelphia the largest such community in the North. Most of the black population lived in and around the Lombard Street area, where they had their own businesses, schools, churches and social institutions.[44] It was from these ethnic communities that many volunteers were drawn for military service. Philadelphians raised a number of ethnic-based commands, like those composed of Irish immigrants, principally McMullin's Rangers (1861), recruited out of the rough and tumble Moyamensing Hose Company; the 24th Pennsylvania Volunteers (hereafter PV); the 69th PV (Philadelphia Brigade); the 116th PV (Irish Brigade); the Irish Dragoons, or 13th Pennsylvania Cavalry; and many Irish were found distributed throughout most of the city-based regiments mixed in with other immigrants or the native born.

The German community furnished the 27th PV, the first ethnically German unit; the 73rd PV, 74th PV, 75th PV, 98th PV, 5th Pennsylvania Cavalry and the 2nd Pennsylvania Heavy Artillery.

The Jewish community at the time of the Civil War was small in proportion but nonetheless devoted to the cause of the Union. Most were immigrants from German-speaking lands in Europe, and they identified closely with the German community. Most joined ethnic German units, serving gallantly in the army and navy.

The Rosengarten family, of the famous chemical company (now Merck) founded by father George, was represented by four sons who served in the army. Major Joseph G. Rosengarten was a hero at the Battle of Fredericksburg, serving with Meade's Pennsylvania Reserves, and was later an aide to General Reynolds. After the war, he became a prominent member of Philadelphia society and a noted author. His brother Adolph G. Rosengarten commanded the 15th Pennsylvania Cavalry and was killed at Stones River in a gallant but hopeless charge on the enemy.

Max Einstein and Max Friedmann both commanded their own regiments in the early part of the war: Einstein, the 27th PV, and Friedmann, the 5th Pennsylvania Cavalry. Einstein was later named a U.S. consul and diplomat to Nuremberg.

William Durst was a sailor on board the USS *Monitor* and was a veteran of the famed fight between the *Monitor* and the *Merrimac* (CSS *Virginia*). "When volunteers were called for, he sprang to his duty with death staring him in the face," stated Admiral Worden himself, who maintained that Durst was a man of distinguished bravery whose services should have earned him the Medal of Honor.[45]

The French were represented in the Corps d'Afrique and 114th PV.

The smaller African American community of Philadelphia, starting in 1863, provided recruits wholly or partially to the Black 54th Massachusetts Volunteers and eleven United States Colored Troops regiments, trained at Camp William Penn.[46]

There was a scattering of immigrants from other ethnic backgrounds who contributed to the war effort and gallantly performed military service. From Cuba came Adolph (Adolfo) Fernandez Cavada and his brother Frederick (Federico) Fernandez Cavada. Adolph served with distinction in the Army of the Potomac from Fredericksburg to Gettysburg and was a "special aide-de-camp," or staff officer, to General Andrew A. Humphreys, having enlisted in the 23rd Pennsylvania Volunteers, "Birney's Zouaves." Frederick Fernandez Cavada served with distinction in the 114th Pennsylvania Volunteers, "Collis's Zouaves," as regimental commander and was captured at Gettysburg. After the Civil War, both became actively involved in the War of Cuban Independence from Spain, and Frederick became commander in chief of all Cuban revolutionary forces but was captured and executed. Many of his former friends and comrades with whom he had served in the Union army, including Generals Meade and Grant, attempted to obtain his release, but without success. Adolph was also killed fighting for Cuban independence. The Cavada brothers, natives of Cuba and residents of Philadelphia, fought for both their adopted and native countries and paid a "last full measure of devotion" for their native land.[47]

A Polish officer, Captain Stanislaus Mlotkowski, served as commander of Independent Artillery Battery A, Pennsylvania Volunteer Artillery. Mlotkowski had fought in the wars of independence in Poland and had immigrated to Philadelphia. He enlisted in September 1861, and his

Camp Ballier, 98th PV. A sketch of the training camp of the 98th PV German regiment raised in Philadelphia. The camp was named for the organizer of the unit and its commander, General John Ballier. *GAR Museum Collection.*

command was assigned to duty at Fort Delaware. He served honorably until mustered out of service on June 30, 1865.[48]

Frederick George d'Utassy helped to organize the famous Garibaldi Guard, or 39th New York Volunteers, though he was living in Philadelphia at the time. D'Utassy had been a Hussar officer in the 1848 Hungarian War of Independence. He came to Philadelphia after his release from prison in Austria and joined the Union army. New York's Garibaldi Guard was organized with the help of d'Utassy who became the first commander of the unit with the rank of colonel. The guard was allowed to display three flags: the Union flag, Garibaldi's Italian flag and also the Hungarian tricolor, since many in the Garibaldi Guard were Hungarians. D'Utassy's two brothers, Carl and Anton, also served in this regiment. After the war, Colonel d'Utassy supported himself teaching piano in Philadelphia.

Gabriel De Korpornay was an exiled Hungarian who arrived in the United States in 1844. He served in the U.S. Army as captain in the Mexican War and later on the frontier. At the outbreak of the Civil War, he became lieutenant colonel, and later colonel, of the 28th Pennsylvania Volunteers. He was a competent commander but was discharged for disability in 1863 and died in Philadelphia of the effects of service in 1866.[49]

This is just a small sampling of the commanders of Philadelphia-based units who were foreign born and immigrated to the Quaker City, and volunteered for service in the cause of preserving the Union.[50]

First Philadelphia Volunteers to the Warfront
and the Baltimore Riot

In the first days of excitement after the bombardment of Fort Sumter, the press was full of stories of volunteer troops assembling, mustering and drilling in anticipation of war service. None was more prominent than the "Washington Brigade." The *Philadelphia Inquirer* reported on April 16 that the Washington Brigade was busily engaged in recruiting and drilling at Ladner's Military Hall, a militia rendezvous and beer hall at Third and Green Streets, an area inhabited by many German and Irish immigrants. There was great excitement at these headquarters. General William F. Small, the commander, was expected to take his troops to Washington that week; the brigade had been accepted for service by the War Department. Military Hall was crowded to overflowing with volunteers, and new organizations were forming for immediate service. The officers all expressed their ability to be ready to move by the close of the week.[51]

About midnight on Friday, April 19, the Washington Brigade, consisting of two regiments—the 1st Regiment "Monroe Guards," with six companies of American-born volunteers, and the 2nd Regiment, "Washington Guards," composed of five companies of German immigrants totaling close to 1,200 men—along with the 6th Massachusetts Regiment, which had arrived the previous evening en route for Washington, had departed by train for the capital. They were met with an enthusiastic reception as they entrained at the Broad and Prime Street Station. A short time before departure of the train containing the Philadelphia Volunteers, the Massachusetts militiamen had left the Girard House and marched to the Philadelphia, Wilmington

National Guards Hall. A sketch showing the armory of the National Guards militia on Race Street below Sixth Street (now the site of the National Constitution Center). *GAR Museum Collection.*

and Baltimore Railroad Depot (hereafter PW & B) and boarded the cars for Washington behind the Philadelphians. The train left Philadelphia for Washington via Baltimore. The Massachusetts regiment was uniformed and well equipped, but the Philadelphians were mostly not uniformed and unarmed. While crossing the Susquehanna River at Perryville, Maryland, the Massachusetts militia was shuttled to the front of the long train, displacing the Philadelphians. The 6th Massachusetts, therefore, reached Baltimore in the lead cars and exited first and, while marching from one depot to the other, was obstructed by an angry mob of Secessionists. In the fight that ensued, four Massachusetts soldiers were killed and dozens were wounded; a number of civilians were likewise left dead after the troops were forced to fire into the crowd. Estimates of the dead reached over 25 civilians. The troops, however, managed to reach the Camden Street Station and passed on southward.

The Philadelphia companies were left in the rear cars. They were stoned inside the cars by the angry mob. In his report of the affair, General Small stated that his Pennsylvanians behaved gallantly and many sprang from the cars upon their assailants and engaged in hand-to-hand combat with them. It was impossible, however, to distinguish friends from foes, as the mob was composed of a mixture of Union men and Secessionists who were fighting among themselves. The Pennsylvanians could not be distinguished from the citizens. Lack of proper weapons made retaliation futile, and one volunteer, George Leisenring, a young German immigrant from Saxony, then residing in the Northern Liberties–Kensington section, was so severely stabbed while sitting in his car that he died a few days later in

Above: *Depot of the Philadelphia, Wilmington & Baltimore Railroad.* A sketch showing the main depot of the PW & B Railroad, the major avenue for transportation to points south and toward the warfront. *GAR Museum Collection.*

Below: Pennsylvania Hospital at Eighth and Spruce Streets. It is the oldest hospital in America, founded in 1751. It treated the first casualties of the war and witnessed the first death of a Philadelphia volunteer. *GAR Museum Collection.*

Pennsylvania Hospital, becoming the first Philadelphia and Pennsylvania fatal casualty of the war.[52]

The officers and men, Small added, conducted themselves with the utmost courage. He stated that even regular army troops could not have behaved better. A majority of the Washington Brigade returned on the night of April 19, reaching the depot at Broad and Prime Streets after eleven o'clock. Twenty-eight members of the force became separated from the rest of the command, and according to the statement by Samuel Baker, a volunteer, after fleeing northwest about twenty-two miles from Baltimore, his group was arrested by some Secessionists. They were marched across the county to Bel Air, Maryland, and placed in jail. They suffered threats of bodily harm and even hanging. On the following day, however, they were released and escorted by local militia to the Pennsylvania line, from where they proceeded to Philadelphia.

In order to avoid further bloodshed, the chief of police at Baltimore had urged the men to return home to Philadelphia. Philadelphians, upon learning of this outrage, were incensed. Several days later, the Buena Vista Guards, one of the companies that had been attacked, presented to city councils a "Rebel" flag that they had captured in the Baltimore riot.[53] After this experience, Northern soldiers were sent south via steamer around Baltimore, the route being Havre de Grace to Annapolis to Washington.

The Baltimore riot caused intense resentment in Philadelphia and called forth strong expressions of indignation from most citizens. The event increased activity at the recruiting stations, and enlistments grew after the attack.[54] Philadelphia now devoted itself, with characteristic energy, to the duty of providing the government with soldiers properly armed and equipped as fast as they were needed. In the course of the war, the city was represented in nearly 150 regiments, battalions, batteries, cavalry troops, independent units and other detached units (including emergency troops not called outside of the state), the majority of which were raised entirely locally. In addition, many Philadelphia companies served in commands of other states, as well as thousands of sailors, marines and regular army recruits.[55]

The effect of war upon business in Philadelphia in the early months of the struggle was a source of great anxiety among larger employers. At the establishment of Matthias W. Baldwin & Co., where 80 locomotives had been built in the preceding year, matters were nearly at a standstill. Many of the workers had been discharged, and plans were considered for turning the plant into a factory for shot and shell. Unexpectedly, however, the national government ordered many engines, and the "war railroads" required many more. Between 1861 and 1865, Baldwin turned out 456 locomotives, many of them the heaviest and most powerful ever constructed.

At the shipyards, machine shops, textile mills and factories of all types, government contracts soon afforded abundant employment. Philadelphia workmen were able to provide heavy and light artillery, swords, rifles, camp equipage, uniforms and blankets in great quantities. This activity continued throughout the period of the war.[56]

During the early months of the war, many Philadelphians were eager to enlist. In the Fourth Ward of the city, Captain William McMullen, a staunch local Democratic politician and Irish immigrant who had served in the Mexican War, was organizing a group of one hundred picked men as rangers, or scouts. A young merchant, wealthy and well educated, came to him and begged to be permitted to join the group even as a private. Because the ranks were already filled, the captain agreed to accept him if at the next drill some recruit would resign. Accordingly, the following day the young man presented himself at the drill field and first offered $25, then $50, and then $100 to anyone who would resign, thus permitting him to march with Captain McMullen. Not a man stepped forward to accept the proposal, and the disappointed patriot finally was informed by a sergeant in the group that even $1,000 would be insufficient to purchase the place of the poorest in the company—so enthusiastic were they all to take part in the conflict.[57]

Because so many of the volunteers enlisted without making adequate provision for their families while they themselves were absent in the service, a petition was submitted to the residents of the wards of the city in which everyone was invited to record subscriptions for the relief or employment of volunteers' families. Not only was aid given to recruits from the city itself, but it was also tendered to volunteers who entered from other parts of the state. Soon after Lincoln called for recruits, the Young Men's Christian Association offered its mammoth tent, which it used for the purpose of holding public worship and was conveniently situated on Broad Street near the Academy of Music, as a reception center and temporary accommodation for troops in transit through the city.[58]

To help volunteers who arrived in Philadelphia, and who had not been mustered into service, John B. Budd, of 1317 Spruce Street, offered to furnish daily at noon a dinner to ten or twelve men who otherwise would have had difficulty in obtaining food. To prevent imposition, this worthy gentleman required a written order from the captain or commander of the respective regiments or companies of which his hungry guests would soon become members.[59]

From the amount of pay received monthly by the majority of volunteers, and later by drafted men, it is little wonder that many left behind them families dependent upon public or private relief. The monthly pay for a private in 1861 was thirteen dollars per month, plus food, clothing and equipment. The officers were required to provide their own uniforms and equipment. So that every soldier might enjoy clean attire, the *North American* newspaper suggested that each company going into service should take along washerwomen, if the men wanted clean clothes.[60] According to paragraph 124 of the U.S. Army regulations, each company was entitled to four washerwomen who were allowed one ration a day, and in addition to this compensation for any washing they did, they were entitled to a small salary paid by the officers and men.

Not to be outdone in patriotic activities by their husbands and brothers, many Philadelphia women volunteered to sew for the national government. At the Girard House Hotel, which Governor Curtin chose for a military depot, as it was then standing vacant due to the competition of the more popular Continental Hotel across Chestnut Street, a notice was posted stating that women were needed to sew uniforms. In the Girard House, the government established a military clothing depot under the supervision of Robert L. Martin, assisted by Captain George Gibson. It was expected that one thousand garments a day could be produced, including such articles as underwear, sack coats, greatcoats and trousers. Here, as well as at the Schuylkill Arsenal, women were employed sewing uniforms on piecework, but many fashionable ladies also offered their services, especially in those early days when uniforms were desperately needed.[61]

After the first Philadelphia troops left for Washington on that fateful Thursday and early Friday morning, April 18 and 19, a number of businessmen met in the Board of Trade rooms to discuss the organization of a company for the military defense of the city. At that time, it was thought that many of those who enrolled would eventually go into active service wherever they were needed even though the terms of enrollment related only to service in the city. Of the approximately fifty men who joined at this first meeting, the majority were merchants and professionals within the legal draft limit, or under forty-five years of age. They were men who felt unable to leave the city immediately for distant service.

Quickly formed, this organization became known as the Home Guard and was increased to include every adult male not needed elsewhere and not physically disqualified. Immediately, agitation commenced in every ward of the city to organize a Home Guard unit within each one's respective limits.

According to the authority conferred on him by councils, on April 20, 1861, Mayor Henry appointed Colonel (later General) Augustus J. Pleasonton to be commander of the Home Guard with the rank of brigadier general of volunteers.[62] General Pleasonton was authorized, under the direction of the mayor, to organize his force into various units of cavalry, artillery and infantry.

The Home Guard Medical Department was placed under the supervision of Dr. John Neill, and Moyamensing Hall was equipped to serve as a hospital not only for sick and wounded members of the Home Guard but also for all such men in the United States service.[63]

Various groups joined the guard in a body, among them the Maennerchor Vocal Society of Philadelphia, composed of Germans. This group, under the command of Captain John A. Koltes, a veteran of the Mexican War, was organized as a rifle company and prepared for active service as part of the Home Guard.[64]

The uniform for the guard consisted of a single-breasted frock coat of cadet gray with a standing collar and buttons of the branch of service to which the regiment belonged; the pantaloons were made of the same material as the coat. The cap, cut on the army pattern, was of drab color, trimmed with a rosette of red, white and blue. Regiments of "young guards" were allowed to substitute the cap for the regulation army hat. These uniforms, many of which were provided by the members themselves, cost from six dollars to twenty dollars, depending upon the financial status and personal taste of the individual. The uniforms were to be worn habitually so that in case of alarm the officers and men could dash at once to their armories without stopping to change their clothes.

In order to enable the Home Guard to become more proficient in military duties, a number of Philadelphia merchants agreed to close their businesses at four o'clock in the afternoon each business day of the week with the exception of Saturday, when they would close at three o'clock for the period between April 15 and July 15, 1861. This was done so that their employees might have an opportunity to drill and obtain military training.

Although the Home Guard was maintained during the entire four years of the war, its activity depended upon the threat of danger from Rebel invasions. This occurred several times, and at the Battle of Gettysburg, a number of companies of the Home Guard were mobilized to defend their state from the enemy.[65]

Political Opposition to the War

D espite the outbreak of rebellion and increasingly bloody and brutal
war, including threats of invasions, Philadelphians were at first neither
unequivocal Unionists nor Republicans. A majority of Philadelphians had
been traditionally supporters of the Democratic Party. Many Democrats
and those who actively supported the rebellion were called "Copperheads."
This was in part due to proximity to the South and because Southerners
enjoyed close family, social and economic ties to Philadelphia. Those
Democrats who were loyal to the country and opposed the rebellion, and
enlisted to preserve the Union, were called "War Democrats." As the conflict
progressed, many people grew increasingly alarmed at the slaughter and
expense. They sought arbitration and peace at whatever cost. With such
growing encouragement, the Copperheads became more outspoken in their
opposition, and lively political debates erupted in the city. In the fall of 1862,
the National Union Party, without making any reference to "Republican," a
fusion of Republicans and War Democrats, nominated a full party ticket for
city elections headed by Alexander Henry for mayor.[66]

The election on October 14 was carried out in an orderly manner, and the
victory went to the National Union Party. Mayor Henry received a majority of
5,088 votes, but the rest of the party ticket only won a majority of about 3,000.[67]

At the state level, however, Democrats were successful in electing their
candidates by a majority of approximately five thousand. In celebration of this
victory as well as for gains in other states, the Democrats held a large jubilee
celebration in Independence Square the evening of October 30, 1862.[68]

A photo of the headquarters of the bastion of anti-Lincoln Democrats among the city elites, the Philadelphia Club stands on Thirteenth and Walnut Streets. *GAR Museum Collection.*

Several Democratic clubs were formed in the city to raise funds for their candidates and to provide a place where strategy could be planned, treasonous pronouncements made and campaigns organized. One was called the Central Democratic Club, and a rival later emerged called the Keystone Democratic Club. It was in response to these and similar groups in support of the rebellion that gave rise to the Union League, a firm and loyal supporter of the president, administration and war effort.[69]

The following March 1863, Congressman Vallandigham, a leader of the Copperheads, arrived from Ohio and was serenaded by enthusiastic followers at the Girard House Hotel, where he was staying while in Philadelphia. However, when he attempted to express his ideas concerning arbitration and peace at a mass meeting, he was frequently interrupted by unsympathetic hecklers in the crowd. On June 1, 1863, the Democrats held another large meeting to protest his arrest and court-martial on charges of "implied treason," which they declared violated the Constitution. Bitter speeches asserted that the correct and legal remedy was an appeal to the ballot box and not to the use of force, which would cause more harm than good.[70]

After Lincoln was re-nominated for election by the Republican Convention held in Baltimore in June 1864 and his opponent, former Major General George B. McClellan, was nominated in Chicago in August, active campaigning in Philadelphia began in earnest. The Republicans held a mass meeting in Independence Square to ratify the nomination of Lincoln, and the Democrats held a similar meeting at the same place a week later to endorse McClellan.[71]

These two gatherings set the precedent for various political meetings held throughout the city. Marching clubs were organized for both parties.

These clubs held torchlight processions in the streets of Philadelphia, and members frequently proceeded to stone one another whenever two or more different groups chanced to meet in the rowdy sections of town. On October 29, 1864, the Democrats held a procession reputed to have been six miles in length. The Republicans were worried over the final outcome of the election, and they had cause to fear, as their party seemed to be losing ground. However, the successful course of the war helped sway the voting public. On September 5, 1864, Sherman reached Atlanta. By November, the campaign in Virginia seemed more hopeful, and Philadelphia returned a majority for Lincoln of 11,762 votes. The state majority was somewhat smaller in proportion to that of Philadelphia.[72]

The seemingly irreconcilable political differences between the rival parties led to bitter divisions, even among members of the same family. Epithets, verbal and written abuse, insults and ridicule were regularly unleashed from both sides. Both parties for the most part were loyal to the Union but differed in their interpretation of the Constitution and public policies.

The Democrats supported the rights of the South and were fully in support of their practice of slavery. The Republicans, on the other hand, initially sought to eliminate the expansion of slavery from the South to the new territories being organized into states. Some Republicans, a minority in Philadelphia and elsewhere in the North, were in favor of the total abolition of slavery. Most Philadelphia Democrats opposed Secession but were also similarly opposed to many of the severe measures the Lincoln administration introduced to help prosecute the war, such as press censorship; suspension of the right of habeas corpus, which allowed arrests without right to trial; and the draft. Many Democrats mistrusted Lincoln and his policies and grew to feel that the war was really being fought to free the slaves rather than preserve the Union.[73]

Many immigrants to Philadelphia adhered to the Democratic Party and its promises of financial support. Most of the Irish were staunch in their allegiance to the party and were fearful of freed blacks migrating to the city and inundating the unskilled labor market, thus creating stiff competition for jobs and consequent loss of their livelihoods.[74]

Many of the Democrat leadership were composed of the old moneyed and propertied elite families, many of whom had settled Philadelphia with William Penn. They were well educated and conservative in their political views. Men like Charles Biddle, the Ingersolls, Peter McCall, William B. Reed, Richard Rush, Richard Vaux and George Wharton were from old, originally Quaker, families, had served in city government or in Congress and were lawyers, businessmen and entrepreneurs.[75]

The essence of their opposition is best stated in a speech by Charles Biddle, a West Point graduate and Mexican War veteran who had helped raise a regiment, the "Bucktails," and served for a time in the field as colonel. While serving in Congress, Biddle made a speech on March 6, 1862, warning about the damage any elimination of slavery would have on the country. Biddle stated:

> *I desire to see a speedy termination to the war...I am a northern man with northern principles...I would leave to my children the Union that our fathers left to us...When I see how deeply Providence has rooted the institution of slavery in this land, I see that it can be safely eradicated only by a gradual process, in which neither the civil nor the military power of the government can intervene...Emancipation can only be safely reached through state action, prompted by conviction and the progress of natural causes.*

This statement sums up, in general, the Philadelphia Democratic Party's view on slavery. They mistrusted blacks and sought compromise and conciliation on the issue with the South. They saw the Republicans as the radicals and revolutionaries who were bent on the destruction of the Union. Some of the more extreme Democrats, however, suggested that Pennsylvania should join the Confederacy. Prominent Philadelphian William B. Reed wrote a pamphlet that advocated disunion and supported the recognition of the Confederacy. Some Democrats even resorted to persuading men not to enlist in the military and pledged assistance to the Confederacy. Famous Philadelphian Pierce Butler had inherited plantations in Georgia, had expressed treasonous remarks in public and had even been imprisoned in Fort Lafayette, located in New York Harbor, for his views. He spent the war years quietly in Philadelphia and returned to his plantation in Darien, Georgia, after the war. His famous wife, the British actress Fanny Kemble, became an ardent abolitionist after a trip to her husband's plantations in 1838 led her to write and publish the *Journal of a Residence on a Georgia Plantation*, a detailed and critical exposé of Southern plantation life.[76]

Confederate successes on the battlefield up to 1863—in addition to war weariness in the North, the enormous cost of the war in lives and treasure and the administration's resort to extralegal measures on the homefront, capped by Lincoln's Emancipation Proclamation—prompted the Democrats to plan all-out efforts in 1863 to unseat Republicans from the state and city offices. They founded an organization, the Central

Democratic Club, to counteract the Union League and to work against Republicans in the elections. In an earlier state convention of 1862, the Democrats had stated their position clearly: "The Party that seeks to turn the slaves of Southern states loose to overrun the North and enter into competition with the white laboring masses, thus degrading...their manhood by placing them on an equality with Negroes in their occupation is insulting to our race and merits our emphatic condemnation...This is a government of white men, established exclusively for the white race." They also blamed the war on Northern reformers, stating, "Abolitionism is the parent of Secessionism."[77]

Reverend Chauncey C. Burr, in a convoluted argument, lashed out at Lincoln in a meeting at the Democratic Club, stating, "Abraham Lincoln is a greater traitor than Jefferson Davis. What has Jeff Davis done? He has merely infringed on our territorial jurisdiction. He has not struck at the Constitution."[78] Burr further maintained that if Lincoln's abolition policy was to continue, Davis would fight for the liberties not only for the South but for the North as well.

Philadelphia remained calm throughout the invective of the Democrats and their attempt to disrupt the course of the war effort and even thwart enlistments. Even the frightful draft riots seen in New York were avoided in Philadelphia due in large part to the active engagement of Mayor Henry and his police force at any potential threat to civic peace and prosperity. Additionally, General Charles Cadwalader was assigned to the command of the city and the military establishment on July 14, 1863. Cadwalader, though a Democrat, was a strict Union man who had much experience in controlling riots, as evidenced by his role in ending the Nativist riots in 1844.[79]

Despite their best efforts, the Democrats were overwhelmed in the election of October 1863 when their candidates were defeated. Control of city councils passed to the Union Party, a fusion of Republicans and War Democrats. The Democrats also resorted to lawsuits filed in federal courts to contest administration policies, but these attempts met with defeat as well. They even resorted to the reissue of Episcopal bishop John Henry Hopkins's treatise in support of slavery based on a biblical analysis, "Bible View of Slavery," originally published in 1861. This attempt was also thwarted by opposition from all Philadelphia clergy. The Democrats were chastened but undaunted and were quiet opponents of Lincoln and the war until its conclusion. In July 1864, the Central Democratic Club was replaced by the Keystone Club, a more moderate group.[80]

Philadelphia lawyer and diarist Sidney George Fisher wrote aptly of the campaign of the Democrats against the Lincoln administration and emancipation:

> *The Democrats in their speeches and their press (the Age) have denounced the war and its motives…gloried in every Rebel victory, mourned over defeats, vilified the North, abused officers of the government and above all President Lincoln on whom they have lavished every epithet of scorn and contempt; he was a usurper, a tyrant, a blackguard, a ruffian, a buffoon, a gorilla, and his administration was worse than an eastern despotism. They were permitted to do this without check or molestation, thus refuting their own charges.*[81]

Only in Lincoln's assassination was the vitriol of the Democrats somewhat muted, but even then some dared to criticize the Great Emancipator even while his body lay in state. One incident found prominent Philadelphia Democrat and party leader Charles Ingersoll attempting to visit his brother Edward in jail. Edward had pulled a pistol on an army officer. The officer and a large crowd had met Ingersoll at the train station and threatened him with violence. Edward had only recently delivered a speech in New York where he expressed sympathy for the Confederacy and supported Secession—this on the day before Lincoln died, a victim of assassination. In trying to push through an ugly mob at the jail, Charles was attacked and badly beaten. The police were largely in support of the mob and barely intervened to save his life. Edward was eventually released and left town, and Charles recovered but never again played an active role in politics.[82]

Abraham Lincoln in Philadelphia

Lincoln's first recorded visit to Philadelphia occurred while he was an attendee at the 1848 Whig National Convention. "In my anxiety for the result," he wrote, "I was led to attend the Philadelphia convention."[83] The convention met at the Chinese Museum at Ninth and Sansom Streets. On Friday, June 9, 1848, the delegates selected General Zachary Taylor, the hero of the Mexican War, as its presidential candidate, and as vice presidential candidate Millard Fillmore, then comptroller for New York. That evening, convention delegates massed in Independence Square, the area immediately behind Independence Hall between Chestnut and Walnut Streets, for a campaign rally that party leaders called a ratification meeting. Lincoln was a probable attendee.[84]

The passage of the Kansas-Nebraska Act was a call to action for Lincoln, and from then onward, the Declaration of Independence became his call to action. Lincoln won the presidency in 1860, running on a party platform that supported the principles of the Declaration of Independence.

In February 1861, in the midst of a national crisis and even death threats, Lincoln as president-elect traveled east from Springfield, Illinois, on his way to Washington, D.C., to his inauguration. At the invitation of the city councils and mayor, his train arrived in Philadelphia at 3:45 p.m. on Thursday, February 21, 1861, at the Kensington Station of the Philadelphia and Trenton Railroad, Front and Montgomery Streets. Nearly 100,000 people turned out on that cold February day to welcome the newly elected leader as he rode three miles in an open barouche from the depot to the

Flag Raising by Lincoln at Independence Hall. A lithograph from *Harper's Weekly* showing the scene at Independence Hall when Lincoln raised the flag with the first star for Kansas on February 22, 1861, prior to his inauguration. *GAR Museum Collection.*

Continental Hotel on the southeast corner of Ninth and Chestnut Streets. Lincoln and his procession reached the hotel only three blocks west of Independence Hall just after 5:00 p.m.[85]

In 1861, the Continental Hotel was one of the finest in the United States. The ornate hotel had opened one year earlier and could host one thousand guests in its seven hundred rooms. It boasted an elevator, a freestanding stairway from the lobby to the second floor and a 165-foot second-floor promenade that opened to a second-floor balcony. Lobby, shops, private rooms and dining rooms occupied the first two floors. Clearly Philadelphians expected the president-elect, a man born in humble surroundings, to stay in a place appropriate to his high station.[86]

Immediately after his arrival at the hotel, Lincoln and the mayor of Philadelphia, a Lincoln supporter, appeared on the hotel balcony to address the crowd that filled the street below. The mayor officially welcomed the president-elect to the city. One newspaper later reported that as Lincoln responded, he held his hat in front of him with both hands, and from time to time he elbowed the onlookers who overflowed on the balcony in order to maintain his place. Lincoln spoke of Independence Hall and the Declaration of Independence. "I shall do nothing inconsistent with the teachings of those holy and most sacred walls…All my political warfare has been in favor of the teachings coming forth from that sacred hall. May my right hand forget its cunning and my tongue cleave to the roof of my mouth, if ever I prove false to those teachings." Lincoln declared, "There is no need of bloodshed in war…the government will not use force unless force is used against it."

That evening at the hotel, Allan Pinkerton and Frederick W. Seward separately informed Lincoln that there was a plot to kill him when he passed through Baltimore the next day. On January 30, 1861, President Samuel M. Felton, of the Philadelphia, Wilmington and Baltimore Railroad Company, invited Pinkerton, a well-known detective of Chicago, to Philadelphia and engaged his services to assist in safeguarding the railroad against threats of sabotage in Maryland. Pinkerton placed a number of his men along the line. One of these detectives, Timothy Webster, joined a disloyal company of cavalry at Ferryman's, Maryland. It was through this source that Pinkerton learned the details of the proposed murder of Lincoln while en route through Baltimore. After President-elect Lincoln arrived at Philadelphia, a messenger summoned Norman B. Judd, of his party, to a conference with Pinkerton. Later in the evening, Pinkerton was introduced to Lincoln and told him of the plot. It was difficult to convince Lincoln that the danger was real. He insisted upon proceeding, with his entourage, to Harrisburg at once after the ceremony of raising the flag at Independence Hall early the following morning.

The next morning, on Washington's Birthday, February 22, 1861, Lincoln and his seven-year-old son, Tad, rode in an open carriage three blocks down Chestnut Street to Independence Hall. The First City Troop, National Guards militia, Washington Grays, Garde Lafayette, minutemen and other militia units accompanied and escorted the presidential party. An unfortunate incident was the refusal of General Robert Patterson, commander of a division of Pennsylvania militia to participate, due to his political opposition to Lincoln. Patterson was a staunch Democrat. At 7:00 a.m., after more than nine years of rhetoric imbued with the words of the Declaration of Independence, Lincoln entered the Assembly Room of Independence Hall.

The room was a patriotic shrine that had been redecorated by the city. The Liberty Bell sat in the corner on an octagonal pedestal that was decorated with flags and the names of the signers of the Declaration of Independence. A sculpture of George Washington stood near the center of the east wall, flanked by portraits of William Penn and the Marquis de Lafayette. A chair said to have been used by John Hancock during the signing of the Declaration of Independence and a block allegedly used for the first reading of the Declaration stood along the outer walls.

After welcoming remarks by the president of the select council, Lincoln was expected to address those in attendance. Lincoln was exhausted by the past eleven days of travel, the crowds, the pushing, shoving and chaos. His right hand was swollen and partially dysfunctional from shaking so many hands. He had only just learned of a plot to assassinate him, and in the meantime, he had had little sleep. He had not known that he would be called upon to speak inside the hall. His words were extemporaneous but based on years of oratory and thought. His voice was low and barely audible.[87]

I am filled with deep emotion at finding myself standing here in the place where were collected together the wisdom, the patriotism, the devotion to principle, from which sprang the institutions under which we live…All the political sentiments I entertain have been drawn…from the sentiments which originated, and were given to the world from this hall in which we stand. I have never had a feeling politically that did not spring from the sentiments embodied in the Declaration of Independence. I have often pondered over the dangers which were incurred by the men who assembled here and adopted that Declaration of Independence—I have pondered over the toils that were endured by the officers and soldiers of the army, who achieved that Independence. I have often inquired of myself, what great principle or idea it was that kept this Confederacy so long together. It was not the mere matter of the separation of the colonies from the mother land; but something in that Declaration giving liberty, not alone to the people of this country, but hope to the world for all future time…If this country cannot be saved without giving up that principle—I was about to say I would rather be assassinated on this spot than to surrender it…My friends, this is a wholly unprepared speech. I did not expect to be called upon to say a word when I came here—I supposed I was merely to do something towards raising a flag. I may, therefore, have said something indiscreet, but I have said nothing but what I am willing to live by, and, in the pleasure of Almighty God, die by.[88]

The president-elect walked out of Independence Hall through the Chestnut Street door, mounted the wooden platform and faced a huge crowd assembled on Chestnut Street. Lincoln stood, bareheaded, holding his top hat in his left hand, while Tad Lincoln stood to his left. Abraham Lincoln addressed the crowd in brief remarks and then raised a large thirty-four-star flag, the first to honor the admission of Kansas to the Union. Later, some realized that the flag was a last-minute addition and had the incorrect number of stars at thirty-five. This flag was reported to have been made by sailors aboard the USS *Hartford*, docked at the Philadelphia Navy Yard. As the flag rose above Independence Hall, it caught a breeze and unfurled to the wind.

Later that day at the state capitol building in Harrisburg, Lincoln told the Pennsylvania legislature that the success of the flag-raising ceremony that morning in Philadelphia augured well for the Union. "When, according to the arrangement, the cord was pulled and it flaunted gloriously to the wind without an accident, in the bright flowing sunshine of the morning, I could not help hoping that there was in the entire success of that beautiful ceremony at least something of an omen of what is to come."[89]

At the conclusion of the reception at the state capitol, a meeting was held at the hotel, where Agent Pinkerton urged Lincoln and his advisers to abandon the Northern Central Railroad train, scheduled to travel to Baltimore, and alter his plans by returning to Philadelphia. In a carefully planned ruse, Governor Curtin called at the hotel in a carriage, ostensibly to carry Mr. Lincoln to his residence. This was a decoy. The only member of his traveling party who entered the carriage was Colonel Ward H. Lamon. Unobserved, the president-elect boarded a special train, which was hurried back to Philadelphia at night. At the same time, employees of the telegraph company drove two miles out of the city and grounded the wires of the telegraph line. No dispatches went out of Harrisburg that night. Under these precautions, Lincoln's special train reached the West Philadelphia station late in the evening, but too soon for immediate connection with the train for Washington.

The funeral cortege of Lincoln in Philadelphia on April 22, 1865, as it processed up Broad Street on its way to Independence Hall for a lying in state. *GAR Museum Collection.*

The closed carriage containing Mr. Lincoln and Colonel Lamon, together with Allan Pinkerton and Superintendent H.F. Kenny of the PW & B Railroad, sitting with the driver, proceeded down Market Street, up Nineteenth Street to Vine Street and thence down Seventeenth Street to the depot at Broad and Washington (then called Prime Street). Chairs for the party had been arranged by "Mrs. Warne," one of Pinkerton's agents. It was reported to the conductor that one of the passengers was an "invalid gentleman" who should be admitted to the rear of the coach and have a chair. The other seats were occupied by Pinkerton and his agents. Officials of the company, including George Stearns (later a U.S. Army colonel), remained on guard throughout the night. So carefully were the plans executed that none of the train employees from either line was aware that Mr. Lincoln was on board. Colonel Thomas A. Scott, waiting anxiously through the night at Harrisburg in company with Colonel Alexander K. McClure, was overjoyed to receive, soon after 6:00 a.m. on February 23, a dispatch from Washington assuring him of the safe arrival of the president-elect.[90]

Colonel Thomas A. Scott, who was then vice-president of the Pennsylvania Railroad, acted at the time as a staff officer of Governor Curtin. On April 27, 1861, he was appointed, by the secretary of war, superintendent of railways and telegraphs, his immediate duties being the restoration of transportation between Annapolis and Washington.[91]

Finally, and tragically, in April 1865, Abraham Lincoln was brought a final time to Independence Hall after his assassination. His funeral train arrived at the Broad and Prime station just before 5:00 p.m. on Saturday

UNION LEAGUE NOTICE!

The Members are requested to meet at

THE HALL,

COR. OF FOURTH AND FEDERAL STS.

ON SATURDAY AFTERNOON,

AT 2 O'CLOCK,

For the purpose of proceeding to Philadelphia, and participating in the obsequies of our late President

ABRAHAM LINCOLN

Members will appear in Dark Clothing, White Gloves and Crape upon their Left Arm. *Badges* and *Gloves* can be procured at the League Room.

All Loyal Citizens who sympathize with us, and desire to participate are invited to join us.

BY ORDER OF COMMITTEE.

SAMUEL HUFTY,

April 21, 1865.   CHAIRMAN.

A copy of the poster from the Union League that announced the death of Abraham Lincoln on April 15, 1865, and preparations for his funeral. *GAR Museum Collection.*

evening, April 22, 1865. The procession that met his funeral cortege wound through the streets of Philadelphia until it reached the Walnut Street gate of Independence Square at 8:00 p.m. Sixty red, white and blue calcium lights illuminated the area. A military band played funeral dirges as muffled bells tolled throughout the city and minute guns boomed from various locations. After the catafalque came to a halt, the honor guard carried the casket into the south entrance of Independence Hall from Walnut Street. Members of the Union League with whom Lincoln had a special relationship lined the walk on both sides. The white-gloved men, dressed in black with mourning bands on their left arms, removed their hats.[92]

In the Assembly Room where the Declaration of Independence had been signed eighty-eight years earlier, Lincoln's body lay in state amidst the elegant trappings of mourning, including flowers, black crepes and wreaths. One of the cards on a wreath spoke of Lincoln's dream that he had mentioned at his last cabinet meeting one week earlier, on April 14, 1865. Lincoln interpreted his dream as an omen that great news would soon come. The card read, "Before any great national event I have always had the same dream. I had it the other night. It is of a ship sailing rapidly." And in a symbolic gesture, Philadelphians placed the Liberty Bell at Lincoln's head so that all who passed by could read its inscription: "Proclaim Liberty throughout all the land, unto all the inhabitants thereof."[93]

Philadelphia Civil War
Military Hospitals

The city of Philadelphia played a large and pivotal role in the treatment of the sick and wounded, becoming, by war's end, the largest center for medical care in the United States. In addition to being a hub for medical education, it was located at the nexus of many lines of transportation. These facts made Philadelphia indispensible as a center for medical treatment. Eventually, there were over ten thousand hospital beds available throughout the city. Referrals were also made to civilian hospitals for special services. Due to its geographical position, Philadelphia received patients both by ship and by rail from the nearby camps and battlefields. Consequently, the hospitals were nearly always kept full. The greatest tax on their facilities, however, came after great battles, such as Antietam or Gettysburg, when the city was so crowded with suffering men that the hospitals were unable to care for them all and many were lodged in firehouses and churches. The Methodist Church at Broad and Christian Streets, the Presbyterian Church at Broad and Fitzwater Streets and Saint Theresa's at Broad and Catherine Streets were the most frequently used. Although Philadelphia hospitals received a greater proportion of wounded and sick soldiers than the general hospitals elsewhere, the percentage of deaths was the lowest in the army medical department.[94]

During the war, there were twenty-four military hospitals, plus branches, at one time or another, with smaller hospitals that also treated troops. Following the Battle of Gettysburg, Assistant Surgeon General James R. Smith informed Pennsylvania governor Andrew Curtain that five thousand beds within the city were available to men wounded in that battle. In the next few weeks, more than ten thousand soldiers were transferred from Gettysburg to Philadelphia.[95]

On January 1, 1866, the Philadelphia branch of the United States Sanitary Commission, a civilian organization chartered by Congress to give aid and badly needed volunteer services to troops, reported that approximately 157,000 soldiers and sailors were cared for in Philadelphia military hospitals during the course of the war. Over 6,000 of the sick and wounded died. But this was a smaller proportion than in all the other Northern states.[96]

Philadelphia also hosted specialty hospitals, most notably the Turner's Lane Hospital, where prominent physician Dr. S. Weir Mitchell was in charge. Here, Dr. Mitchell and his colleagues studied nerve disorders and injuries, such as paralysis, spasms and epilepsy (considered a nervous disease at the time). Detailed case histories were essential to such research and to medical care in general.[97]

The first casualties of the Civil War were brought to Pennsylvania Hospital. These were the men of the Washington Brigade who had been attacked in Baltimore on April 19, 1861. Their wounded were brought

U.S. General Hospital at Broad and Cherry Streets. The hospital was situated in the former depot of the Reading Railroad. *GAR Museum Collection.*

back to Philadelphia to the PW & B Station on Broad and Washington. At that time, Pennsylvania Hospital was the closest hospital to that depot. The hospital was founded in 1751 by Benjamin Franklin and Dr. Thomas Bond to care for the "sick, poor and insane of Philadelphia." It is still located at Eighth and Spruce Streets. Pennsylvania Hospital's surgical expertise brought hundreds of casualties to its wards for special treatment. The War Department paid the hospital a fee for each serviceman it treated.[98]

Some Philadelphia military hospitals reused older buildings. For instance, Haddington Hospital near Sixty-fifth and Vine Streets, with two hundred beds, was housed in an old hotel. Most of the hospitals had fewer than five hundred beds, but two of the largest military or general hospitals in the country were located in Philadelphia. These were West Philadelphia, or Satterlee General Hospital, with more than four thousand beds, and Mower General Hospital, which was located on the Reading Railroad line in Chestnut Hill. The latter was designed by John McArthur, the architect of the present city hall. It could accommodate four thousand patients. These new hospitals were constructed using the "pavilion system." Since bad air was thought to spread infection, the wards had large windows and extensive ventilation systems.[99]

Most of the military hospitals were either installed in an existing building felt to be suitable for the purpose or were constructed on open ground using the pavilion system of long, narrow, pavilion-like structures as wards constructed of lumber usually 160 to 170 feet long and 24 feet wide. Also constructed were a laundry, nurses' rooms, offices, a guardroom and a knapsack room where soldiers' gear could be stored. The hospital was usually built on higher ground with good ventilation, breezes and woods for shade, along or near creeks or wells for good, clean water and near to a transportation network.

Satterlee General Hospital was an example of the pavilion style. Satterlee was constructed with fourteen parallel pavilions, each being 167 feet by 24 feet, which projected from each of the corridors at 21-foot intervals. There were at its height of service thirty-six wards in the hospital, twenty-eight wards in the wooden barrack-style buildings and eight wards in the tented campground that could be supplied in times of great necessity. The construction of the hospital was completed rapidly in less than forty days.

There were eleven attendants to each one hundred patients in the wards. There were thirty-five medical officers on duty, including eighteen medical cadets. Each ward, in theory, had a surgeon, a Sister of Charity, a ward master, three male nurses and a medical cadet assigned. If a surgeon was not available, then an assistant surgeon would take over.[100]

Satterlee General Hospital. A contemporary sketch of the giant hospital complex in West Philadelphia. *GAR Museum Collection.*

Hospitals required many and varied medical personnel, surgeons, nurses, apothecaries, clerks, guards, musicians, administrators and mechanics, cooks, laundresses and a host of others. At the start of the war, most nurses were male, since women in Victorian society were not yet accepted as caregivers for men who did not belong to their families. Gradually, however, female nurses, including Catholic nuns, became more common, either as paid workers or as volunteers.[101] Organizations of volunteers, such as the U.S. Sanitary Commission and the U.S. Christian Commission, contributed greatly to patient care, donating money, supplies and labor. The Great Central Sanitary Fair of 1864 raised large sums of money for the Sanitary Commission's work.

Each hospital was placed under the supervision of a surgeon in chief who had complete control over its management. He was assisted by assistant surgeons, as well as medical cadets, who were frequently medical students who volunteered their services; nurses, male and female; a ward master; support personnel; invalid soldiers of the Veteran Reserve Corps (VRC) who could perform light duties; and sundry other personnel, such as the military band and a chaplain to minister to the patients' spiritual needs.[102]

Satterlee was one of the largest hospitals in the country. Located in a West Philadelphia neighborhood near the intersection of Forty-second Street and Baltimore Avenue, its sixteen-acre grounds ran north to Forty-fifth and Pine Streets. The hospital featured a library, reading room, barbershop and printing office that printed its newspaper, the *Hospital Register.*

Water was obtained from the mill creek that was located nearby. The hospital was opened for patients on June 9, 1862. It was named Satterlee in honor of General Richard Satterlee, MD, a military surgeon from New York. With a capacity of three thousand beds in the permanent facility and one thousand more in tents, it was the largest military hospital in the United States until the opening of Mower General Hospital in Chestnut Hill. More than sixty thousand soldiers and sailors were cared for at Satterlee Hospital before its closure on August 3, 1865. Clarence Clark Park is the present location of the parade ground and tent portion of the facility. The park contains a memorial to this hospital, a granite rock from Devil's Den at Gettysburg.

Dr. Isaac I. Hayes, the famous Arctic explorer, was appointed surgeon in charge. Although rigid military discipline was enforced here, everything possible was done to make the patients comfortable. Forty-two Catholic Sisters of Charity and women from the Ladies' Aid Society, Penn Relief Association and the Ladies' Association for Soldiers' Relief were in constant attendance in the wards. A library, reading and writing room contained newspapers from various parts of the country, and a billiard room and entertainment hall were also provided. A military band supplied music for daily concerts as well as for dress parades and dirges for the dead.

Satterlee was opened in 1862 by order of Surgeon General William A. Hammond. By May 1864, more than 12,000 patients had been treated. Only 260 suffered deaths, a remarkable accomplishment considering the sanitary conditions of the day. At the height of the influx of patients, mostly after great battles, the hospital could expand to 4,500 beds.

In Stewart Bulkley's reminiscences of Satterlee Hospital during the Civil War, a most interesting account is given of the tenderness and devotion of Mother Gonzaga, mother superior of the Sisters of Charity whose care of the sick and the wounded ever remained memorable. A veteran of the 142nd Regiment of Pennsylvania Volunteers, Bulkley said of the saintly sister:

Mother Gonzaga was a mother to about fifty soldiers in the Satterlee United States Hospital during the years from 1862 to 1865. No matter what the creed, her devotion was ever the same, and not a few soldiers recalled in after years the midnight visits of Mother Gonzaga—as she was called by the men—her silent steps after "taps" and in the dim gaslight were listened for, and with her white-winged head-dress she flitted from bed to bed to soothe and cheer the suffering soldiers. She was one of the purest and loveliest of women, and the mention of her name with that of old Satterlee Hospital is only a fitting tribute to her gentle memory.

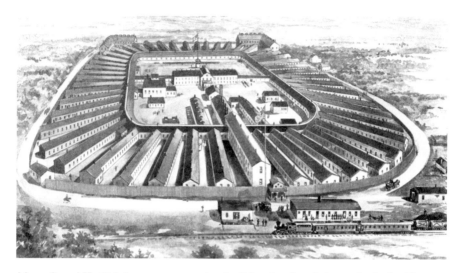

Mower General Hospital. A contemporary sketch of the giant hospital complex in the Chestnut Hill section of Philadelphia. *GAR Museum Collection.*

At Forty-second Street and the Schuylkill River, back of Woodlands Cemetery, there was, in 1862, a steamboat landing, where the sick and wounded were brought. From there they were carried in carts and ambulances manned by patriotic firemen and other manner of conveyances to Satterlee Hospital.[103]

Mower General Hospital was located between Abington and Springfield Avenues, County Line Road and the Chestnut Hill track of the Reading Railroad and was erected by the same contractor who built Satterlee Hospital. Like it, Mower was of lumber, rough cast on the outside. With a capacity at first of 2,820 beds, later more than 4,000 beds were made available in fifty wards. The hospital opened on January 17, 1863. Today, the former hospital site is at the Chestnut Hill Village Apartments, adjacent to the current Wyndmoor Railroad Station. The surgeon in chief was Dr. J. Hopkinson. The hospital had a full band and drum corps furnishing daily music. The hospital was technologically very advanced and boasted a very low rate of death.

John MacArthur Jr., the designer of Philadelphia City Hall, laid out plans for Mower Hospital and other new-style army hospitals. Mower was named for Thomas Mower, an army surgeon. The hospital was one of the largest and most innovative in the Union. Its design could limit the spread of infection by sealing off wards and centered on an administrative area with barracks, dining halls, surgeries, kitchens, mortuary, etc. Wards radiated out as spokes on a wheel with about fifty to one hundred beds per ward.

Patients were brought directly from the battlefield by trains using special hospital cars converted from sleeping cars. This terrible journey was known among the servicemen as the "seven circles of hell to heaven on earth," a journey lasting days or even weeks. The railroad also carried families of the patients, hospital workers and volunteers. Nearly three thousand people visited the hospital each week.

An existing freshwater supply of the Chestnut Hill Water Company was used (the stone water tower on Ardleigh Street still stands today). Mower occupied a tract of twenty-seven acres extending from County Line (Stenton Avenue) to Germantown Avenue, Springfield Avenue to Abington Avenue, and was built on the highest level point in Philadelphia.

The hospital was laid out in a geometric pattern. Tramways extended in the wards to bring medical supplies and food in carts with flanged wheels. Mower contained butcher shops, a guardhouse, a chapel, a library with 2,400 volumes, an operating theater and the dead house/mortuary. There were many advanced conveniences, including gas lighting, indoor plumbing, constant hot water and ventilation.[104]

Additional, though smaller, military hospitals were opened around the city to accommodate the large numbers of sick, wounded and debilitated men arriving every day. These included the McClellan Hospital located at Wayne Junction, Germantown Road and Cayuga Street, in the Nicetown section of North Philadelphia.[105] Summit House Hospital was located on the west side of Darby Road near Paschalville, a small village in West Philadelphia, four miles from the Market Street Bridge.[106] Haddington Hospital was located in Haddington, a section of West Philadelphia, historically that section of Haverford Avenue between Sixty-fifth and Sixty-seventh Streets. Haddington was initially housed in the Bull's Head Tavern on Sixty-fifth and Vine Streets, placed near the property of the Butcher's and Drover's Association on the southwest corner of Haverford Avenue and the Merion and Darby Roads.[107] Cuyler Hospital was located at the Germantown Town Hall.[108] Broad Street Hospital was located in the old station of the Philadelphia and Reading Railway Company on Broad Street, below Race, and on the southeast corner of Cherry Street, east of Broad.[109] Citizens' Volunteer Hospital was supported and financed entirely by the private donations of citizens. Foremost in extent and capacity among the centrally located hospitals, this charitable establishment was located opposite the depot of the Philadelphia, Wilmington and Baltimore Railroad.[110] Christian Street Hospital was located in the old Moyamensing Hall, on the south side of Christian Street, below Tenth Street. The building had also served as the police station for the Second Ward.[111]

Turner's Lane Hospital, sometimes referred to as the "German" Hospital, was located at Twentieth and Norris Streets in North Philadelphia west of Broad Street. The Union army rented it from the German Hospital of Philadelphia from 1862 through 1866. A special study of the diseases of the nerves caused by wounds was conducted at this hospital by famed surgeons S. Weir Mitchell, W.W. Keen and Jacob A. DaCosta. Here, they undertook research on "irritable heart" (neurocirculatory asthenia) in soldiers; this research was of landmark importance in clinical medicine.[112] Hestonville Hospital was situated in the West Philadelphia area called Hestonville on Lancaster Avenue near Fifty-second Street and Merion and the Pennsylvania Railroad at the Park Hotel near the Monroe Engine Company. Master Street Hospital was located in a manufacturing building on the northwest corner of Sixth and Master Streets. Islington Lane Hospital was known as the "Smallpox Hospital" because cases of the disease were transferred there from other hospitals. George Street Hospital occupied the building of the Order of American Mechanics at Fourth and George Streets. Fifth Street Hospital was established in the buildings of the Dunlap carriage factory at Fifth and Buttonwood Streets. Race Street Hospital was used temporarily and occupied the National Guards Armory on Race Street below Sixth Street (now the site of the National Constitution Center). Twelfth Street Hospital was located at Twelfth and Buttonwood Streets. Filbert Street Hospital was located at the State Arsenal Building, on the southeast corner of Sixteenth and Filbert Streets (now the site of JFK Plaza). The lower floors of the building were used as a depot for army uniforms. In February 1863, this was converted to a convalescent facility. After the war, it became the Soldiers' Home. Dr. S. Weir Mitchell's novel *In War Time* described this hospital and its operations. South Street Hospital was originally a silk-dyeing factory and was located at Twenty-fourth and South Streets backing onto Naudain Street. This hospital was often called the "stump hospital" because of the large number of patients with amputations. St. Joseph's Hospital occupied temporary buildings erected on the property of the large Catholic hospital of the same name at Seventeenth Street and Girard Avenue founded in 1849. Catherine Street Hospital was located at Eighth and Catherine Streets. The hospital was conveniently located near the main PW & B Station and was of great service to passing troops. Wood Street Hospital was the site of a former paper factory. It was one of the earliest military hospitals in Philadelphia, located at the northeast corner of Twenty-second and Wood Streets. The Officers' Hospital, or Camac's Woods, was located near the corner of Eleventh and Berks Streets. Camac's Woods Hospital was founded perpendicular to Turner's Lane on the east side of Broad Street (now on the campus of Temple University). The hospital opened in 1862. It was a facility owned by Dr. Camac, who had converted his own home to a hospital, and was later moved to Twenty-fourth and Chestnut Streets. The Episcopal Hospital was located at Front and York Streets. Cooper Shop Soldiers' Home and Hospital was located in city-owned buildings at Race and Crown Streets, on the north side of Race Street between Fifth and Fourth Streets, one-third of the way down the street. The street was removed in 1941. This was a home and hospital for debilitated and discharged soldiers who could not get home from Philadelphia. It was founded through the tireless efforts of the volunteer nurse Anna M. Ross, who died on December 22, 1863, from overwork and exhaustion. The Union Volunteer Refreshment Saloon Hospital was located near the Refreshment Saloon at the Navy Yard at the foot of Delaware and Washington Avenues, opposite Old Swede's Church. The hospital backed up to the wall of the navy yard. It accommodated the sick and ailing soldiers of regiments passing through the city. This was one of the first hospitals for wounded and sick soldiers and sailors. During times of great need and large numbers of wounded after great battles, Broad Street churches and firehouses were also used as hospitals.

The U.S. Army Laboratory facility was located on the northeast corner of Sixth and Jefferson Streets in a factory building. It was established under the direction of Surgeon General William A. Hammond in the summer of 1863 to produce medicines and medical supplies for the army and navy under the direction of noted scientist Professor John Maisch. Here a staff of chemists and other experts prepared supplies needed for the medical and surgical requirements of the armed forces.

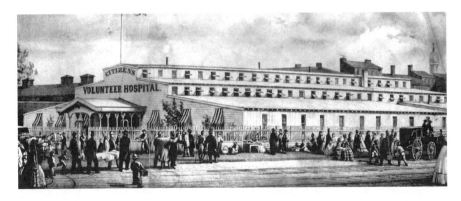

A contemporary photo of the Citizens' Volunteer Hospital, funded by voluntary donations. It was located at the northeast corner of Broad and Washington, across the street from the PW & B Depot. *GAR Museum Collection.*

The "Invalid Corps" was founded by the government and later designated the Veteran Reserve Corps. The corps was recruited from men of military service who were sick or wounded but were still fit for garrison and guard duty. Under the direction of the provost marshal, twelve companies of these troops were formed at the several army hospitals in Philadelphia. Through the efforts of Colonel Richard H. Rush, Lieutenant Colonel George W. Gile, formerly of the 88th PV, was appointed to command. The "Invalid Corps" was composed of two classes: the more able-bodied companies were employed on provost duty and as guards; those in the second class were assigned as hospital clerks, cooks and male nurses.[113]

Benevolent and Volunteer
Service Organizations of Philadelphia

THE UNITED STATES SANITARY COMMISSION

The most benevolent and generous of the many civic organizations formed for the assistance of the soldiers and alleviation of their sufferings during the Civil War was the United States Sanitary Commission, which originated with a group of military and civilian men and women in New York City, led by the Reverend Henry W. Bellows. This association was given official status by the secretary of war on June 8, 1861, and later by Congress.[114]

Branches of the commission were formed in every large Northern city. Large donations of money and supplies were constantly placed at the disposal of the commission, coming from every corner of the loyal states. The officials and committees volunteered their time and served without pay. The Sanitary Commission undertook the collection and forwarding of supplies and comforts to the troops at the front and assisted in the relief work among the sick and wounded, especially after battles. A general hospital directory was published by a Bureau of Information, located in Washington, in order to enable friends and relatives to find soldiers in the army hospitals. A claim's agency and pension agency were maintained without cost to the soldiers.

More than forty Soldiers' Homes were established, having a daily average of 2,300 patients. Hospital inspectors constantly visited every segment of the army. Hospital trains were operated by the Sanitary Commission over the railroads, and hospital ships were employed on the seas. As far as possible, the commission supplied food, medicine and clothing to prisoners of war held in the South.[115]

In Philadelphia, the local branch was located at 1307 Chestnut Street and received large monetary donations, as well as supplies, 80 percent of which was sent outside the city. The local commission also provided a "lodge" at Thirteenth and Christian Streets for the support and shelter of soldiers.[116]

GREAT CENTRAL SANITARY FAIR

Many organizations for soldiers' relief in Philadelphia united to sponsor the Great Central Fair on behalf of the Sanitary Commission in June 1864. This Great Central Fair was probably the greatest purely civic act of voluntary benevolence ever attempted in Philadelphia. To assist the work of the Sanitary Commission, large fairs were held in all the great cities of the North. Philadelphia's fair was held in an enormous temporary building covering the whole of Logan Square (now Logan Circle). Many of the large businesses and commercial houses and all of the street railway companies contributed one day's receipts, and many workers donated a day's pay to the project. With the funds obtained, the immense building was erected, with its booths, smoking lounge, picture galleries and brewery. To stock the booths and galleries, thousands of contributors poured their treasures into the

Great Central Fair. A sketch from *Harper's Weekly* showing the Great Central Sanitary Fair on Logan Square, held in June 1864. The Great Central Fair was held to raise funds for the benevolent work of the Sanitary Commission. *GAR Museum Collection.*

structure. The fair opened on June 7 and remained open until June 28. The governors of Pennsylvania, New Jersey and Delaware participated in the opening ceremonies, and President and Mrs. Lincoln and son Tad visited the fair on June 16, 1864. After his visit, President Lincoln was hosted at a dinner held by the members at the Union League at the first League House at 1118 Chestnut Street. After the fair closed, all remaining articles were sold at auction. The fair not only proved very attractive but was also immensely successful, raising the enormous sum of $1,261,822.52, which was donated for the general work of the Sanitary Commission to aid in soldiers' relief.

According to Charles J. Stille, who wrote a memorial history of the fair for the Sanitary Commission, "This great hall had all the vastness of the Cathedral's long drawn aisles and its moral impressiveness as a temple dedicated to the sublime work of charity and mercy." Various "departments" were organized along the corridors of this city of mercy.[117]

Local businesses, individuals and institutions donated their products, services and valuable items to sell or raffle to support the patriotic cause, and the fair exhibited a wide array of goods, artifacts and curiosities, all under one gigantic roof. A magnificent collection of paintings was loaned by private collectors and museums, filling the northern corridor. A great variety of displays and amusements were provided to entice visitors.

The cost of the undertaking was largely derived from popular subscriptions and donations.[118] Over the several weeks of the fair, more than 250,000 visitors were recorded at an admission price that varied from fifty cents to one dollar.

The New Jersey and Delaware Branches of the Sanitary Commission were also involved and invited to participate in the noble work.

An exciting aspect of the fair was the ongoing competition to vote for favorite generals then serving in the field and to raffle off valuable treasures to raise additional funds. As the fair progressed, the voting was continually announced based on the purchase of a ballot, allowing the purchaser to cast a vote for each item. Even the generals noted the competition and commented on the contest.[119] At the conclusion of the fair, the results were announced and the prizes awarded. Voting results announced the following winners: General Meade was the winner of the magnificent sword with 3,442 votes out of a total 5,541. General Hancock won the horse equipments with 116 votes out of 212. General Birney won the camp chest with 308 votes out of a total of 385. The silver vase was won by Mr. Edward D. James, a citizen, with 4,939 votes. The imported leghorn ladies' bonnet was won by Mrs. General Burnside with 296 votes, with Mrs. General Meade a close second with 285 votes.[120]

THE UNITED STATES CHRISTIAN COMMISSION

Another important organization for relief work during the Civil War was the Young Men's Christian Association of Philadelphia, which began its operations almost simultaneously with the operations of the armies of the United States at the outset. It soon ceased to be a merely local organization and developed into the United States Christian Commission. At first its headquarters were in New York, but they were removed to Philadelphia in 1862 and remained there during the war. During the four years of the war, large sums of money and an enormous amount of supplies were disbursed by the commission.[121]

On November 15, 1861, delegates from fourteen branches of the Young Men's Christian Association met in New York City and organized the commission, electing George H. Stuart, a distinguished citizen of Philadelphia, as permanent chairman. Philadelphia, therefore, became the center of the national movement for the moral and spiritual welfare of the soldiers. Of the nearly five thousand agents of the commission eventually sent to the army, the first group was composed of fourteen members of the Philadelphia association.

For a long period, the government army officers and many of the chaplains tolerated, but did not heartily assist, the commission's agents. Authority to visit and work among the soldiers was officially granted in some instances and refused or revoked in others.

Along with its moral message, the commission began to provide material comforts, especially to the sick and wounded. In November 1863, an arrangement was made with the Confederate authorities that enabled the commission to send food, medicine and clothing to Union prisoners of war. It was not until September 1864 that an order was signed by General Grant giving the representatives of the Christian Commission full privileges in the camps of the army.

In the years of its existence, the commission performed much benevolent work. The Philadelphia offices of the Christian Commission were located at 1011 Chestnut Street, where assistance was given to soldiers, sailors and visitors seeking relatives in the hospitals. During the war years, the local YMCA also provided a large tent on Broad Street near the PW & B station for the use of the army recruits and volunteers on the way to the warfront. The Christian Commission established cordial relations with the United States Sanitary Commission, and they cooperated in the cities, camps, on battlefields and on the seas—in fact, everywhere—in the important work to which both organizations were devoted. The officers of the Christian Commission were George H. Stuart, president; Joseph Patterson, treasurer; and Reverend W.E. Boardman, secretary.[122]

PHILADELPHIA-BASED CIVILIAN ASSOCIATIONS FOR AID AND COMFORT OF THE SOLDIERS AND FAMILIES

During the war, numerous patriotic and benevolent associations were founded in Philadelphia. Many of them were connected with the churches, while others were of secular origin, but all provided some form of assistance to the soldiery of the Union cause. The services of a large proportion of the devoted men and women cannot be adequately estimated. In some instances, printed reports were made, copies of which have been preserved, and these afford an outline of many helpful deeds these groups accomplished.

The Women's Pennsylvania Branch of the United States Sanitary Commission was organized on February 25, 1863. The special work of this grass-roots organization of women was the relief of soldiers' dependents and the gathering of supplies for the men in the field.[123]

Probably the first local association of women who "wanted to help" was the Ladies' Aid Society of Philadelphia, which was organized in April 1861 "to provide garments for soldiers, work in hospitals and take care of soldiers' families." Its mission covered a broad field of patriotic services, and it did excellent work in furnishing volunteer aid and supplies both locally and to those serving in the field. Those most active were Mrs. Joel Jones, president; Mrs. Stephen Colwell, treasurer; and Mrs. John Harris, secretary.[124]

The women of Philadelphia were so eager to find beneficiaries among the soldiery that the whole country was not too large. For instance, the ladies of St. Luke's Episcopal Church sent, in May 1861, nine hundred pairs of shoes to the Union Missouri Volunteers.[125]

In December 1861, the Soldiers' Relief Association of the Episcopal Church was formed. On July 28, 1862, a number of ladies met at the office of Edward Brady, Esq., 135 South Fifth Street, and formed the Ladies' Association for Soldiers' Relief. Mrs. Mary A. Brady became president and Mrs. M.A. Dobbins treasurer. At first, this association devoted its efforts to providing special dinners to the occupants of the local army hospitals. Later, it seems to have made a specialty of the Sixth Corps. One of the most successful relief expeditions that ever went out of Philadelphia, from the soldiers' point of view, was welcomed in the camps of those Philadelphia warriors when Mrs. Brady and her associates appeared one day at the front with a wagonload of good plug and smoking tobacco. The ladies of this association hastened to the bloody fields of Antietam and Gettysburg and there, amid sickening surroundings, imitated the English nurses who had, but a few years before, followed Florence Nightingale to the Crimean War. On May 27, 1864, Mrs. Brady died at her home, 406 South Forty-first Street in West Philadelphia, as a result of her persistent labor in the cause to which she had been so long devoted.[126] The Penn Relief Association was founded "to assist sick soldiers in and out of hospitals and to aid their families." The officers and Executive Committee included many women who belonged to the Society of Friends.[127]

The first institution in the United States to receive and care for children of men who had enlisted, and of deceased soldiers, was the Northern Home for Friendless Children and Associated Institute for Soldiers' and Sailors' Orphans, located at Twenty-third and Brown Streets. This institution was aided liberally through the efforts of Mrs. Elizabeth Hutter and by Dr. Albert G. Egbert, a wealthy oil operator of Mercer County, Pennsylvania. Over 1,300 children of soldiers were housed and educated at this home. After the war, General Meade took an active role in the support of the institution and its educational program.[128]

The Lincoln Institution was founded in order to provide a home for the sons of soldiers who had fallen in battle. General George G. Meade was active in this charity and became its first president. The institution was located on Eleventh Street, below Spruce.[129]

After the war, in 1873, the Educational Home for Friendless Boys was opened at Forty-ninth Street and Greenway Avenue. It was a branch of the Lincoln Institution and was later merged with it and became part of the Pennsylvania Orphans' School system. At these well-conducted homes, hundreds of boys were educated and sustained while learning trades and sent out into the world well equipped to be successful citizens. At a later period, the management admitted Indian boys and girls to both institutions.

A modest but popular enterprise of war days in Philadelphia was the Soldiers' Reading Room maintained, for several years, on Twentieth Street below Market Street, in a building formerly the Brickmakers' Baptist Church. Here soldiers were always welcome to come and rest, read and relax. The organization was a precursor to the future USO of more modern times. A considerable library of books, magazines, games, files of newspapers from many cities and writing material, a piano and a smoking room were at the free disposal of all soldiers and sailors. Hot lunches were provided for five cents, or without charge if occasion required. Lectures were given in the evenings, and religious services were offered on Sundays. The average attendance was about one hundred soldiers per day.[130]

The Ladies' Association of West Philadelphia was active in raising money for soldiers' families. Prominent ladies involved were Mrs. John Cotton, Mrs. Thomas Hunter, Mrs. John Sweeney and other ladies of distinguished families.

The Union Temporary Home was established to provide a shelter for the children of soldiers in the field of men who had enlisted.

In 1864, the Ladies' First Union Association was active, with rooms at 537 North Eighth Street, in feeding and providing for a large number of the families of soldiers.[131]

Among other groups founded by patriotic organizations wishing to lend material and spiritual support for the soldiers and sailors and their families were the Freemasons' Soldiers' Relief Association at 204 South Fourth Street, the New England Soldiers' Relief Association on Chestnut Street near Thirteenth and the Hebrew Women's Aid Society. The free black community of Philadelphia also formed similar groups to assist the colored volunteers, their families and recently freed slaves from the South. These included the Colored Women's Sanitary Commission, with headquarters at 404 Walnut Street. The distinguished officers were Mrs. Caroline Johnson, president; Mrs. Arena Ruffin, vice-president; Reverend Stephen Smith, treasurer; and Reverend Jeremiah Asher, secretary, who later served as chaplain of the 6th U.S. Colored Troops and died in service. There were also the Colored Union League and Freedmen's Relief Association. Many of these volunteer service organizations continued their work to the close of the war and even into the postwar period.[132]

Southwark Refreshment Saloon Movement

The Camden and Amboy Railroad was the major route from New York and New England to the South. Rail traffic from New York and New England came through New Jersey on the railroad and was ferried over the Delaware to the foot of Prime Street (now Washington and Delaware Avenues). The ferries landed at the foot of Washington Avenue next to the Philadelphia Navy Yard. Passengers disembarked and took horse-drawn cars up Washington Avenue to Broad Street. At that point, travelers bound for the South would enter the imposing terminal of the Philadelphia, Wilmington and Baltimore Railroad to reembark for transportation to Baltimore and Washington. It took approximately nine hours to travel from New York to Philadelphia, but it was the most efficient transportation method for the day.

When large numbers of troops began to make this journey with transit through the Southwark district of Philadelphia south of Washington Avenue, they had already been on the road for some time, and they were tired, thirsty, hungry and sometimes sick. No amenities had been provided by the military. The local families of Southwark saw the poor condition of the troops and took pity on them. Many were the wives or relatives of navy personnel or navy yard workers or in the local factories, and they were sympathetic to the plight of the volunteers. Soon, these willing angels of mercy were bringing food and drink from their own homes to distribute to the men before they marched on to the station one and a half miles away at Broad and Prime for transportation south to an uncertain future.

Union Volunteer Refreshment Saloon. A contemporary lithograph of the arrival of troops at the Union Volunteer Refreshment Saloon at the foot of Delaware and Washington Avenues. *GAR Museum Collection.*

Out of this spontaneous gesture of civic kindness and hospitality grew the Southwark Volunteer Refreshment Saloons—two institutions founded through volunteer efforts of local citizens to care for the troops as they passed to and from the front.[133] The Cooper Shop Refreshment Saloon was founded in a two-story brick building on Otsego Street about fifty yards south of Washington Avenue, near the Camden Ferry, and the Union Volunteer Refreshment Saloon was located on Swanson Street a short distance below Washington Avenue at Delaware Avenue. During the course of the war, millions of servicemen, both Union and Confederate prisoners, were lovingly cared for by both of these prominent benevolent civic institutions.[134]

The Refreshment Saloons were conveniently located near the tracks to the depot at Broad and Prime. Both institutions would soon become known throughout the East wherever soldiers wrote home describing the work being done and the help and comfort they had been given. Both institutions developed from committees formed by a few women and ably assisted by sympathetic business and civic leaders. In May 1861, seeing a group of hungry troops waiting for transportation, volunteers set about providing the men with food and coffee, thus originating the idea of service upon which the refreshment saloons were based. Being unable to accomplish all the work themselves, the women enlisted the help of their husbands and friends, who wholeheartedly cooperated.

These ambitious and thoughtful men and women soon realized that it would be necessary to find some building in which to provide for the hungry soldiers. In this effort, William M. Cooper and his business partner, Mr. Pearce, kindly offered the use of their manufactory shop to the committee. Hostilities had interrupted their business, and the partners turned their attention to the new enterprise occupying their facility that soon demanded most of their time and efforts.

Likewise, Barzilai S. Brown, a grocer and fruit dealer who worked as a distributor, offered a small boat shop owned by James Grim on Swanson Street, below Washington Avenue, as a "free refreshment saloon for soldiers or Union Refreshment Saloon." This was at first referred to as "Brown's," being so called in letters written to their home newspapers by some grateful soldiers. It first opened on May 27, 1861.[135]

It was these patriotic men and women, their friends and the residents of the Southwark neighborhood who began to collect provisions for the refreshment saloons, bringing them first from their own homes and later from the homes of their neighbors and donors. Before long the storekeepers, butchers and grocers in the vicinity were supplying the refreshment saloons with food, and women from the neighborhood brought provisions that kept the saloons well supplied throughout the war. Both institutions received no government funds.[136]

The first recorded instance of troops being fed in a body was on the morning of May 27, 1861, when the Cooper Shop fed Colonel Louis Blenker's entire 8th New York Regiment, one thousand men strong. After the hearty breakfast, all the soldiers drew up in line and cheered both the Philadelphia ladies and the Refreshment Saloon.

The meals usually served consisted of beef, ham, bread and butter, sweet and white potatoes, pickles, tea and coffee and sometimes cake or pie. Barrels of coffee and fifteen thousand cooked rations were often made in one day. The large fireplace in the building was used to prepare one hundred gallons of coffee per hour. The hungry soldiers of entire regiments from the northeastern states had a way of swarming from the ferries at Washington Avenue wharf at most inconvenient hours, but the good people of Southwark were always ready for them.[137]

Religious services were usually held on Sunday afternoons at the refreshment saloons and were attended by large numbers of citizens and soldiers. Music was provided by regimental bands and by the choirs from downtown churches.

From time to time, various souvenirs and curiosities were sent by grateful soldiers to the saloons from the South and other places. Among such mementos was a rough board boat in which two slaves had been picked up in Chesapeake Bay; a piece of the woodwork had been bored through by a rifled cannonball. Also included were a musket taken as a souvenir at Fort Beauregard and a cutlass snatched from a Confederate naval officer. One soldier, wounded in the head by a Rebel, had shot his assailant dead and, seizing the sword that inflicted the cut, sent it back to be exhibited at the saloon.[138]

In the fall of 1863, the captured Confederate ram *Atlanta* was loaned to the Union Committee and exhibited to the public at the foot of Washington Avenue. A modest admission charge added greatly to the funds of the saloon.[139]

As the work progressed, improvements were made and the number of volunteers increased, and the accommodations extended until it was possible to feed one thousand men in an hour.

The Union and Cooper Shops became friendly rivals in their goodwill. The need was great, and both organizations and their volunteers cooperated in supplying the troops with articles the men might need.

In order to avoid delay when large numbers of volunteers were to be fed, each organization appointed several men to a committee for the reception of soldiers. This committee saw to it that an equal number of the troops were sent to each saloon. An arrangement was made with the railroad company transporting the troops whereby the company would forward to the committee notice by telegraph several hours in advance of the arrival of the train bearing troops.[140] Out on Washington Avenue, there was a large flagstaff, and at the foot was placed a small cannon covered, when not in use, by a box embellished with patriotic insignia. When a troop train left Jersey City, a telegram was sent to the refreshment saloons, and the gun was fired to notify the local lady volunteers, often busy at their own homes, to hurry to the large sheds and make ready for the arrival of the troops. It was the business of small boys to watch upriver for the coming of the ferries.

When the ferries were sighted, thronged with hungry men, every youngster rushed "up the tracks," and the cannon was fired a second time. This trusty little cannon was credited by contemporary newspapers with a remarkable record. It had been cast at the Springfield Armory and went with the U.S. Army to Mexico, but it was captured by the Mexicans at Veracruz, and they remounted the gun at the ancient fortress of San Juan d'Ulloa. Later, it was recaptured from a Mexican gunboat, sent to Philadelphia and sank on the receiving ship *Union* in the Delaware River. It was recovered and placed among the curios at the navy yard. When the war began, it was used for the defense of the railroad bridge at Perryville, Maryland, and was finally loaned to the committee of the Union Volunteer Refreshment Saloon. It was popularly dubbed at this period of its service "Fort Brown," in honor of the originator of the Union Refreshment Saloon. It was the first to thunder out the news of the surrender of General Lee on the night of April 9, 1865. After the war, it was preserved and displayed among the trophies of Schuyler Post, No. 51, GAR, in Philadelphia into the twentieth century. It is now believed to be kept at Fort Mifflin.[141]

When the volunteers arrived in smaller groups of fewer than two hundred, one saloon working a full twenty-four hours would entertain all the arrivals. The next day, the other saloon would take over in turn. When this schedule was in effect, the cycle commenced at six o'clock in the evening. When more than two hundred appeared, the group of men would be divided and an equal number directed to each saloon. The staff was sent alternately to the Union and then to the Cooper Shop. No matter at what hour the volunteers arrived, they would always find some of the committee in attendance.[142]

In addition to supplying food for the troops, the saloons also established their own hospitals. Dr. Andrew Nebinger, who for three years gave his services freely despite having a large private practice, was the surgeon in charge of the hospital founded by the Cooper Shop. From time to time he was assisted by his brother, Dr. George Nebinger. Miss Anna M. Ross, a beloved unmarried civic activist and volunteer for many relief causes, was the impetus behind the hospital, supervising the women of the neighborhood as they waited upon sick and sometimes wounded soldiers. At first, the second story of the Cooper Shop Refreshment Saloon was used as the hospital, and donations to carry on the work were procured by Miss Ross and female volunteers.[143]

The Union Refreshment Saloon Hospital was placed under the care of Dr. Elias Ward. It contained, at first, fifteen beds and was one of the first military hospitals opened in the city. Later, more spacious quarters were occupied on the opposite or west side of Swanson Street. Dr. Ward continued at this post of duty throughout the war, and it was due to his efforts that this hospital, which ministered to thousands of sick and wounded soldiers, was recognized as a regular government establishment.

So successful were the volunteers in soliciting funds that the new institutions soon came to be recognized as model hospitals. Miss Dorothea Dix, the supervisor of the U.S. Army Nurse Corps and visitor to the refreshment saloons, commended them highly and contributed a number of books to the libraries.[144]

By early 1862, the hospitals had been expanded to accommodate more patients, and apothecary shops were attached. The work and materials for these structures were nearly all contributed by a large number of businesses and individual donors. The rooms were clean, well lighted and well ventilated, and the female volunteers strove to achieve as homelike an atmosphere as possible. When a patient, completely recovered, left the hospital, not only was he supplied with a testament and other religious tracts but his clothes were also exchanged from a supply of underclothing, hosiery, mittens, handkerchiefs, towels and blankets kept for this purpose.[145]

On May 17, 1863, Robert P. King, president of Mount Moriah Cemetery, donated to the Union Refreshment Saloon a large burial lot in which the committee could bury any soldier who might die while in the hospital. Later, the Cooper Shop Soldiers' Home was also permitted to use this lot when a soldier died. However, of all the soldiers admitted to the hospital, comparatively few died, as can be ascertained from the records. In 1862, the first year in which the establishment was open, 159 patients were treated; the following year, 305 were helped; in 1865, 85 were admitted, 79 discharged and 2 died; during the fourth year, 12 patients died and 291 were discharged. The hospital closed in the autumn of 1865.[146]

The gratitude of the soldiery for the splendid treatment extended to them was expressed in thousands of messages and letters of thanks, many of which were printed in distant newspapers, and the fame of patriotic Philadelphia soon spread all over the East. There is hardly a memoir or regimental history that does not extol the virtues of the kindness and hospitality of the citizens of Philadelphia who contributed so much so freely without any government subsidy during the entire period of the war and even afterward.[147]

> *The ladies of the Refreshment Saloons Committees, on many a wintry night, when they have waited to welcome, with kind words, the nation's defenders, and to serve food to revive their weary frames, have been repaid for their labor by the grateful thanks and "God bless you!" of the noble patriots, and these soldiers have, without exception, exclaimed, "If ever Philadelphia needs defenders she will find them in the men whom their kindness has succored!"*[148]

At emergencies such as the Gettysburg invasion, the ladies replied: "If the hour of danger ever threatens we will remember your promise. Soldiers, that hour has come. Shall they not find you to have forgotten? Shall they welcome you again to our city as the defenders of their homes and fire-sides, or shall they wait in vain?"

Another soldier who passed through the city and had been entertained at the refreshment saloons later wrote in his memoirs: "The soldiers entertain a high regard in Philadelphia. Nowhere else that I have been are soldiers

Inside the Union Volunteer Refreshment Saloon. A contemporary lithograph of the inside portion of the Union Volunteer Refreshment Saloon. Here, many soldiers and sailors were fed and cared for while passing through the city. *GAR Museum Collection.*

treated with so much consideration and respect as there. The rations served there are of a quality good enough for the most fastidious, and that peculiar air: 'Good enough for soldiers seems to be entirely wanting among these benevolent people.'"[149]

The Cooper Shop Soldiers' Home was chartered by the Court of Common Pleas for the county of Philadelphia on February 15, 1862. The purpose of this home was to aid or house discharged veterans from the army and the navy and to take care of those who were disabled, sick or otherwise in need of assistance and could not reach home unassisted. The managers found a suitable building, one that previously had been used as a hospital, on the northwest corner of Race and Crown Streets (present-day Race Street between Fourth and Fifth Streets on the north side midway between both streets). The committee purchased adjacent buildings from the state, and city councils generously permitted the use of another structure that belonged to the city. The first money, $2,400, for the establishment of such a home was raised by means of a fair conducted by the female volunteers of the Cooper Shop under the direction of Miss Anna M. Ross.

After it was open, any soldier passing through Philadelphia could obtain meals and lodgings there. Three years later, by an act of legislature, the Cooper Shop Soldiers' Home was permitted to merge with another similar institution, the Soldiers' Home of Philadelphia, and the two became one organization in the spring of 1865.[150]

Many thousands of Southern refugees, freedmen and Confederate prisoners were also beneficiaries of the kindness of the refreshment saloons. In fact, an announcement appeared in the Great Central Fair's newspaper, *Our Daily Fair*, and in the newspaper of the Union Refreshment Saloon, the *Fair Record*, which informed the public that visitors to the fair, then in progress in June 1864, would see a large number of Confederates from Vicksburg, then being guarded through the city en route to Fort Delaware. These unfortunates were, however, well fed upon reaching the ever-bountiful refreshment saloons.

Near the close of the war, some prominent citizens, including the distinguished lawyer, and war veteran Joseph G. Rosengarten, founded a committee to help former Confederate soldiers find employment. It was called the Association to Procure Employment for Rebel Deserters who have taken the Oath of Allegiance to the United States. For this purpose the sum of $2,875 was raised. Green meal tickets to be presented at the Union Volunteer Refreshment Saloon were issued to many of these refugees, but the larger part of the fund was eventually turned over to the institution.

Daily Bible classes were also conducted in the spacious chapel provided for that purpose, and in the evenings musical entertainments were provided for the men. Although the Cooper Shop Refreshment Saloon closed on August 28, 1865, its Soldiers' Home continued to operate until 1872.

Another school for returned veterans similar to that set up in the Cooper Shop Soldiers' Home was established by the Reverend John Long at the Christian Street Hospital, of which he was chaplain, in January 1865. Here the soldiers were taught the workings of the telegraph and similar manual occupations.[151]

In April 1866, the home and its functions moved into a three-story brick building at Sixteenth and Filbert Streets. This building, formerly a state arsenal, had been used as the Filbert Street Hospital during the war and later the Convalescents Hospital. The state allowed the institution the use of the building without charge. The first floor contained the office, laundry, library, matron's room, dining hall, kitchen, bakery and storerooms; on the second floor were dormitories, an infirmary and an apothecary's shop. The home maintained a school for soldiers that, in addition to reading, writing and arithmetic, gave its pupils vocational training. When a veteran was discharged he received a certificate stating that he was competent to earn his own living.[152]

Benevolence of Volunteer Firemen

No one responded more promptly to the country's call in April 1861, and throughout the war, than the members of the volunteer fire companies of Philadelphia. At that time there were eighty-seven volunteer companies in existence. Firemen were numerous in all of the regiments recruited in the city, and some entire commands were composed of the firefighters, including the greater part of the 23rd PV, "Birney's Zouaves," and the entire 72nd PV, or Baxter's Philadelphia "Fire Zouaves." The firefighters were also well represented on the many warships built and manned in Philadelphia.[153]

Even those who remained at home contributed significantly to the war effort. They volunteered for the Home Guard and the Emergency Militia but continued to fight fires in the city during the war and offered the use of their horses for any emergency service. Twice in the course of the war, at the request of Fire Chief David M. Lyle, the Hibernia Engine Company sent its powerful steam engine, with a detail of men, to Fortress Monroe and Washington for use of the military.[154]

The first organization of Philadelphia firemen who served in the field was Captain William McMullen's "Rangers," a company recruited from the Moyamensing Hose Company for the three months' service under General Robert Patterson in the spring of 1861.[155]

The total number of Philadelphia firemen who served in the Union army between 1861 and 1865 is estimated at approximately eleven thousand.[156]

A noteworthy accomplishment of many of the fire companies was the volunteer ambulance service they established. With money subscribed by the firemen and their friends, thirty-five ornate ambulances were built and maintained at the firehouses. These vehicles were kept in constant readiness for use. Upon the arrival of hospital ships or trains filled with wounded and invalid soldiers, the electronic call "9-6" was sent out and repeated and bells were rung in the fire towers, and immediately, the ambulances sped for the riverfront or the depots. As an example of their service, in the five days before Christmas 1862, the ambulances carried 2,500 patients from the Citizens' Volunteer Hospital alone to other hospitals throughout the city.

A great rivalry existed between the fire companies in the decoration of their handsome vehicles. In fact, even after the war, the old ambulances were kept as venerated souvenirs, displayed at exhibitions and pulled in parades.[157]

When the casualties of battle were brought to the city in great numbers, the firehouses became temporary hospitals. Many of the dead of the 72nd PV Regiment who fell at Antietam and Gettysburg were exhumed from graves on the fields where they had fought by their brother firemen and given burial in the home cemeteries.

In *Lossing's History of the Civil War* is a report that Philadelphia ambulances carried to the hospitals over 120,000 sick or wounded soldiers without cost.[158]

The Union League of Philadelphia

After many months of seemingly endless war and ever larger casualty lists, many citizens had begun to grow weary. This emboldened certain disloyal elements in the city, largely from the conservative fringe of the Democratic Party, who began to openly support the Southern rebellion and worked actively against the war effort and the Lincoln administration. Some of these individuals belonged to the social elite of the city. This disturbing situation was discussed and addressed by a group of prominent, loyal citizens. They decided to meet and invite other loyal men to gather at the residence of Mr. Benjamin Gerhard, at 226 South Fourth Street, to promote the formation of an organization whose purpose was to support the Union, its preservation and the war effort. This group was quickly dubbed the Union Club. Referring to this group years afterward, George H. Boker, a founder, wrote:

> So timid and hesitating was the beginning of the Union Club that the notice to certain gentlemen to meet in Mr. Gerhard's house seemed to contain no authority for the assemblage. The receivers of the notes of invitation were informed merely that there would be a meeting of loyal men for a patriotic purpose. There was no signature to these notes, and from the context one might have inferred that Mr. Gerhard, had abandoned his house to the use of his friends.[159]

A sketch of the newly opened Union League House in May 1865. The Union League still uses the same edifice, though expanded over the years, located at 140 South Broad Street. *GAR Museum Collection.*

Several meetings were afterward held at private homes, and these meetings seemed to revive the historic Wistar parties instituted by Dr. Caspar Wistar in his home on South Fourth Street in 1798. At one of these early meetings, held at the residence of Dr. John F. Meigs on December 27, 1862, the title of the "Union League" was adopted for use of the group, which had grown considerably. The first formal meeting of the Union League was held in Concert Hall at 1219 Chestnut Street on January 22, 1863.[160]

In the meantime, the former residence of Mr. Hartman Kuhn, at 1118 Chestnut Street, had been leased by the league for use as its headquarters. (This house, which afterward became the Baldwin Mansion and still later Keith's Theater, stood on the site now occupied by a row of modern shops.) According to reports, the members kept a supply of sturdy hickory axe handles on hand for use in the defense of the League House and possibly also against Rebel soldiers should they enter Philadelphia.[161]

The first elected president of the Union League was William Morris Meredith, then serving as attorney general of the state. The membership

Union League Memorial Tablet. A sketch of the memorial in the hall of the Union League House commemorating the units raised by the Union League for Civil War service. *GAR Museum Collection.*

had grown to 536 members by 1863.[162] The first League House was opened to members on February 23, 1863, and the Union League immediately became a powerful center of support for the Union cause and war effort. In fact, a national movement was launched based on the Philadelphia Union League's mission and resulted in the creation of hundreds of similar leagues throughout the loyal states. After the war, they were revived by the freedmen and their supporters and established in the South. This was received with contempt by many of the former Southern Confederate supporters, and these loyal leagues became prime targets of the Ku Klux Klan and other anti-black groups.

One of the first committees formed by the Union League was the Military Committee, which was established to raise funds to assist in the recruitment, organization and equipping of volunteer units for army service. The members of the committee formed a virtual who's who of the socially prominent Union men who were in support of the military and the Union. Many had sons and relatives then serving in the armed forces.[163]

As an inducement to secure recruits, the Union League offered a bounty of $300 to each volunteer soldier, expending funds on bounties totaling hundreds of thousands of dollars.

In early June 1863, league members met and agreed to form a committee to assist in the recruitment of Colored Troops. As a result, a large number of league members formally petitioned the government for permission to raise black regiments. Thereafter, the army established Camp William Penn, just beyond the Philadelphia city line, where African American volunteers from the region were gathered to train and organize under the command of Lieutenant Colonel Louis Wagner of the 88th Pennsylvania Volunteer Regiment. Wagner became an active member of the league after the war. The Union League, through its Military Committee, assisted in this enterprise by spending over $33,000 on equipment, uniforms, bounties and support for their families. Each regiment at muster into Federal service was presented with a stand of colors also funded by the league.[164]

Many prominent civic leaders supported the wartime activities of the Union League, and especially the effort to recruit Colored Troops. Frederick Douglass, the best-known black abolitionist, was often a guest of the league and gave impassioned speeches there in support of its work. Douglass spoke effectively on July 1, 1863, during the Gettysburg emergency when the first colored volunteers were enlisting.[165]

During the period of the war, the Publication Committee also issued many patriotic circulars and pamphlets in support of the war, as well as the *Union League Gazette*, of which 560,000 copies were printed and distributed.[166]

The Union League also supported veterans by caring for sick, wounded and disabled men and their families after their discharge and establishing a bureau to assist them in finding employment. This effort continues unabated to the present time through the work of the Armed Services Council.

On May 11, 1865, the Union League moved into its new house at 140 Broad Street, which it has occupied to the present time.[167]

A bronze tablet placed in the corridor of the Union League House and two bronze figures of soldiers stand on pedestals in front of the Union League building on South Broad Street as memorials to the veterans' of war service in the history of this influential and patriotic organization.[168]

Civil War Philadelphia Railroad Transportation

During the four years of war, Philadelphia railroads played a conspicuous part, constantly transporting a steady stream of men and supplies to the South and returning with wounded Union soldiers and Confederate prisoners. As soon as hostilities commenced, the Philadelphia, Wilmington and Baltimore Railroad stationed men to guard its bridges and to act as a military corps. To allay suspicion, the men were set to work whitewashing bridges, of which some received six or seven coats, but it was reported that this precaution prevented rust from forming. In April 1861, the line was taken in charge by the Federal government through an agent in Philadelphia, and all equipment under government control, as well as troop trains, was sent out as quickly as possible. An uninterrupted route to Washington was nearly completed by April 25, 1861.[169]

It was on this railroad line that an armored car was first used. Built by Baldwin Locomotive Works, the tank-like car consisted of a railroad car made of boiler iron. In the interior of the car, cannon were set on a pivot, which enabled them to be fired through portholes. For the protection of the train, this mounted battery was located in front of the locomotive.

The North Central Railroad, which was soon controlled by the Pennsylvania Railroad, sent patrols along the southern border of the state as a safeguard against Rebel raids. The Philadelphia and Reading Railroad, occupied in carrying coal from the upstate Pennsylvania coalfields down to the river terminals for the navy, was taken over by the government in the summer of 1864 to assure continuous transportation of the vital fuel during strikes by the miners.

All the railroads in and around Philadelphia were generous in their contributions toward the relief of soldiers' families, military hospitals and orphans' homes and in their purchases of government bonds.[170]

WARTIME SERVICE OF THE RAILROADS

In 1861, Philadelphia's rail connections with the South consisted of the PW & B, the Pennsylvania, the Northern Central and the Cumberland Valley Railroad, which led into central Pennsylvania. The importance of these lines, from a military standpoint, was recognized long before the outbreak of the war, and some were caught in the middle of the conflict on several occasions. Although the burden of responsibility was heavy and constant, the officers of these lines worked nobly to support the Union throughout the war. This patriotic attitude of the railroad officials had already been exhibited in the safe conduct of President-elect Lincoln to Washington from Harrisburg via Philadelphia on the night of February 22, 1861.

Realizing that some of the disloyal element in Maryland might attempt to damage railroad property, President Samuel M. Felton, of the PW & B, organized a select force of about two hundred men to guard the bridges and act, if necessary, as a military body. A train was kept in readiness to concentrate them at any time. Immediately following the transportation of the 6th Massachusetts Regiment and the unarmed Washington Brigade of Philadelphians under General Small into Baltimore, ending in the Baltimore Riot, the mayor and police commissioners of Baltimore ordered the destruction of the railroad bridges. The work was entrusted to a force under the charge of Isaac R. Trimble, formerly a superintendent of the railroad company, later a Confederate general.

As a result, on April 20, a number of bridges were burned. All telegraph wires leading from Baltimore were cut. It required twenty-four days of hard work to repair the damage. In the meantime, troops and supplies were carried from Perryville, where the PW & B, railroad terminated at the Susquehanna River, and via Havre de Grace on the large transport steamer *Maryland*, the Philadelphia ice boat and other vessels, to Annapolis, Maryland, and then to Washington via the B & O Railroad.

With the occupation of Baltimore by a Federal force under General B.F. Butler and the arrest of the pro-Southern leaders, the Union sentiment of the city again returned and brought peace and stability once again. The only further damage done was in July 1864 by a raiding party known as "Gilmour's Guerillas," which partially burned the Gunpowder River Bridge and a few cars.

The PW & B Railroad was destined to become the greatest military transportation hub in history up to that time. This modern rail connection between Philadelphia and Baltimore was created in the 1830s by the consolidation of several connecting railroad companies to link the two cities. An iron bridge proved too expensive to build; consequently, the Susquehanna River terminal was changed to Perryville on the north and Havre de Grace on the south side and would be connected by a ferry. By 1838, the lines had been completed, and utilizing the ferry system offered efficient through service to Baltimore and back to Philadelphia. The terminals at the Broad and Prime Streets Depot in Philadelphia and President's Street Station in Baltimore linked the cities and also offered connections to the Baltimore & Ohio's Baltimore–Washington branch and other railroads between Philadelphia and New York City. The PW & B quickly became a strategic link in a network of railroads handling a burgeoning rail service along the Washington-Baltimore-Philadelphia–New York corridor.

This strategic position benefited the cause of the Union during the Civil War. The line was crucial to the war by steadily funneling troops and war materials from the Northeast to the warfronts and the capital. The rail line also played a significant role in the war's first bloodshed. On April 19, 1861, an angry mob of Southern sympathizers in Baltimore attacked Union troops who were attempting to transfer from the President Street terminal to the Baltimore & Ohio's Camden Station. In what became known as the Baltimore or Pratt Street Riots, four Massachusetts militiamen and one Philadelphian were killed, and as many as twenty-five citizens were killed by the troops.[171]

Thomas A. Scott was granted a leave of absence from the Pennsylvania Railroad in 1861 in order to serve the government as assistant secretary of war. He was thirty-seven years old and endowed with great energy, as well as experience. It was his task to facilitate the movement of troops by rail and to establish telegraphic service in the field. At his insistence, the first military telegraph station in America was opened in the office of Governor Curtin at Harrisburg, April 17, 1861, by William Bender Wilson, who later became manager of military telegraphs at Washington.[172]

Scott was given a commission by President Lincoln as colonel of the District of Columbia Volunteers. Among the young men summoned to Washington to aid him was Frank Thomson, who was not yet twenty years old but was well versed in the line of work assigned to him. Under the orders of Colonel Scott, he organized the Military Telegraphic Corps, the first auxiliary of its kind in the world, from among the dispatchers of the Pennsylvania Railroad. It was the duty of this corps to maintain the important lines used by the armies in the field in serviceable condition.[173]

The Northern Central Railroad, in which the Pennsylvania Railroad soon afterward acquired a controlling interest, was operated as a separate corporation. Other managers of the different lines were induced to cooperate with Superintendent Enoch Lewis and Division Superintendent Samuel D. Young, of the Pennsylvania System, in maintaining a mounted patrol along the southern border of the state as a safeguard against raids. The members of this patrol made constant use of a telegraph line extending from Chambersburg to Bedford, keeping the railroad officials at Harrisburg and, through them, the War Department fully informed of movements by the enemy. It was due to the energy of the Northern Central officials that the five companies of militia from the interior of Pennsylvania, known now as the "First Defenders," were promptly and safely conveyed to Washington on April 18, 1861, being the very first volunteers to arrive after Lincoln called for troops for the defense of the capital.[174]

Until the start of the Civil War, the railroad had never been a factor in military campaigns. The constant destruction and rebuilding of tracks and bridges by the enemy in the earlier part of the war made it essential to use experts familiar with the work of rebuilding. In April 1862, the secretary of war called on Herman Haupt of Philadelphia, an engineer and graduate of West Point who had previously occupied the position of the Pennsylvania Railroad's first general superintendent. He was appointed chief of construction and transportation, with the rank of colonel. In recognition of invaluable services rendered the government, Colonel Haupt was promoted to the rank of brigadier general in September 1862. General Haupt and his subordinates performed heroic service in many times of need and danger.[175]

Prominent among the railroad men who served in this branch of the army were W.W. Wright, of the Pennsylvania Railroad staff, who became General Sherman's chief of construction on the campaign through Georgia and the Carolinas; General Adna Anderson; and E.C. Smeed. It was with the cooperation of such practical engineers that, under the active personal supervision of Colonel Thomas A. Scott, Colonel D.C. McCallum, successor to General Haupt, was able to transport the 11th and 12th Corps of the Army of the Potomac in September 1863 after the Battle of Gettysburg. He moved this force of twenty-two thousand men, with all of their equipment and supplies, to the support of Grant and Sherman's armies of the Western Theater from their base at Catlett's Station, Virginia, to Georgia and Tennessee, over a distance of nearly 1,200 miles in eight days.[176]

William J. Palmer, private secretary in 1861 to President John Edgar Thompson of the Pennsylvania Railroad, resigned to take command of the famous "Anderson Troop" of cavalry. In 1862, he recruited this force to a full regiment and took command of the 15th Pennsylvania Cavalry, which he continued to lead to the end of the war.[177]

A number of high-ranking officers in the Federal army left work with the railroads for service to their country and had outstanding achievements in their military career. One of the most famous Philadelphia railroad men was George Brinton McClellan, of the Ohio and Mississippi Railroad Company, a former captain of the regular army who succeeded General Scott as commander of the U.S. Army.[178]

The patriotism and devotion to the Union of the Philadelphia railroad workers and officials are illustrated in a circular issued to all employees by the Philadelphia and Reading Railroad, proposing to them to devote one day's pay in each month to the purchase of government bonds, with the interest to be reinvested until the close of the war. This request was generally complied with.

The Railroad companies voted large sums of money to the relief of soldiers' families. The Philadelphia and Reading Railroad performed valuable service throughout the war by the rapid transportation of troops and actively providing coal at its tidewater terminals for naval use. When considerable disruptions occurred among the immigrant miners in the coal regions, and in resistance to drafts, it required the stationing of troops in those sections of the state. Some front-line troops were lost to the front.[179]

Through at least a portion of the war, the official envelopes of the Pennsylvania Railroad bore the popular insignia of cannon and flags. The subscriptions made at various times by the Pennsylvania Railroad for the help of the Great Central Sanitary Fair and the military hospitals were substantial. The railroad also made donations for homes for orphans of deceased soldiers and sailors.[180]

The Philadelphia railroad depots during the course of the war consisted of: New York line depots—Kensington Depot and the Walnut Street Wharf; Baltimore and Washington Line Depot—Broad and Prime Streets; Pennsylvania Central Depot—Thirtieth and Market Streets; Philadelphia and Reading Depot—Broad and Callowhill Streets; West Chester and Media Depot—Thirty-first and Market Streets; Philadelphia, Germantown and Norristown Depot—Ninth and Greene Streets; and North Pennsylvania Depot—Third and Thompson Streets.[181]

The railroads played a significant role in transporting troops, citizens and manufactured goods and war material, as well as the returning veterans, both living and dead, who were welcomed home in a respectful and fitting manner.

War Industries and Manufacturing

At the outset of the Civil War, Philadelphia was a major hub of commercial enterprise, manufacturing, transportation and heavy industry in the nation. By 1860, the city boasted of 6,314 manufactories, including 525 in textiles, 649 in iron and steel and 1,523 in garments and apparel. Over 17 percent of the laborers in Philadelphia worked in manufacturing areas.[182] Despite a number of economic crises that preceded the outbreak of war—such as the loss of Southern markets, a persistent recession, the loss of hard currency and accompanying bank closures, falling stocks of goods, unemployment and uncertainty—most businesses adapted. The flurry of activity as the call for troops and the contracts for arms, clothing and equipment bolstered the economy.[183]

Prior to Secession, Philadelphia had enjoyed substantial trade with the Southern states. These ties were now severed with economic losses and the creation of uncertainty. But quickly, the city's manufacturing base adjusted, and an upswing in government work and contracts brightened the outlook. Just weeks after Lincoln's election, the *Public Ledger* was already reporting that the city manufacturers seemed undisturbed by the state of affairs, and optimism prevailed on the economy.[184]

Philadelphia firms began to manufacture military goods in great quantity, especially in shipbuilding and engine machinery along the Delaware River. Thomas Potter made knapsacks, employing over 2,400 workers. Clothing and uniform production increased. Henry Simons produced wagons, gun carriages and ambulances. The North, Chase & North Foundries produced shot and shell. Sheble & Fisher pitchfork and rake factory converted to producing swords and bayonets, and Van Dyke Lamp Company turned out one thousand pairs of cavalry spurs per day. Baldwin Locomotive Works on the southwest corner of Broad and Spring Garden ramped up production to keep up with the demands of the military railroad, erecting new shops and foundries and adding workers during the war.

William Horstmann & Sons, one of the largest prewar military regalia, uniforms and military goods firms, expanded its business exponentially, even spinning off the manufacture of certain types of goods to subcontractors, such as the making of battle flags for military units. Two former craftsmen at Horstmann left to create their own firm, Evans & Hassell, which then competed with Horstmann for contracts to make regimental battle flags. Charles Stokes, a textile manufacturer, turned to military contracts and produced army trousers. He humorously ran advertisements in the press asking: "What is the use of a great *seat of war* for a *standing army?*" He promised that his establishment made *"breeches to cover the rear!"*[185]

The development of a massive and efficient system of organized supply of manufactured goods was perfected during the war by Philadelphia-raised Quartermaster General Montgomery C. Meigs. His competent efforts created the impetus that led to the manufacture of all the numerous items necessary to the management of the war and marshaled private industry to rise to fill the contracts to supply the goods needed. Many military items were also manufactured at the Philadelphia Quartermaster Depot, known as the Schuylkill Arsenal, at Grays Ferry. This facility was managed for the Quartermaster's Department by Colonel George H. Crossman. Crossman and Meigs, after an initial period of ramping up and inefficiency, were able to establish a very efficient system of contracting that led to the ability to completely outfit military units for service as they were needed. In this system, the state apparatus cooperated closely with the U.S. Army to outfit the volunteers as they came into service.[186]

Philadelphia also featured a large pool of willing laborers, many of whom were skilled in their crafts. Although the war forced declining real wages after adjustment for inflation, there was never a shortage of work. Labor was also supported by a benevolent community that provided funds and support for the families of workers who entered military service. A budding labor movement was also established in Philadelphia that would grow stronger in the postwar years.

There were also dangers at home in the workplace. Accidents were common, and the city faced a tragedy on March 29, 1862, when Professor

Jackson's cartridge factory on Tenth and Reed Streets in Southwark blew up. The explosion killed seven workers, including two women and the owner's son, and wounded over sixty-five. Sparks, as well as body parts, were thrown onto homes in the vicinity in a horrible tragedy, as recorded in the press.[187]

Practically every kind of product, goods and provision was manufactured in Philadelphia on government contract. Some of the largest and most noted firms included Alfred Jenks Company at Richmond and Franklin Streets in Bridesburg, which produced thousands of Springfield pattern rifled muskets; Francis Jahn, which produced swords; Thomas Sparks, which made bullets and shot; and Bush Hill Iron Works, which produced naval Dahlgren guns. The list is long and laced with the names of commercial manufacturers who turned to the production of military items. This was in addition to the government arsenal and armories. The navy yard employed close to three thousand workers building or repairing ships. The Frankford Arsenal produced shot, shell, mini-ball cartridges and percussion caps in enormous quantities. The Schuylkill Arsenal Quartermaster Depot continued to produce vast quantities of uniforms, camp equipage (cooking implements, tentage, tent poles, canvas, etc.), harness and saddles and leather goods. Lead production, cordage, lumber, brewing and sundry other items necessary to an active military campaign were also produced in Philadelphia factories.[188]

Philadelphia companies also produced an array of items and goods needed by the Quartermaster in quantity. Items such as flags, banners and guidons, brass musical instruments, medical supplies, surgical instruments, artificial limbs for amputees, medicines, boots and shoes, as well as leather goods for military uses, were turned out on contract by the factories and firms of Philadelphia to meet the needs of individuals and entire commands. There were such a large number of textile mills operating in Germantown producing clothing, uniforms, blankets and hosiery that the term "Germantown Goods" signified the prowess of that sector of production.

Even the fanciful needs of the soldier and the citizen were met by the tripling of beer brewing, whisky distilling and entertainment, including the new CDV (carte de visite) photograph fad that was so popular during and after the war. Frederick Gutekunst had a photographic studio on 704 Walnut Street that rivaled Matthew Brady's studios. Also, food production was a major industry, supplying sugar, hard bread and canned goods to the troops. In short, there was really no item that could not be supplied to the military or homefront by Philadelphia manufacturers.[189]

These manufacturers profited greatly during the war from government contracts, tariff protection and flexible methods in production and markets. The large increase in wartime production led to increased capital investment, especially in textiles, iron and steel industries, during the war and sustained afterward into peacetime. Wartime commander Colonel William Gray, for example, went from manufacturing swords to gas fixtures after the war.[190]

Financing the War

Closely related to the importance of the industrial output at home was the necessity to finance the growing needs of the war. While the men were away fighting, those who remained at home soon became aware of the enormous amounts of money required to support the war in the field and the federal and local governments at home. This task was accomplished by the persistent efforts of Jay Cooke. In January 1861, the Philadelphia financier, with his brother-in-law, William G. Moorhead, organized the firm of Jay Cooke and Company. This firm was brought to the attention of the new secretary of the treasury, Salmon Chase. After successfully selling some of Chase's earliest loans, Cooke was offered the position of assistant treasurer of the United States in Philadelphia soon after the outbreak of the war. Cooke initially refused this offer, admitting that his main object was the selling of government notes and bonds. About the middle of May 1861, the state legislature, sitting in an extra session, passed an act that called for the organization of an army for state defense, to be designated as the Pennsylvania Reserve Volunteer Corps, or Pennsylvania Reserves. In order to equip and maintain this command, the legislature had authorized a $3 million loan at 6 percent interest. As the state credit was low, due to previous and somewhat reckless expenditures for internal improvements, it was thought that the loan could not be sold at par, a condition included in the act. However, Mr. Cooke intervened and volunteered to sell the loan at par, which he thought was possible. Accordingly on May 28, 1861, Governor Curtin

Jay Cooke's Bank was located on South Third Street next to the old Girard Bank. From here, Cooke helped to finance the war effort. *GAR Museum Collection.*

commissioned the firms of Jay Cooke and Company and Drexel and Company to organize the work, and in a little over two weeks the entire loan was sold, much to the surprise and gratification of the governor.[191]

Jay Cooke again visited the Philadelphia bankers after the disastrous defeat of the Union army at the First Battle of Bull Run in June 1861 in an effort to secure additional money for the government to be advanced for a period of sixty days. The lenders were asked to take their payment not in hard currency but in "seven-thirty" government notes. These were treasury notes that ran for three years with an interest rate of 7 3/10 percent per annum, or $7.30 a year on each $100.00. The earliest seven-thirty bond issue Jay Cooke made famous by continuous and extensive advertising. During this period, Secretary of the Treasury Chase—whom Cooke had known through Chase's friendship with Cooke's brother William, an influential newspaper editor in Ohio—held various conferences in Washington, Philadelphia and New York that resulted in the formation of the Associated Banks, a group of banks in those three cities that agreed to advance $50 million to Chase and the government and to follow this loan with additional ones in October and December, if the rebellion persisted. In all, they promised to loan the government $150 million, an enormous sum for the times.[192]

One of the most popular locations for the subscription of seven-thirties in Philadelphia was Cooke's office, which he opened at 114 South Third Street, next to the old Girard Bank. As the war continued and constantly demanded additional funding, the banks found it difficult to keep their agreement to pay $50 million more dollars. When the December payment came due, with the result that the hard currency system collapsed, Secretary Chase found it necessary to issue paper money, called greenbacks, to pay the debt.

While Philadelphia citizens were purchasing seven-thirty bonds, the newspapers warned their readers to guard against what was termed a "new method of swindling." Certain guilty parties obtained a number of bonds of the seven-thirty loans and, after cutting off the coupons, endeavored to sell the bonds at par or at a slight reduction to unsuspecting purchasers, who discovered sorrowfully that bonds minus coupons paid no interest to the holder.

Early in 1862, while the country remained on a paper money basis and inflation became rampant, Secretary Chase unsuccessfully attempted to sell another issue of bonds called "five-twenties." These bonds, bearing interest in gold, were so designated because they might be redeemed in five years and must be redeemed in twenty years. Offered at par in greenbacks, which only paid forty to ninety cents in gold, the bonds proved to be unpopular until October 1862, when Jay Cooke was made the sole national agent. By the end of the following March, the daily subscription rate was estimated to be $1 million. It had been planned to close the loan when the sum of $500 million was procured, and the date set for the end of the sales period was January 21, 1864. However, before the machinery that Mr. Cooke had created could be stopped, an additional $11 million worth of bonds was sold, making the total amount for the loan $511 million.[193]

Throughout the war, the efforts of Cooke and other private financiers such as A.J. Drexel continued unabated on the national level and contributed immensely to the successful financing of the war effort, thereby making Cooke, Drexel and the others very wealthy men.

Training Camps

Volunteers were often recruited into a unit at local sites set up in towns and cities. After a man enlisted by signing a muster roll, undergoing a cursory physical examination and being sworn into service, he was sent to a military camp for the particular unit, usually set up on open spaces in the vicinity. The new recruit was supplied with a uniform and assigned to a tent. Now began an extended period of indoctrination into army life and routine.

Army regulations called for the camps to be laid out in a fixed grid-like pattern, with officers' tents at the front end of each street and enlisted men's tents aligned along a company street, facing opposite one another. The camp was set up with the color line, or line for formation to the rear of the tents, and the line of field and staff at the other end. Regulations also defined where the mess tents, medical area and baggage trains should be located. This was the usual pattern when in training at the outset of enlistment, but frequently at later periods of service, when such regularity was not feasible or possible due to time constraints, field campaigning, weather conditions or hilly or narrow terrain, it often became impossible to meet army regulations. The campgrounds themselves were picked by the quartermasters and placed on open ground, with shade nearby, a source of water, proximity to transportation and, if possible, away from the distractions of the public. Such characteristics were not always possible, and the campsites were often abysmal, where rain and storm produced thick mud in winter and spring and dust and heat in the summer.[194]

Troops were housed in canvas tents. At the beginning of the war, the army supplied the Sibley tent, named for its inventor, Henry H. Sibley, who later became a Confederate general. It was a large cone of canvas, eighteen feet in diameter, twelve feet tall and supported by a center pole. The tent had a circular opening at the top for ventilation and a cone-shaped stove for heat. Although designed to fit a dozen men comfortably, army regulations assigned up to twenty-four men to each tent, leading to cramped, uncomfortable quarters. When closed, there was little or no ventilation and the air inside the tent became foul and fetid with the odors of men who bathed infrequently.[195]

Other tents were also issued, such as the A-frame or wedge tent whose design dated back to the Revolutionary War period and, later, the "dog" tent, with two six- by six-foot wedges, which were buttoned together and shared by two men. In wartime service in winter, crude wooden huts were built with an inner fireplace and canvas roof.[196]

In training camp, the average soldier's day began at 5:00 a.m. in the summer and 6:00 a.m. in the winter, when he was awakened by reveille. After the first sergeant took the roll, the men ate breakfast they prepared themselves or grouped together in an informal mess. The troops were then drilled for as many as five sessions per day. Here the rookie troops learned how to march, the manual of arms and how to perform various maneuvers. Drill sessions lasted approximately two hours each and, for most men, were exercises in tedium. One soldier described his days in the army like this: "The first thing in the morning is drill in the manual of arms and evolutions of the line. Then drill, and drill again. Then drill, drill, a little more drill. Then drill, and lastly drill."[197]

In the intervals between duties, soldiers cleaned the camp, built roads, dug trenches for latrines (called sinks) and gathered wood for cooking and heating. Finding clean water was a constant goal; the lack of potable water was a problem that led to widespread disease. While in fixed camps in towns and cities, the soldiers were relatively well fed and supplied. Sutlers, or merchants authorized by the army, were also available to supply their needs for a hefty price. Supplies became limited when troops went on the march or campaign and supplies could not reach them in the field. Then the troops were forced to live off the land.

Boredom was rampant, and the days in camp tended to drag on endlessly. The sheer tedium of camp life led the men to attempt to find recreational outlets. "There is some of the orneriest men here that I ever saw," wrote a new recruit, "and the most swearing and card playing and 'fitin' [fighting] and drunkenness that I ever saw at any place."

When not drilling or performing routine duties such as guard mount, the troops read, wrote letters home and played a variety of games, including baseball, cards, boxing matches, checkers and chess. Although most commanders attempted to control vice in camp, both gambling and drinking were rampant, especially after payday. Army regulations prohibited the purchase and use of alcohol by enlisted men, and soldiers who violated the rule were punished, but the men found ways around it. When not drinking or gambling, some men escaped the tedium of daily army life by visiting prostitutes who often followed the troops. Thousands of prostitutes thronged the cities in the war zones and clustered about the camps.[198] After a certain amount of time spent learning how to "soldier," it often came as a relief to receive marching orders to proceed for assignment at the front.

There were a large number of army camps created in Philadelphia to train the huge influx of volunteers. Most of these camps were set up on open spaces on the edge of the city. Early in the war, even the city parks were used as camping grounds. Thus, Washington Square, Franklin Square, Logan Square and even Center Square (city hall today) were employed for regimental camps. Many of these grounds were being used as baseball fields, racetracks or for agricultural fairs. So many training camps, known as "camps of instruction," were established in the open fields along Ridge Avenue that the name "Champs de Mars" (military training ground in French) was given to the two-mile stretch extending from Columbia Avenue (today Cecil B. Moore Avenue) to Robin Hood Dell in East Fairmount Park. Here, the regimental camps and noteworthy events during the war were more numerous than in any other portion of the city.[199]

The largest military camp in Philadelphia was Camp Cadwalader, located along Islington Lane (now Twenty-second and Diamond Streets) east of Ridge Road fronting on Twenty-second Street, and across from several large cemeteries (Glenwood, American Mechanics and Odd Fellows), now removed and replaced by the Johnson Housing Project. A large number of regiments were organized and trained here. In fact, this became known as the Civil War Plaza due to the many regiments trained here, as well as the fixed cantonment that became Camp Cadwalader. One of the more memorable incidents of the war at this site was the large battle flag presentation to five newly organized regiments on December 5, 1861, by the governor, Andrew G. Curtin, and other dignitaries. At the ceremony were gathered many prominent citizens, officers and a large assembly of family members and friends of the soldiers, as well as a huge crowd of spectators. Pennsylvania state battle flags were presented in a moving ceremony to the 58th, 67th, 90th and 91st Pennsylvania Volunteer Infantry Regiments and the 6th Pennsylvania Cavalry, Rush's Lancers.

Later, this camp became a permanent point of assemblage and the most important military rendezvous in the city. Recruits were housed here, and regiments organized and mustered into service. This camp consisted of an extensive group of barracks and other buildings enclosed by a high board fence with a platform around the edge manned by the guard. At times, the camp was very overcrowded, and later it was severely criticized by soldiers and the public. A camp of guards was also maintained here to keep order, the guards coming chiefly from the Veterans Reserve Corps, a force of invalid soldiers who could perform light duties. Many volunteer regiments were mustered into service here, and a large number of the returning commands were sent here to be mustered out of the army.

Early on, a series of military training camps was similarly established along Islington Lane along the Schuylkill River in open areas west of Girard College. Camps Edwards, Ballier and Wallace were located on Islington Lane opposite the old Odd Fellows Cemetery.

Camp Chase was the site of Edgar Gregory's 91st PV regiment. The regiment's recruiting headquarters, however, were at the Girard House hotel on Chestnut Street downtown. The camp was on the Darby Road, about three-quarters of a mile below Gray's Ferry Bridge in West Philadelphia. The location of the tent camp had "a fine growth of trees" on the east, "ample drainage" to the south and a large space in front of the tents for drill and parades. On September 29, 1861, religious services were held in camp at 4:00 p.m., with a Reverend Seiz officiating and "crowds of visitors" in attendance. A "benefit" was held for the regiment at the Academy of Music in the middle of October 1861. In November, they took part in a procession honoring Colonel Edward D. Baker, recently killed in action at Ball's Bluff.[200]

On November 3, two privates had a fight, which Colonel Gregory broke up. An early newspaper article described the 91st PV as "a splendid regiment," with men who "are not only above the average in size, but are also well disciplined, obedient and steady." All men were ordered to report back to camp on December 24, 1861, from a Christmas furlough in order to share a Christmas dinner at the Union Volunteer Refreshment Saloon. The regiment left camp on January 21, 1862, and proceeded under orders to Washington.[201]

The *Inquirer* reported on camp life and encouraged citizens to visit the camps, which it promised "cannot but prove interesting." Those who desired to witness drill were told to attend at 6:30 a.m., 12:00 p.m. (every other day) and 6:30 p.m. The cars of the Ridge Avenue Railroad left from Second and Arch Streets and proceeded up Ninth Street to Ridge Avenue and then directly to the camps.[202]

Philadelphia during the Gettysburg Campaign

FORTIFICATIONS

Sometime after the outbreak of the Civil War, a proposal was made that the city should prepare for the danger of a possible attack. Accordingly, a few small defensive earthworks were erected at various defensible places, but they were never occupied by troops. They were situated as follows: a redoubt on the hill in East Fairmount Park at the intersection of the main drive from Lemon Hill and Girard Avenue; at the head of the Girard Avenue Bridge (the embankments were leveled at the close of the war); a small half-moon artillery redoubt on the north side of Gray's Ferry Road, between the Schuylkill Arsenal Depot and the Schuylkill River, on the eastern side; a redoubt on the rocks formerly known as the Cliffs, on the west side of the Schuylkill, near the end of the railroad bridge at Gray's Ferry (the fort and the rocks were eliminated by the railroad after the war); an earthwork on the north side of Market Street west of the Schuylkill River, on the rise of the hill west of Thirty-sixth Street; an earthwork on Chestnut Street (south side) east of the junction with Darby Road; and an earthwork on Lancaster Avenue near Hestonville, West Philadelphia.[203]

Local Defenses in June 1863

During the Confederate invasion of Pennsylvania in June 1863, a real threat existed to Philadelphia. Accordingly, a Committee of Defense was authorized by city councils to establish fortifications for defense and improve those that had already been started, defending the principal approaches to the city from the west. The positions of these earthworks were determined by officers of the United States Coast Survey stationed in Philadelphia under Professor Alexander Dallas Bache.[204]

They were located as follows: on the south side of Chestnut Street, east of the junction of Darby Road, east of the Schuylkill River, near the Schuylkill Arsenal; west of the Schuylkill River, below Gray's Ferry Bridge; at the east end of Girard Avenue bridge; in Hestonville, near Lancaster Avenue; and on School House Lane, above Ridge Avenue in East Falls. The largest of these works, located at the falls of the Schuylkill and known as Fort Dana, was created by a force of seven hundred city workers from the gasworks, as well as volunteers from the vicinity and the clergy.[205] Fort Dana was constructed during the panic caused by Lee's invasion of Pennsylvania at the end of June and into early July 1863. It was the largest of the several redoubts hurriedly built to protect the city. No guns were ever mounted, as the threat receded after the Battle of Gettysburg, though two two-hundred-pound Parrott cannon were ordered. No names were given to the other works.[206]

The danger ended with the Union victory at the Battle of Gettysburg and repulse of the Confederates. Several of the redoubts remained for a number of years after the war as reminders of the strenuous and, as some critics thought, unnecessary labors of the public, which had been panicked at the time.

After the war, the projecting bluff where Fort Dana had been constructed was quarried for stone and was slowly removed, though the position can be imagined if one visits the present site on the campus of Philadelphia University near the old Ravenhill Academy.[207]

Arsenals

The following were the federal arsenals and installations where military weapons, ordnance, uniforms and equipment were manufactured and stored.

Frankford Arsenal

The Frankford Arsenal is located along the Delaware River and Frankford Creek in the Bridesburg section. It was opened in 1816 on 20 acres of land purchased by the federal government. The grounds originally contained 2 stone buildings but later grew to over 234 buildings on 110 acres at its heyday during World War II. During its long history, it served as nerve center for U.S. military ordnance, shells, cannonballs and small-arms ammunition design, manufacture, research and development until its closure in 1977. The old arsenal was sold in 1983 and is now a private business park.[208]

At the outbreak of the Civil War, the arsenal's commander was Captain Josiah Gorgas, a native of Pennsylvania. He soon resigned in deference to his Alabama-born wife and joined the Confederate States Army and was promoted a brigadier general and chief of ordnance. In May 1861, when an effort was made to equip several three-month or ninety-day regiments from stores contained at the Frankford Arsenal, the officers protested at the antiquated, unusable muskets offered to their men.[209]

At the end of the Civil War, the arsenal employed over one thousand workers. It served as a major site for the storage of weapons and artillery pieces and a depot for the repair of artillery, cavalry and infantry equipment; repair and cleaning of small arms and harness; the manufacture of percussion caps, powder and ammunition, especially the Minié ball; and the testing of new forms of gunpowder and time fuses. During the Gettysburg Campaign, the arsenal provided tens of thousands of muskets and vast supplies of ammunition for Pennsylvania's Emergency Militia regiments. Among the innovations extensively tested at the arsenal were the Gatling gun, an early form of machine gun, and other innovations in ordnance.[210]

Schuylkill Arsenal

This depot was originally built as a U.S. Navy powder magazine. The arsenal became an ordnance depot in 1814. Later, the arsenal became a military textile (uniform) depot after 1818. The name of the Schuylkill Arsenal was changed in 1873 to the Philadelphia Depot of the Quartermaster's Department, United States Army. It was later renamed Philadelphia Quartermaster Depot in 1921. New buildings were built in 1942, and the old complex was later closed. Presently, the site is occupied by the Gray's Ferry PECO power generating plant, but the surrounding wall and some of the original buildings still stand. The facility evolved into the present-day Defense Supply Center of Philadelphia, serving all branches of the military.[211]

During the Civil War, more than ten thousand seamstresses and tailors were hired to make uniforms, clothing and equipment for Union troops. Philadelphia troops, for the most part, were equipped with supplies from the two United States arsenals in the city, especially with supplies of uniforms, blankets and various types of equipment manufactured for the Union armies in Philadelphia.[212]

ARMORIES

There were also a number of state, city and individual unit armories located in and around Philadelphia. At the outbreak of the war, there was great excitement in the city, and concern for defense was raised. Therefore, an ordinance for the protection and defense of the city was passed, along with a resolution appropriating public halls for military purposes and a resolution recommending citizens to form companies for the purpose of drilling. The ordinance for the defense and protection of the city was prefaced by a preamble, which declared:

> *At this unparalleled crisis in our national affairs, it is eminently proper that the city of Philadelphia should be placed in a condition of defense against any attack that might be made. And as arms and other munitions of war may be required here for the proper equipment of the Home Guard that are at our own disposal and can be used, should the occasion arise, for our own defense. Serving also as a means of drill to such companies as might wish to practice, and thus be well prepared at any moment to respond to their country's call as efficient artillerists.*[213]

A total of $50,000 was appropriated for the purchase of arms or other munitions of war for the use of a Home Guard or any company that may thereafter be formed for the defense of the city. One week afterward, $200,000 was added to the appropriation. The question of armories for the city military establishment became important. The city was in possession of two large market houses in the neighborhood of Broad and Race Streets. It was determined to put these buildings to military use. By ordinance of

City Armory at Broad and Race Streets. It was from this armory that many city units were uniformed and equipped for military service. *GAR Museum Collection.*

November 14, 1861, these premises, one of them at the southwest corner of Juniper and Race Streets and the other on the east side of Broad Street, below Race, were appropriated to the use of the Home Guard, under the direction of the mayor and the Committee of Defense and Protection. A budget of $3,000 was appropriated to pay for the necessary alterations. The building on Race Street was appropriated to arsenal purposes and the storage of cannon. The first piece placed in that building was a cannon with full equipments and ammunition presented to the city by a citizen, James McHenry, then residing in London. A few days afterward, two rifled guns were presented to the city by James Swain, also a native of Philadelphia and residing abroad. They were manufactured in Prussia and, when received, were placed in the Race Street armory.

Several of the militia units of the city also owned their own armories, which they used for meetings, drill, social gatherings and storage of gear. This included the National Guards, which had purchased in 1857 a lot of ground on the south side of Race Street, between Fifth and Sixth (now the National Constitution Center). A large, three-story brick building was erected, occupying the entire lot and imposing in appearance. This was the National Guards Hall. There were rooms for officers' regimental headquarters, and reading, writing, drilling, dressing, meeting and storerooms. On the second floor was a large hall with a high ceiling, occupying nearly the whole space from Race Street to Cresson's Alley. This hall was used for drill and other regimental purposes, inspections and occasionally as a public hall for lectures, fairs, concerts and meetings. It also featured accommodations for troops and, during a portion of the war, was occupied as an army hospital.

The First City Troop also built and owned an armory on the west side of Twenty-first Street at the corner of Ranstead Street. This armory was constructed in 1863. Later, this armory was replaced by the turreted, castle-like structure that stands there now. Frederick Ladner owned a "military hall" in the Northern Liberties neighborhood on Third Street and Brown. Although this building was used as a restaurant and beer hall catering to the German populace of the area and as a concert hall, it also served as an armory and meeting place for militia units, especially the German Rifle Regiment, later to become the 98th Pennsylvania Volunteers.

Many other units gathered, enlisted and rendezvoused in hotels and halls all over the city. They used the nearby parks, squares and public grounds to drill for marching and inspections.[214]

FORTS AND PRISONS

Fort Mifflin next to the Philadelphia Airport was one of the strategic harbor defenses for Philadelphia. During the Civil War, Fort Mifflin held both Union and Confederate prisoners as well as civilian prisoners. The civilian prisoners were held for draft evasion, bounty jumping and treasonous antiwar activities.

A sketch from Taylor's *Philadelphia in the Civil War* depicting Fort Mifflin, a Federal fort in Philadelphia near the present airport. *GAR Museum Collection.*

At its maximum, Fort Mifflin held 215 prisoners, and the overflow was sent to Fort Delaware, farther down the Delaware River on Pea Patch Island opposite Delaware City. A Reverend Dr. Handy was arrested for calling the Union flag an "emblem of oppression." He had refused to take an oath of allegiance and was imprisoned at Fort Mifflin for fifteen months. A large number of civilians were arrested in the infamous "Fishing Creek Confederacy" campaign in Columbia County, Pennsylvania, in August 1864 and imprisoned at Fort Mifflin in wretched conditions. They were arrested under the provisions of the controversial suspension of the writ of habeas corpus provision of the Lincoln administration. The writ was suspended ostensibly to eliminate resistance to the draft.

There were a number of military executions at Fort Mifflin during the war. The most notorious case was that of the fort's most famous prisoner, Private William H. Howe of Company A, 116th PV. He was arrested for desertion after he received a severe wound in battle and was sent home to recuperate. But he overstayed his leave, and during his apprehension, a provost guard was murdered. Howe was condemned by court-martial and ordered executed. Howe apparently led an attempted escape of two hundred prisoners from Casemate #5. He was afterward placed in solitary confinement in Casemate #11 in February 1864. Howe was held at Fort Mifflin from January 1864 until April 1864, when he was transferred to Eastern State Penitentiary, a public prison, from which he was returned to Fort Mifflin on the day of his execution, August 26, 1864. He was held in the fort's wooden guardhouse, just steps from the gallows where he was to be hanged. Howe wrote to President Lincoln twice in his own hand, as well as to the commanding officers of his regiment, seeking clemency for a "brave soldier." All attempts failed, and Howe was hanged as a murderer and deserter.

Howe was one of four men executed at Fort Mifflin, but he has the distinction of being the only person ever executed by the army for which tickets to the execution were sold to the public. Inside Casemate #11, where Howe was held, his handwritten signature can still be clearly seen on the wall.[215]

Philadelphia-Based Military Units

PHILADELPHIA UNITS OF THE THREE-MONTH (NINETY-DAY) SERVICE

President Lincoln's first call for troops to assist in suppressing the rebellion was made on April 15, 1861. He called for seventy-five thousand volunteers to serve for ninety days. Each state was given a quota to fill proportionate to its population. Pennsylvania's quota was originally sixteen regiments. Due to patriotic fervor and enthusiasm among the male population desiring to enlist, this number was later raised to twenty-five regiments.[216] Philadelphia eventually raised eight regiments of infantry, one company of artillery (Commonwealth Artillery), one troop of cavalry (First City Troop) and one independent company of rangers (McMullin's Rangers) and sent them to the front.

There was almost universal support for the war effort, even among the various ethnic communities. In the black community, there was less enthusiasm while blacks could serve in the navy but were ineligible for army service. This was changed in 1863 with the enlistment of Colored Troops.[217] The German community sent one regiment (21st Pennsylvania), and the Irish sent the 24th Pennsylvania. The small French community sent two companies of Gardes Lafayette, who served in the 18th Pennsylvania Regiment as Companies C and D. They were recruited by Captain Joseph Archambault, a venerable veteran of Napoleon's army. He issued a call to his "confreres": "Comrades: Our country of adoption is attacked in its

Artillery Corps, Washington Grays. Monument to the militia unit that formed a part of the 17th PV and later the 21st and 49th PA regiments of the Emergency Militia. The monument now stands in front of the Union League. *Author's collection.*

Constitution and its laws. Our duty is to aid the Government constitutionally elected, to maintain the Union. We appeal to our countrymen and others to come and increase the ranks of the 'Gardes Lafayette,' so as to be ready at the first call for any contingency."[218]

The eight infantry regiments, cavalry troop, artillery company and independent company of rangers furnished by Philadelphia under the first call of the president served three months or ninety days. The units were all mustered into service in mid- to late April and discharged in July and August 1861. The units raised at this time included the 17th Regiment, Infantry Pennsylvania Volunteers. The regiment was originally called the First Regiment of Artillery. This organization included a number of old Philadelphia militia units such as the Washington Grays, Philadelphia Grays, National Artillery and State Guards. It was the first Philadelphia regiment to reach Washington.[219]

The 18th PV was the old First Regiment Infantry Pennsylvania Militia. This regiment included a number of old militia companies, including the State Fencibles, Washington Blues, Minute Men of '76, National Grays, Gardes Lafayette and Zouaves.[220] The 19th PV was also called the National Guards Militia.[221] The 20th PV was known as the Scott Legion, another old and respected militia battalion. The men were clad in the gray militia uniform of the Mexican War.[222] The 21st PV, the German Rifle Regiment, also included a number of German militia companies and shooting clubs.[223] The 22nd PV was known as the Philadelphia Light Guard.

The 23rd PV was originally formed in the Pennsylvania militia. This was the first fully equipped Philadelphia unit to leave for the scene of war. The 23rd

Parade of the National Guards Regiment. A *Harper's Weekly* lithograph depicting the Chestnut Street parade of the 19th PV National Guards after return from the ninety-day service in Virginia in 1861. *GAR Museum Collection.*

formed part of a force of Union troops composed of regulars and volunteers that met the Confederates at an early action at Falling Waters, West Virginia, on July 2, 1861, and shared with the First Troop, Philadelphia City Cavalry, also present, the honor of participating in the first skirmish of the Civil War in which Pennsylvania troops were engaged; it was fought south of the Potomac River. It claimed the honor of being the most heavily engaged unit from Philadelphia in the three-month service.[224]

The 24th PV was composed largely of men of Irish birth or descent. The command included the Irish Volunteers, Hibernia Greens, Emmitt Guard, Meagher Guard, Jackson Guard, Shields Guard, Patterson Light Guards and United Guards.[225]

In addition to the infantry units raised in the ninety-day service were the Commonwealth Artillery Company, which was sent to reinforce the small garrison of regulars at Fort Delaware, and the First Troop Philadelphia City Cavalry, the elite cavalry force composed of the sons of the leading families of the city. The troop was attached to the Second Regular Cavalry, under Colonel George H. Thomas (later major general). They were provided at Philadelphia with regulation U.S. cavalry uniforms. At Falling Waters, the troop was engaged with the enemy and had the distinction of being the first body of Pennsylvania cavalry under fire during the Civil War.[226] Finally, there was McMullin's Rangers, a company of Irish "toughs" organized chiefly from the membership of a fire company. The Rangers were engaged at Falling Waters and in the skirmish at Bunker Hill, West Virginia, on July 15, 1861.[227]

The approximate number of officers and men from Philadelphia in the three-months service of 1861 comprised about 5,700.[228]

THE THREE-YEAR REGIMENTS—
VOLUNTEER INFANTRY

The men who enlisted in the three-year regiments/units, especially in the first calls made by the government and without the inducement of a bounty, made up the backbone of the U.S. Army during the course of the Civil War. They were often paid irregularly, their pay was often docked for missing equipment, which they had sometimes been ordered to discard, and they received a meager allowance for difficult, dangerous and demanding service. The average monthly pay of commissioned officers in an infantry regiment, not including additions for rations, servants and forage for a horse, was $58.75 per month. The enlisted men really received a little more than $13 per month.

Three years away from the ordinary exercises of life was a handicap for the discharged soldier, and many found a return to civilian life difficult. The three-year volunteers did not figure out the cost—they "accepted" an opportunity to fight to preserve the Union and ultimately to free an enslaved race.[229]

Under a general order dated June 25, 1863, able-bodied volunteers who had served more than nine months in the United States forces, and who could pass the mustering officer, were eligible to reenlist as veteran volunteers for three years' service.[230] The three-year regiments recruited in the first call of the government in 1861 were later called upon again to reenlist for another term starting in December 1863, as the expiration of their service loomed. The loss of so many veteran troops promised to be a great impediment to the further prosecution of the war. Thus, a campaign was launched to induce the troops to reenlist. The inducements included a month's pay in advance and generous bounties of a premium of $402, payable in installments at specified intervals. It also provided that the full sum be paid to the veteran who was honorably discharged at any time prior to the full term of his enlistment. A thirty-day furlough home was also guaranteed, and the men could keep the regimental organization, officers and noncommissioned officers intact. They were also given the coveted designation of "Veteran Volunteer," as well as a stripe to wear on their uniform. Some units did reenlist and served to the end of the war, but many others chose not to and were discharged after the full three-year term, often leaving the battlefield to be mustered out and sent home.

Out of all enlistments, 72 percent were for the term of three years. The average constant field strength of the Union armies, volunteers and regulars during the war was approximately one million men. This figure does not include the militia serving as state troops.[231]

SECOND CALL FOR THREE-YEAR SERVICE TO AUGMENT THE REGULAR ARMY

On May 3, 1861, Lincoln called for forty-two thousand recruits to serve for three years to augment the regular army. Each state was similarly assigned a quota distributed proportionately. This quota was quickly filled by those who had not been able to enter the ninety-day service in 1861. Philadelphia (with a large mixture of volunteer companies from throughout the commonwealth) supplied four regiments, the 26th through 29th Pennsylvania Volunteers. In fact, these units were the very first of the three-year volunteers, who would become the backbone of the Federal volunteer army.

Citizens desirous of recruiting a body of men received authority either from the War Department or the governor and began to recruit in their communities until such time as they had accumulated a sufficient number to be mustered into service as a company or even a regiment. (Ten companies formed a regiment.) These units bore state authority and were registered under the state name and assigned a sequential number or designation. The enlisted men normally elected their company officers, often the man who had recruited them. The governor commissioned the field and staff officers, often simply endorsing the efforts of the men most responsible for gathering the troops.[232]

A fine example of this volunteer system was the 28th Pennsylvania Volunteer Infantry Regiment. This regiment was recruited by noted Mexican War hero and Democratic politician John W. Geary. It drew recruits from throughout the state but assembled and was trained and mustered in Philadelphia. The regiment contained fifteen full companies out of a reported sixty-two companies that requested to be joined to the 28th PV. Later, the number of companies in a volunteer regiment was limited to ten. In the fall of 1862, any amount of companies greater than ten in a regiment were transferred to new units as a nucleus of a new regiment or consolidated into the existing companies. The last five companies of the 28th PV, for example, were joined together with three new companies to form the 147th PV, with a former commander of the 28th, Ario Pardee Jr., as the new colonel.

In subsequent years of the war, when new calls for additional troops were made, usually new regiments were created rather than resupplying the old veteran commands. This was frequently done as a political gesture by the governor to reward political supporters with high ranks in the volunteer service. This system proved to be very unwieldy and inefficient and led to the gradual loss through attrition of the most experienced veteran commands.[233]

THIRD CALL FOR THREE-YEAR SERVICE IN THE VOLUNTEER ARMY FOR 500,000 MEN

In late September 1861, the War Department finally turned over full control of recruiting to the state government. The Federal War Department determined manpower needs. State officials managed the regimental and unit organizations. City officials such as the mayor and city councils in Philadelphia appropriated funds to use as bounties to spur enlistments, support the families of soldiers, provide for local defense and provide any needs where the Federal government could not assist. The local community also banded together in civic volunteer associations and as individuals to collect goods for the soldiers and provide needed services such as volunteering in hospitals, sewing parties, scraping lint for bandages and collecting goods for the troops.[234]

FOURTH CALL FOR THREE-YEAR SERVICE IN THE VOLUNTEER ARMY FOR 300,000 MORE MEN

Due to some foolish decisions in Washington to manage the supply of troops against an anticipated early end of the conflict and to minimize the enormous costs of adding additional troops that might not be needed, then Secretary of War Simon Cameron had instructed the Northern governors not to send any more regiments unless they were called for. His successor, Edwin Stanton, sent out a telegraph on April 3, 1862, ordering the Federal recruiting offices closed.

In the early summer of 1862, the government was forced to make another call for volunteers to replace the many casualties suffered in fighting battles in the recent spring offensives and general hard service over the last year. Again, the War Department issued each state a quota of troops to fill, with authority under the control of the governor. The North was demoralized from the never-ending casualty lists in the papers, and the early enthusiasm for military service had waned. Recruiting was slow and sluggish, and the Federal authorities threatened a draft or conscription to fill the vacant slots. Local governments now resorted to cash bounties to spur enlistment. Bounty funds were launched by citizens, mostly of the higher social classes. Philadelphia was able to fill its quotas without a draft, but only after the generous bounties were offered.

Lincoln wrote to the governors, "Fully concurring in the wisdom of the views expressed to me in so patriotic a manner by you in the

Frank Leslie's lithograph of *Recruiting for the Bucktails*, depicting the frenzy surrounding recruiting efforts attempting to attract new recruits to the regiment. *GAR Museum Collection.*

communication of the 28th day of June, I have decided to call into the service an additional force of 300,000 men. I suggest and recommend that the troops should be chiefly of infantry." The formal call for fresh troops was made July 2, 1862.

Pennsylvania governor Andrew G. Curtin reported on August 20, 1862, that volunteers were coming in rapidly and that with the use of the power of the draft as an incentive, the entire quota of the state could be furnished without conscription.

The three-year regiments/units identified closely with Philadelphia formed a large force of close to 100,000 men who bore a large part of the fighting during the war, and they became the veteran troops who brought victory to the Union and an end to slavery.[235] These units included the 23rd PV (Birney Zouaves), which was designated as the 23rd regiment in succession of acceptance into state and federal service. Its commander, David Bell Birney, sought permission and, in an unprecedented occurrence, was granted the continued use of the regiment's earlier service designation from the ninety-day call.[236] The 26th PV was the first unit from Pennsylvania mustered into Federal service for three years. The regiment was made up of the volunteers of the 1st Regiment, Washington Brigade, which had gone out as the first Philadelphians called to the defense of the capital but had been stopped in Baltimore by the riot there on April 19, 1861.[237]

The 27th PV was the second unit from Pennsylvania mustered into Federal service for three years. It was made up of the volunteers of the German 2nd Regiment, Washington Brigade, which had likewise gone out as the first Philadelphians called to the defense of the capital but had been stopped in Baltimore by the riot. The 27th was destined to serve gallantly in both the Eastern and Western Theaters of operations, as were the 28th and 29th PV, as well as several other Philadelphia units.[238]

The 28th PV was also known as the Cold Stream Guard and the American Highlanders.

In June 1861, Colonel John W. Geary began the organization of the 28th PV regiment. Geary uniformed and equipped the regiment at his own expense. Geary afterward was promoted general and commanded the famous White Star Division in both Eastern and Western Theaters of Operations. He was elected to two terms as governor of Pennsylvania after the war. The original uniform was Pennsylvania militia gray, but the regulation blue was afterward adopted.[239] The 29th PV (Jackson Regiment) was recruited entirely in Philadelphia in May, June and July 1861. The heavy expense of recruiting and of uniforms and subsistence was borne by the officers. The uniforms were of Pennsylvania militia gray cloth. It was the third of the five Philadelphia infantry regiments destined to win acclaim in both the Eastern and Western Theaters of operation.

THE PENNSYLVANIA RESERVE VOLUNTEER CORPS (PRVC)

The rapid formation of troops for service by Pennsylvania in the spring of 1861 deprived the state of its uniformed militia. The legislature, under an initiative by Governor Curtin, enacted a law on May 15, 1861, providing for the formation of a body of troops to be employed for state defense against internal disorder and invasion. It was also provided that this "Reserve Corps" should be subject to call by the Federal government if needed. Thus was formed a force for state service, composed entirely of Pennsylvanians, which may be considered a forerunner and genesis of the Pennsylvania National Guard. Thirteen regiments of infantry, one regiment of cavalry and one regiment of artillery aggregating approximately fifteen thousand soldiers were recruited and were soon assembled in camps of instruction at Easton, West Chester, Harrisburg and Pittsburgh, respectively. Philadelphia was represented by twenty companies of infantry and four companies of artillery, in which were enrolled over three thousand men. Most of the Philadelphia contingent was sent to the camp of rendezvous and instruction at Easton named Camp Washington to be organized, trained and equipped.

At first organization, the Reserve Corps was intended for service in defense of the state and was designated numerically by its sequence of organization in the corps. Later, the Reserve Corps was tendered to the Federal government and was accepted and mustered into Federal service. At that time, it received its numerical designation in the "Pennsylvania Line." This necessitated the change of number for some regiments that had previously been mustered, causing some confusion.

The command of this Pennsylvania Reserve Division was offered to, and accepted by, Colonel George A. McCall, a native of Philadelphia and a veteran officer of the United States Army who had retired and was residing on his farm in Chester County. He was given a state commission as major general and proceeded to organize the force.[240]

After the First Battle of Bull Run, responding promptly to the urgent call of the president for troops to defend Washington, the entire Reserve Corps was mustered into the United States service for three years. It was not until the reserve regiments were encamped at Tenallytown, Maryland, at Georgetown Heights, that they were organized into three brigades. Major General George A. McCall, having received his commission from the United States government, selected as his brigade commanders Brigadier Generals John F. Reynolds, George Gordon Meade and E.O.C. Ord, all graduates of West Point.[241]

The record of the Pennsylvania Reserves in the Civil War forms a brilliant chapter in the annals of the commonwealth. The Reserves acted as "shock troops" in many of the hotly contested battles in the first three years of the war. In addition to General McCall, Generals Reynolds and Meade commanded the corps in battle. The last commander of the corps was General Samuel Wylie Crawford, who led the remnant of the division in its heroic fight at Gettysburg.[242]

A CDV photo of Major General George G. Meade, commander of the victorious Army of the Potomac at Gettysburg. *Author's collection.*

In the critical days just before the Battle of Gettysburg, when newspapers of other states were reproaching Pennsylvania because of its inability to defend its state borders from invasion without help from outside, the editor of the *Philadelphia Inquirer* wrote, on July 1, 1863:

> *At the first call to defend the National Capital, Pennsylvania's valleys overflowed with volunteers, and the excess was embodied into a military organization armed, equipped and maintained out of her own treasury. Then she was capable of defense. But when McDowell's army was*

overthrown at Bull Run, the National authorities called again for instant help, and Pennsylvania contributed her only State Corps to the defense of the Nation, for the whole war, fifteen thousand nine hundred men, Infantry, Cavalry and Artillery.

That body is known to history for its brilliant fighting in almost every great battle of the Eastern Theater of operations as the Pennsylvania Reserves.[243] At the close of their term of service, in the summer of 1864, the Reserves were accorded great honors at Harrisburg and Philadelphia.

The Philadelphia units were the 31st PV, or 2nd Reserves. The men had been lavishly supplied with personal items by Christ Church (Second and Market Streets) before they embarked for service. There was also the 34th PV, or 4th Reserves.[244]

The 68th PV (Scott Legion) was largely composed of members of the "Scott Legion" Militia.[245]

THE "CALIFORNIA" REGIMENTS, LATER KNOWN AS THE "PHILADELPHIA BRIGADE"

It is perhaps nowhere as strikingly illustrated in the military records of the volunteer army that commands have had problems and complications in their service than in the case of the four so-called "California" regiments of 1861, which were destined to win fame and glory as the "Philadelphia Brigade."[246]

Early in May 1861, a number of citizens from the Pacific coast who were in Washington decided that California should be represented in the army in the Eastern Theater and urged Edward D. Baker, a Philadelphia immigrant, was then serving as senator from Oregon, to form a regiment in the East to be credited to California. Senator Baker decided to undertake the task, provided that he was allowed to enlist men for three years. At the urging of the president, who was a friend of Baker, the secretary of war addressed Senator Baker as follows: "You are authorized to raise for the service of the United States a regiment of troops (infantry), with yourself as colonel, to be taken as a portion of any troops that may be called from the State of California by the United States, and to be known as the 'California Regiment.' Orders will be issued to the mustering officer in New York to muster the same into service as presented."

Senator Edward D. Baker was, at this time, an imposing figure among the men of the nation. He was fifty years old and of commanding appearance and great eloquence. He was born in London, England, and had immigrated in 1815, with his family, to Philadelphia. The future senator found work as a weaver in a Southwark mill. When he was nineteen years old, the Baker family moved to Illinois, where his career ran parallel with that of his friend and occasional political opponent Abraham Lincoln. Baker became a congressman, forsaking this honor, however, to lead a regiment in the Mexican War. On his return, he was again sent to Congress from Illinois, after which he became associated with Isaac Wistar, of Philadelphia, in a law firm in San Francisco. It was in large part due to his influence that California remained loyal to the Union, despite much intrigue. In December 1860, Colonel Baker was again in Washington as the first senator from the new state of Oregon. When the opportunity came to join the war, he looked to New York City for the material for his projected force. Isaac Wistar, who was an old Indian fighter, advised him, however, to recruit in their mutual hometown of Philadelphia. As a result, nine of the ten companies were raised in Philadelphia and one from New York. As fast as companies were formed they were sent to New York for muster at camp at Fort Schuyler. They were regarded as part of the regular army. They were uniformed in gray, which had been confiscated in New York when ready to be shipped to a Confederate artillery regiment. The 1st California Regiment paraded in Philadelphia on June 29, 1861. Many supposed the men to be actual California soldiers. After a brief stay at Suffolk Park (stadium area today), they were sent south. While in camp at Washington, the regiment was increased to fifteen companies, with the additions coming from Philadelphia. Senator John C. Breckenridge tried to induce a revolt in the camp during the absence of Colonel Baker, but the eloquence of Baker, upon his return, prevailed.

In October 1861, by authority of the president, Colonel Baker increased his command to a full four-regiment brigade. The additional regiments thus credited to California were those of Colonels Owen, Baxter and Morehead, all from Philadelphia, respectively designated the 2nd, 3rd and 5th California Regiments. The 4th California Regiment, as planned, was to be composed of artillery and cavalry. These troops never did serve with Baker's brigade. After the unfortunate action at Ball's Bluff, in which Colonel Baker was killed, Pennsylvania claimed these four regiments as part of its quota, and they became known as the Philadelphia Brigade, Pennsylvania Volunteers. The gray uniforms of the initial regiment, later designated the 71st Regiment, Pennsylvania Volunteers, were discarded for the regulation Union blue, and the men were no longer in danger of being mistaken for Confederates. The Philadelphia Brigade was unique in the history of the Civil War as one of the few organizations of its kind coming from a single city of the North. The story of its achievements and losses forms a stellar record in the annals of the citizen soldiers of the patriotic Quaker City.[247]

The units of the Philadelphia Brigade included the 69th PV, which was composed almost entirely of Irish Americans.[248] The 71st PV was the first and original regiment raised by Edward D. Baker in Philadelphia but credited to the state of California. The 72nd PV, or "Baxter's Philadelphia Fire Zouaves," consisted almost entirely of volunteer firemen of Philadelphia who were spirited, patriotic, brave and prompt in their response to the call of the government to defend the Union, enlisting in large numbers in the three-month regiments. At the end of this term of service, they were equally ready to volunteer "for three years or the war." The regiment of Fire Zouaves that Colonel De Witt Clinton Baxter formed was composed of these hardy types. They were recruited from nearly every fire company in the city. The 72nd Pennsylvania Fire Zouaves were first uniformed in a distinctive and conspicuous uniform of the French Chasseur pattern. These uniforms were discarded in the course of the Peninsula Campaign for regulation blue.[249]

Finally came the 106th PV, or 5th California, many of whose members had served in the Philadelphia Light Guard in the ninety-day service.[250]

Continuing the listing of the Philadelphia three-year volunteers includes the 73rd PV. This regiment was largely recruited from the Philadelphia German community and its rifle-shooting clubs and was originally known as the Pennsylvania Legion.[251] The 75th PV was also recruited entirely from the patriotic German citizens of Philadelphia. Many of its officers had been veterans in foreign armies. Colonel Bohlen, its commander, had served in European armies and as aide to General Worth in the Mexican War.[252]

The 82nd PV was organized in Washington and composed of nine companies from Philadelphia. They saw their entire service with the 6th Corps of the Army of the Potomac.[253] The 88th PV was recruited under the nickname of the "Cameron Light Guards." It rendezvoused at Camp Stokley, located near the Schuylkill River, just below the Wissahickon Creek; this site is now located near East Fairmount Park.[254] The 90th PV was reorganized from the 19th Regiment of the three-month service, and the original militia command from which both descended was the National Guard Militia Regiment.[255] The 91st PV was recruited in Philadelphia during the fall of 1861 and was mustered in December. At Appomattox, the regiment was honored to be assigned to receive the arms and flags of the captured Confederates.[256] The men of the 95th PV, or Gosline's Pennsylvania Zouaves, received as their first uniform the modified French Chasseur pattern, similar to those of the 72nd

PV. This style became known as the Pennsylvania Zouave pattern.[257] The 98th PV, or German Rifle Regiment, was composed almost entirely of German American immigrants from the northern districts of Philadelphia. Company A was the exception; most of whose members were Irish millworkers from East Falls.[258] The 99th PV served the entire war, as its members reenlisted as "veteran volunteers." They served gallantly in the Army of the Potomac and were heavily engaged near Devil's Den at Gettysburg.[259]

The 109th PV, or Curtin Light Guards, saw service in both the Eastern and Western Theaters during the war.[260] The Independent Corps, Zouaves D'Afrique, Infantry PV, included many French soldiers who had served as Zouaves in the Italian campaigns for France and had served earlier with the 18th Regiment in the three-month service. The troop was recruited at Philadelphia by Charles H.T. Collis, who was proposing to serve as a bodyguard to Major General N.P. Banks. The uniform adopted was that of the French Zouaves d'Afrique, which was retained throughout the war by the unit and by the 114th PV Regiment, or Collis's Zouaves, into which it was later absorbed.[261] The single company of Zouaves d'Afrique, which Captain Collis had recruited and led one year before, formed the basis as Company A of this Zouave regiment raised in the summer of 1862 and left the city as

Band of the 114th PV Collis's Zouaves. The band was raised in Germantown and was considered one of the best army bands. It was used as the headquarters band by General Meade. *From the* Germantown Crier.

the 114th PV Infantry on September 1, 1862. An incident in their colorful service happened at the Battle of Fredericksburg, where the regimental band of seventeen musicians was captured with their instruments. The unfortunate musicians were eventually exchanged and, fortunately, were provided with new instruments donated by friends and supporters from Philadelphia. The regimental band remained with the regiment to the end of the war. After Gettysburg, General Meade assigned this unit to his Headquarters Brigade. It is thought that his love of music may have influenced the move, since the regiment had the finest band in the army.[262]

The 115th PV was assigned to the Third Corps, Army of the Potomac, and served in the 2nd New Jersey Brigade, which was, with the exception of the 115th, composed of New Jersey troops.[263] The 116th PV at Harpers Ferry was attached to General Thomas Francis Meagher's famed Irish Brigade and was the only Pennsylvania regiment so attached. The unit was composed of many Irish Americans.[264] The patriotic members of the 118th PV (or "Corn Exchange Regiment," a commercial institution of Philadelphia) took action to form a regiment of infantry and supply its equipment and bounties. This resulted in the rendezvous of the unit at Camp Union, near the falls of the Schuylkill River (East Falls). To accomplish this, the Corn Exchange offered the inducement of a liberal bounty and provided each recruit with articles of comfort not usually furnished by the government. Many of the officers had previously seen service in earlier commands.[265] The 119th PV, or "Second Gray Reserves," was composed, to a large degree, of officers and men from the Gray Reserves Militia. The 119th PV has direct lineage of the 103rd Combat Engineer Battalion of the 28th Division of the Pennsylvania National Guard of today.[266] As for the 121st PV, or Philadelphia Light Guard, most of the regiment was raised in Philadelphia and encamped near Chestnut Hill in August and September 1862. It was assigned to the Pennsylvania Reserves, with which the 121st entered its first battle at Fredericksburg on December 13, losing many killed and wounded. The heroic steadiness of the regiment there elicited special praise from its commander, General Meade. A number of officers and men were mentioned for bravery in special orders, among them Lieutenant Joseph Rosengarten, who saved the colors from capture after the color-bearer had fallen.[267]

The 183rd PV, or "Fourth Union League Regiment," was recruited in Philadelphia and organized under the direction of the Military Committee of the Union League. The 183rd served longest and experienced the most active service of the regiments raised by the Union League. Their camp was established in Frankford but was later located in barracks built on the lot now occupied by the Union League House (at the corner of Broad and Sansom Streets). The command left Philadelphia on February 23, 1864. The 183rd was the last entirely Philadelphia regiment sent to the front. The rookie soldiers were quickly thrown into combat, beginning at the Wilderness campaign. The regiment participated in seven battles, a record for raw troops probably unequalled in the history of Pennsylvania.[268]

The 186th PV was recruited in Philadelphia in the spring of 1864 to act as provost guards (military police). Many of its officers had served in other commands. The regiment was utilized by companies and stationed at various locations in and around Philadelphia throughout its term of service. Elements of this command were sent into the interior of Pennsylvania, to Columbia County, to enforce the military draft and suppress draft resistance during the so-called "Fishing Creek Confederacy" in August 1864. The Fishing Creek Confederacy is not often mentioned in official reports, but it deserves a place in Civil War history and was reported by a correspondent of the *Philadelphia Inquirer* who was witness to the "Invasion of Columbia County" in August and September 1864, a narration of which may be found in *The American Bastille*, by John A. Marshall.

At all times, dating from the first draft, a considerable element of the Pennsylvania population living in remote areas was strongly opposed to military service. In this respect, they held the same attitude as that of the loyal mountaineers of the South, who only became soldiers for the Confederacy under duress. The tasks of the military detachments sent out under the orders of the provost marshals to enforce conscription, capture deserters and break up disloyal gatherings were full of untoward incidents and much abuse.[269]

The 187th PV was employed on provost duty in Philadelphia and at points in the state where disturbances threatened. The regiment acted as a guard of honor on the arrival in Philadelphia and departure of the remains of President Lincoln on April 22 to 24, 1865.[270] The 188th PV was formed from the surplus men of the 3rd Pennsylvania Heavy Artillery, of whom about six hundred volunteered for infantry service. With additional recruits, the command took the field as the 188th PV.[271]

The total number of units with Philadelphia allegiance aggregates forty-five regiments and other units comprising approximately forty-five thousand troops.[272]

Volunteer Artillery

A full regiment of field artillery was authorized, organized and mustered as the 14th Regiment of the Pennsylvania Reserve Corps. When accepted by the government, it was enrolled as the 43rd of the Pennsylvania line, but the batteries never served with the Pennsylvania Reserves. The Philadelphia-based batteries were assigned as occasion required to cooperate with and support any body of troops to which they were assigned.

Out of a large number of recruits gathered at Philadelphia in April 1861, four batteries of light artillery were organized, and as the Philadelphia batteries were armed and equipped by the city, the men were trained for combat. The four Philadelphia batteries—C, D, G and H—were commanded, in the course of the war, by fifteen different captains, and the practice of designating artillery organizations in accounts of battles by the names of their commanders often leads to some confusion.[273]

The total of Philadelphia-based light artillery units comprises approximately 840 troops.[274]

Volunteer Heavy Artillery

The nature of the varied forms of service performed in the course of duty by heavy artillery is best viewed not by listing skirmishes, engagements or battle. Rather, its chief mission was the garrisoning of forts and fortified camps and the operation of the heavy guns mounted there. In the course of the war, however, these so-called Heavies were often found in combat acting as infantry and not infrequently with the navy. The 112th Heavy Artillery PV, or Second Pennsylvania Heavy Artillery, was one of the last Philadelphia regiments in service. It was the largest regiment in the Union army. Garrison duty in forts often made service in a heavy artillery regiment more attractive for some recruits.[275]

The Pennsylvania Marine Artillery, composed of Companies A and B, was assigned to duty at Fort Delaware.[276]

Large elements of the 152nd Heavy Artillery PV or 3rd Pennsylvania Heavy Artillery were composed of Philadelphians. The individual companies, sometimes called batteries, served separately scattered over many campaigns. Company H stationed at Baltimore was unique due to the fact that it was engaged at Gettysburg. At various times it served as a naval detachment, heavy and light artillery, infantry and even mounted cavalry. It served at the

Battle of Gettysburg as field artillery, attached as a battery to the cavalry corps on East Cavalry Field.[277] Pennsylvania Volunteer Independent Battery A (Pennsylvania Heavy Artillery) was recruited from the German immigrant community of Philadelphia and was stationed at Fort Delaware through the three years of its service.[278]

The total of Philadelphia Heavy Artillery soldiers comprises approximately 3,200 troops.[279]

VOLUNTEER CAVALRY

Detailed here are the three-year cavalry regiments from Philadelphia. The city furnished to the Union armies more cavalrymen than any other city with the possible exception of New York. The only body of volunteer cavalry in the field during the three-month campaign of 1861 (First City Troop) and the first volunteer regiment of cavalry mustered into the three-year service were of Philadelphia origin. This branch attracted a large element from men of higher social status and wealth. The mounted service seemed to attract the elites of society.

The volunteer regiments recruited for the cavalry were designated upon muster into Federal service by their numerical order in the Pennsylvania line

Camp Stanton, 19th P.V. Cavalry. A sketch of the training camp of the 19th PV Cavalry Regiment raised in Philadelphia. The camp was named for the secretary of war. The organizer of the unit and its first commander was General Alfred Cummings. *GAR Museum Collection.*

but were always better known and generally called by their sequential order in the cavalry branch.

The Philadelphia-based cavalry units included the 59th PV or 2nd Pennsylvania Cavalry.[280]

The 60th PV or 3rd Pennsylvania Cavalry was also known as "Young's Kentucky Cavalry." The most famous and fearless officer in this regiment was Captain Walter S. Newhall, of the famous Germantown family of sportsmen. He was admired by every cavalryman. In the opening months of the war, he served as an officer under Major Zagonyi in the western army. At the date of his death, he was adjutant general on his brigade's staff. On starting to join his brother, Captain Frederick C. Newhall, of General Pleasonton's staff, on a visit home, he was drowned by his horse falling upon him at a fording place of the raging Rappahannock River. Ever afterward, the Newhall memorial flag was carried with the regimental colors at the head of the regiment. He is buried in Laurel Hill Cemetery.[281]

The 65th PV or 5th Pennsylvania Cavalry, also known as "Cameron Dragoons," was recruited in Philadelphia,[282] as was the famed 70th PV, 6th Pennsylvania Cavalry or "Rush's Lancers." Army commander George B. McClellan expressed the wish that this command should be armed with lances in the European tradition, a weapon not before used by American troops. This suggestion was adopted by the officers. The lances were provided and were carried by the 6th PV Cavalry at the presentation of state flags on December 4, 1861, in which five infantry regiments also participated, and in a street parade on December 6, long remembered as one of the most imposing military displays ever seen in Philadelphia. Thereafter, the regiment was called "Rush's Lancers." It was completely uniformed, equipped and mounted by the Federal government before being ordered into active service.

The unit served with the Reserve Brigade Cavalry Corps, U.S. Regulars (the 6th Pennsylvania Cavalry served with the Regular Army Cavalry units and was called the 6th U.S. Regulars by the division commander, General Buford). The first commander, Colonel Richard Henry Rush, was born in England; his father was at the time United States ambassador to the Court of St. James. He graduated from the United States Military Academy in 1846 and served with the army in Mexico. After his discharge from the colonelcy of the 6th Cavalry, he became commander of the army's Veteran Reserve Corps. He is buried at Laurel Hill Cemetery.

The lance of Rush's Lancers was a weapon nine feet long, with an eleven-inch, three-edged blade. The staff was of Norway fir, with a ferrule and counterpoint at the heel. Each lance bore a scarlet swallow-tailed pennant.

They were made under the supervision of the European officers attached to the staff of McClellan, who suggested the innovation to Rush. The lance was eventually discarded in 1863 and replaced by the carbine, being unsuited for use in the terrain of the South.[283]

The 89th PV or 8th Pennsylvania Cavalry was largely based in Philadelphia. The regiment was recruited in the summer of 1861 and was originally planned as a regiment of mounted rifles.[284]

The 160th PV or 15th Pennsylvania Cavalry was first formed as an independent company known as the "Anderson Troop" in October 1861 by William J. Palmer, private secretary to John Edgar Thomson, president of the Pennsylvania Railroad. It was intended as the headquarters guard and escort to General Robert Anderson, briefly in command of the Army of the Cumberland. Its members, one hundred in number, were carefully selected from the elite of society. The troop was accepted by General Don Carlos Buell, second commander of the army, as his bodyguard. The troop maintained its identity as a separate organization until after the Battle of Stones River, by which time it had become so depleted in numbers that the company was honorably mustered out of service.

In the summer of 1862, Palmer secured authority from the War Department to raise a full regiment, and it became known as the "Anderson Cavalry." In April 1865, the regiment marched to Nashville, completing the longest raid by any cavalry force during the war, about two thousand miles. The 15th was the only independent mounted scouting regiment in the Union army.[285]

Another Philadelphia unit was the 180th PV or 19th Pennsylvania Cavalry. It was the last of the Pennsylvania Volunteer Troops to return home discharged from the service on May 14, 1866. Its first commander, Colonel Alfred Cummings, was the originator of *Cummings' Evening Telegraphic Bulletin*, the initial issue of which appeared in Philadelphia on April 12, 1847. This paper made a specialty of telegraphic news and was perpetuated in the former *Philadelphia Evening Bulletin*.[286]

The total of cavalrymen from Philadelphia comprises approximately ten thousand troopers.[287]

PENNSYLVANIA EMERGENCY MILITIA OF 1862

As a result of the Confederate invasion of Maryland in September 1862 and anticipated incursion into Pennsylvania, Governor Curtin issued a call on the male citizens of the commonwealth to arm and prepare for defense of the state.

He requested the formation of military companies and regiments throughout the commonwealth and ordered drill and instruction. After 3:00 p.m. each afternoon, all businesses were to be closed. On September 10, with the enemy already in Maryland, Curtin issued a general order calling on all able-bodied men to enroll immediately for the defense of the state and to hold themselves in readiness to march upon an hour's notice. They were to select officers to provide themselves with such arms as could be obtained, with sixty rounds of ammunition to the man, and to promise that they should be held for service for such time only as the pressing emergency for state defense should continue.

On the following day, acting under authority of the president of the United States, the governor called for fifty thousand men, directing them to report by telegraph for orders to move and adding that further calls would be made as the emergency should require. The population responded and began to assemble and move to Harrisburg. One regiment and eight companies were sent forward during the night of September 12, and others followed as fast as they could be organized. In the meantime, the militia was concentrating near Hagerstown and Chambersburg, and General John F. Reynolds, who at the time had been commanding a corps in the Army of the Potomac, assumed command of the militia. Fifteen thousand men were pushed forward to Hagerstown and Boonsboro, and some of them even stood in line of battle in proximity to the field at Antietam within sound of the battle. Ten thousand more were posted in the vicinity of Greencastle and Chambersburg, and "about twenty five thousand," stated Governor Curtin, "were at Harrisburg, or on their way to Harrisburg, or in readiness and waiting for transportation to proceed there."

The Union Army of the Potomac's repulse of Lee at Antietam under Philadelphian General George B. McClellan ended the invasion on September 17, 1862. Most of these troops served about two weeks. They were mustered in early September and were discharged after the Battle of Antietam and the end of the threat of invasion had passed in late September.[288]

PHILADELPHIA CONTINGENT

Most of the emergency units saw limited service in the Antietam Campaign. They were largely sent to guard the border of the state and were to be used as a reserve force to thwart any further advance by Lee and his Confederate force. Some units actually advanced close to the battlefield at Sharpsburg,

Maryland, and were within hearing distance of the fighting. Fortunately, the defeat of Lee at Antietam allowed the Emergency Militia to be mustered out and returned home after a short campaign.

The Philadelphia contingent was composed of the 7th Regiment, Pennsylvania Emergency Militia (hereafter PEM), or Gray Reserves; the 8th Regiment, PEM, or Second Blue Reserves; the 9th Regiment, PEM; the 20th Regiment, PEM, or Revenue Guards, which suffered the only known deaths in service in a collision on the Cumberland Valley Railroad, losing four men killed and thirty injured; and the 25th Regiment, PEM, or First Blue Reserves, which was formed from the Home Guard. They were posted on duty guarding the DuPont Powder Works in Wilmington, Delaware. In addition, there was a battalion of Pennsylvania Emergency Militia, the Baldwin Light Infantry, formed from workers at the Baldwin Locomotive Works, Philadelphia. There were two batteries raised in the city, Spencer Miller's Battery and Landis's Battery.[289]

ENROLLMENT ACT OF MARCH 3, 1863

After experiencing enormous losses and a shortage of soldiers, the government resorted to a Federal draft in March 1863. President Lincoln signed the Enrollment Act on March 3, 1863, requiring the enrollment of every male citizen, and those immigrants who had filed for citizenship, between ages twenty and forty-five. Federal agents established a quota of new enlistments due from each congressional district.

Once set, states were responsible to fill the enrollment quota through the enlistment of volunteers or draftees. States tried to avoid the draft, offering instead a considerable amount of money to induce voluntary enlistment. Volunteers received a bounty of $100 from the Federal government, plus state and local bounties. Combined bounties in some locations exceeded $500. This gave way to the practice of bounty jumping—men enlisted, took the bounty, deserted and then enlisted elsewhere to receive another set of bounties.

Even those who were drafted often successfully avoided military service. Many simply failed to report, and there were also exemptions for those with disabilities or who were the sole supporters of dependent family members. Any draftee not excused could hire a substitute, guaranteeing exemption from any future draft, or pay a commutation fee of $300, providing exemption for one draft. The $300 commutation fee soon became the most controversial part of the act, leading to the widespread charge in newspapers and political meetings that the Civil War was "a rich man's war and a poor man's fight." Ironically, the $300 fee was fashioned by Republicans who "saw this as a way of bringing exemption within reach of the working class instead of discriminating against them." Paying for substitutes had a long tradition in European warfare and was employed during the American Revolution. Congress ultimately repealed the use of a commutation fee in July 1864.

Because of the widespread use of bounties to spur enlistment, only a relatively small amount of men were actually drafted. Again, there was serious resistance to the Enrollment Act. Serious riots erupted in New York City and elsewhere, but Philadelphia remained mostly calm, primarily due to the quick and decisive action of the mayor and his judicious use of the police force to nip such behavior before it could occur.[290]

Pennsylvania Emergency Militia of 1863 in the Gettysburg Campaign—Philadelphia Troops

The Confederate army under General Robert E. Lee invaded Pennsylvania in June 1863, an act that resulted in the Gettysburg Campaign.

The scene in Philadelphia in that month was very different from the previous emergency after the Confederates invaded Maryland in September 1862. The sober truth of a bitter war and hard service had possessed the souls of the people of Philadelphia in the early summer of 1863. The color, the thrill and the glory of war were now faded. There were monotonous daily reports of military funerals and of the return of the horribly wounded from the field, shattered in battles and hardened by service. There were signs of yet another draft. The disloyal element of the city became aggressive. They proclaimed the war a failure; they railed against Lincoln and the administration; they held meetings in the shadow of Independence Hall and defied the government in their newspapers.

Many of the depleted Union regiments whose terms of service had ended were passing homeward through the city. Under the tender care of the tired but steadfast men and women of the great refreshment saloons they were, as always, bountifully fed. Now and then a new regiment passed southward, clean and fresh in new uniforms. There were also long gray lines of prisoners limping between their guards down Washington Avenue, bound for internment at Fort Delaware but amazed to find a good meal and kindly

DEFENCE

OF THE

CITY OF PHILADELPHIA

Office of the Mayor of the City of Philadelphia.

BY VIRTUE OF THE AUTHORITY vested in me, by the Act of the General Assembly of the Commonwealth of Pennsylvania, entitled, "An Act relating to the Home Guard of the City of Philadelphia, Approved the Sixteenth day of May Anno Domini one thousand eight hundred and sixty one.

I do hereby require Brigadier General A. J. PLEASONTON, Commander of the HOME GUARD, to order out (and into the service of the City of Philadelphia,) THE WHOLE OF THE SAID GUARD, for the preservation of the public peace AND THE DEFENCE OF THE CITY. And I hereby call upon all persons within the limits of the said City, to yield a PROMPT AND READY OBEDIENCE to the Orders of the said Commander of the HOME GUARD, and of those acting under his authority in the execution of his and their said duties.

In witness whereof, I have hereunto set my hand and caused the Corporate Seal of the City of Philadelphia, to be affixed, this sixteenth day of June, A. D., one thousand eight hundred and sixty-three.

ALEXANDER HENRY,
Mayor of Philadelphia.

BEFORE GETTYSBURG, THE HOME GUARD ON DUTY.
(From a war time poster.)

City Call for Troops, June 1863. A sketch showing a recruiting poster used to exhort citizens to rally to the colors and enlist in the emergency campaign. *GAR Museum Collection.*

attention awaiting them at the same refreshment saloons. Many sought entertainment on the beautiful June afternoons by visiting Fairmount Park to enjoy the concerts by Birgfeld's popular German military band.

The Union League and the fire companies were busy planning for a grand Fourth of July parade, with banquets and fireworks planned for the evening. Meanwhile, the veterans of the Army of the Potomac were serving in the field and on the march, expecting to resist the enemy. But the daily newspaper dispatches told the story of the steady advance of the Confederate army into Pennsylvania.

On June 15, President Lincoln called for fifty thousand emergency troops to be mustered into the national service to serve six months. The earlier call of September 1862 had been "for the duration of the emergency," and many were reluctant to commit to a six-month term of service. This call was immediately followed by another from Governor Curtin, in the course of which he stated, "We must be true to the thirty-five thousand Pennsylvanians who have fallen on the field of battle." On the following day, the mayor summoned the city businessmen to close their places of employment and arm themselves for defense of the city and state.

At the City Arsenal at Broad and Race Streets, rifles, cannon, harness, firearms, uniforms, equipments, tents and commissary stores that had been bought and stored by the city awaited the expected rush of volunteers. As fast as they came with the proper requisitions, they were fitted out and entrained for Harrisburg. In this way, a full company could be transformed from civilians to soldiers in half an hour.

On June 17 and 18, many city units proceeded to Harrisburg. Within the week following, nearly all of the local militia had departed. Several fine regiments from New York and New Jersey, the first of them being the Dandy 7th Regiment of New York City, had crossed through the city and were now on the line of defense.

On June 29, Mayor Henry again issued an urgent call to the citizens:

> *You number more than fifty thousand able bodied men. The means to arm and equip yourselves are at hand. Close your manufactories, workshops and stores before the stern necessity for common safety makes it obligatory. Assemble yourselves forthwith for organization and drill. Spurn from you those who would delude you to inactivity or disaffection. Let no one refuse to arm who will not be able to justify himself before man and God in sight of a desolated hearth or of a dishonored family.* [291]

As he wrote these fiery words, the Confederate cavalry of General Jenkins was within sight of Harrisburg, and another column of raiders also was threatening York, sixty-five miles from Philadelphia, for heavy requisitions of supplies, food and money. The nearest corps of the Union army under General Hooker, who was then still in command of the Army of the Potomac, was forty miles or more distant from the points then reached by the enemy.

But business and manufacturing were very good in Philadelphia in the summer of 1863. A large number of establishments were humming with government contracts. Military goods of all kinds, locomotives, shipbuilding and other undertakings occupied the attention of the working citizens. That day, June 29, 1863, city policemen carried enrollment blanks from house to house, and those who signed were told to go to Independence Square, where the mayor and the commanding general of the Home Guard awaited them. Here, Major General N.J. Dana instructed them how to organize and where to report for service.

The *Evening Bulletin* reported on the effect of the emergency in Philadelphia:

> *On the day when Reynolds took his position at Seminary Ridge and began the main fight, Governor Curtin was in Philadelphia. He communicated to the Philadelphia authorities and to the officers of the Pennsylvania Railroad the principal facts concerning the critical conditions at the State capital and the difficulty of obtaining exact information from the Federal army, now that it was on the point of contact with the advancing forces of the Confederates. It was at this time that he made his memorable speech from the balcony of the Continental Hotel* [at Ninth and Chestnut Streets]; *he exhorted all Philadelphians to spring to arms at once, and some men in after years recalled it as the most impressive in its earnestness that was heard here in the course of the war. This was the speech which produced enough enlistments during the next ten hours to make at least five regiments. Before nightfall the city was in the midst of alarms; all business had come to a standstill, and the report that Reynolds had fallen caused, for the moment, a profound depression.*
>
> *Some dispirited citizens doubted whether the Governor would be able to get back to the Capitol, and the thought of the possibility that it might be necessary to set up the State government in Philadelphia entered many minds.*

Three regiments of Maine troops whose enlistments of nine months had expired arrived in Philadelphia, homeward bound, on July 1, 1863. While dining at the Union Volunteer Refreshment Saloon, the Reverend Thomas

Brainerd, beloved pastor of Old Pine Presbyterian Church, and others appealed to them to remain and assist in the defense of the city. They were offered, by city authorities, fifty dollars each if they would stay ten days. A minority of the men and nearly all of the officers were willing to do so, but the majority refused, and all finally departed northward.[292]

The points designated as rendezvous for citizen volunteers were Commissioners' Hall, at Thirteenth and Spring Garden Streets; the City Armory, Broad Street; the Market House, at Twenty-second and Spring Garden Streets; and Commissioners' Hall, at Thirty-seventh and Market. A stirring instance of the answer made by the people was the appearance of one hundred workers at Independence Hall requesting immediate enrollment. These men were employed at the ironworks of S.V. Merrick & Sons, engaged on machinery for warships. At this great plant at Washington Avenue, three companies of armed and uniformed infantry from the working force were raised and maintained by the firm. The volunteers thus mentioned were promptly sworn in, sent to Harrisburg and became Company K of the 31st Regiment Emergency Infantry.[293]

These Philadelphia-based troops served "for the time of the emergency," or approximately sixty days, from mid-June to mid-August 1863. Among those included the 20th Regiment, Pennsylvania Emergency Militia. This command was formed from the Philadelphia Home Guard Brigade. It was composed largely of workers at the Philadelphia Custom House (now the Second Bank of the United States on Chestnut Street). It had served as the 20th Regiment, Emergency Militia, in the Antietam campaign of 1862. The regiment was assigned to guard duty along the Northern Central Railroad, near York, from which it was forced back by the Confederates at Wrightsville, Pennsylvania. The 20th joined the 27th PEM under Colonel Jacob G. Frick, the First City Troop and some other commands gathering there to defend the Wrightsville Bridge from capture. They had no artillery, and after an engagement with Lee's veterans, Colonel Frick's force was obliged to retreat across the Susquehanna River to Columbia, burning the bridge behind it and thereby saving Harrisburg and possibly Philadelphia.[294]

Other units included the 31st Regiment, PEM; the 33rd Regiment, PEM, or Blue Reserves; and several independent commands such as the Henry Guards, named for Mayor Alexander Henry and composed of officers of the Philadelphia police force.

Landis's Battery and Spencer Miller's Battery were also reactivated. Landis's Battery was engaged in actions against the Confederates on the west shore of the Susquehanna River opposite Harrisburg at Sporting

Hill on June 30 and at Carlisle on July 1, when in the early evening the town was shelled by the Confederate cavalry under J.E.B. Stuart. Miller's Battery was engaged in defending against the approach of Ewell's Confederates toward Harrisburg. At Oyster Point on the west shore of the Susquehanna, a few miles west of the state capital, the battery with its infantry support turned back the invading enemy column. This action, on June 28, 1863, was the most northerly point of conflict in the Civil War.

The First City Troop of Philadelphia under Captain Samuel J. Randall (later Speaker of the House of Representatives) hastened to the defense of the state on the Susquehanna River. The troop was engaged in scouting the roads in the vicinity of Gettysburg and encountered, at several points, advance parties of the enemy. As the Confederates increased, the Union advance retreated. The troop crossed the Wrightsville Bridge after a skirmish with the enemy. A detail of four troopers set fire to the bridge, which was destroyed. On July 2, a detachment of the troop crossed the river on boats and rode to York, there learning of the Union victory at the Battle of Gettysburg.[295]

Philadelphia was elated and relieved at the twin victories of Gettysburg and immediately thereafter the surrender of Vicksburg a day later. The *Public Ledger* on July 8, 1863, stated:

Never since the commencement of the Rebellion were the people of Philadelphia so excited and filled with joy as on the receipt of the official announcement of the surrender of Vicksburg. The news following so soon on the brilliant victory of Gen. Meade electrified everybody. In addition to the spontaneous celebration at the State-House, when the bells were rung and the cannon fired, there were exhibitions of joy of the people all over the city, the news having spread with wonderful rapidity.

At five o'clock that afternoon occurred a most interesting ceremony. Five hundred members of the Union League assembled at their headquarters and, headed by Birgfeld's Band, marched to Independence Square. A large crowd was soon attracted, and the Reverend Boardman invoked the blessing of Almighty God and recognized His hand in the recent glorious victories. Charles Gibbons followed with a patriotic address. At the conclusion of the speech, the band, which had been stationed in the steeple, rendered the hymn of thanksgiving "Old Hundred," and the enormous crowd joined in singing it, producing a most impressive effect.[296]

NINETY-DAY EMERGENCY MILITIA, 1863
GETTYSBURG CAMPAIGN

All the ninety-day regiments of Emergency Militia of 1863 were mustered into the United States service "for the defense of the State of Pennsylvania." Most, but not all, of the troops served their whole term of enlistment. These units included the 32nd Regiment, Pennsylvania Emergency Militia, or Gray Reserves. This unit was associated with the 1st Regiment, Infantry Militia, later serving in the Pennsylvania National Guard. The command assisted in the defense of Harrisburg at Fort Washington on the heights of the western shore of the Susquehanna River. The unit reached Carlisle on the evening of July 1, 1863, accompanied by Landis's Battery, and was subjected to enemy artillery fire by a Confederate battery. One casualty occurred in the regiment. Private Charles W. Colladay, of Company D, was fatally wounded by the fragment of a shell. This soldier is considered to have been killed at a point farther north than any other Union volunteer who died in service during the war.

None of the Philadelphia troops of the ninety-day enlistment was present at the Battle of Gettysburg. The 32nd was sent to Gettysburg after the battle and later was ordered, with the brigade of General Brisbane, to the passes of the South Mountain, in Maryland, and the lower Shenandoah Valley.

Other units included the 40th Regiment, PEM, or First Coal Trade Regiment. The Coal Trade Board of Philadelphia had paid to uniform and arm the 40th and 51st Regiments of 1863 and paid a bounty of twenty-five dollars to each recruit. The 44th Regiment, PEM, or Merchants' Regiment, was mustered into the United States service on July 1, 1863, and discharged August 27, 1863. This command was assisted by the Merchants' Exchange in its organization.

The 45th Regiment, PEM, was known as the First Union League Regiment because it was raised under the auspices of the Military Committee of the Union League, which funded bounties for the men and families and helped to equip the unit. This was the first of a number of units raised by the Union League in support of the U.S. military, the war effort and the national government.

The 49th Regiment, PEM, or Second Corn Exchange Regiment, was partially formed from the Washington Grays. The 51st Regiment, PEM, or Second Coal Trade Regiment, was ordered to Gettysburg following the battle and assisted in the work of removing the wounded, burying the dead and guarding the military materiel left on the field. The 52nd Regiment, Infantry PEM, or Second Union League Regiment, was likewise raised with the assistance of the Union League, as was the 59th Regiment, PEM, designated the Third Union League Regiment.

The 60th Regiment, PEM, was known as the Victualers' Regiment. It performed guard duty at Philadelphia during its term of service. The Victualers' Association was a group of businessmen in the catering business who supported the unit financially.

Also serving in the ninety-day Emergency Militia was the Dana Troop of cavalry under Captain Richard W. Hammell. This command was known as the Dana Troop because it was named for the army commander in Philadelphia, General Dana, and sponsored by his wife. It was organized largely from veterans of the Anderson Troop Cavalry, under the sponsorship of the Military Committee of the Union League. It was the only unit of cavalry sponsored by the Union League. It served on duty in the anthracite coal regions of Pennsylvania.

In addition, there were two independent batteries of Light Artillery, Frishmuth's Battery and Fritzki's Battery. Both were on duty in the Department of the Susquehanna in central Pennsylvania guarding depots, railroads and supplies.[297]

The Emergency Militia force raised in Philadelphia for the Gettysburg Campaign aggregated approximately ten thousand volunteers.[298]

ONE-YEAR TERM ENLISTED REGIMENTS, 1864–1865

The units enlisted for one-year terms were organized to supply a deficit in the combat forces serving at the front due to heavy service and depletion among the old three-year regiments, as well as the discharge of many troops whose period of enlistment had expired and to take the place of the numerous long-term commands on garrison, provost and guard duty whose presence was required at the front. These new regiments were offered the inducements of liberal bounties and the prospect of a quick end to the war. They were largely officered by soldiers with battle experience, and the raw recruits, many of them too young to be accepted at an earlier period, had the advantage of comrades who had experience in past campaigns. When these one-year commands were mustered in, they were fit for service and ready for any assignment required of them, and the fact that most of them experienced little or no fighting was not due to any lack of patriotism on their part.

The Philadelphia contingent comprised the 192nd Regiment Infantry, PV. This unit was recruited largely from officials and employees of the United

States Custom House at Philadelphia. The original 192ⁿᵈ Regiment, formed from this source as volunteer infantry in July 1864, was the basis of the new organization, which was employed in the vicinity of Staunton and Lexington, Virginia, during its term of service without seeing any action.

The 198th Regiment Infantry PV, or 6th Union League Regiment, was destined to have an active part in several of the important engagements in the last year of the war. The unit was composed of many veterans' troops who had previously served, primarily in the Pennsylvania Reserves, and was officered by many of the veteran officer corps of the reserves, including Colonel Horatio Sickel of the 3rd Pennsylvania Reserves.

The 199th Regiment PV, also known as the Commercial Regiment, joined the "Army of the James" in October 1864 on the James River. President Lincoln, viewing an attack by this unit, characterized the action as "a most gallant charge."

The 203rd Regiment PV was recruited in Philadelphia and was intended to serve in the division of Major General David B. Birney as sharpshooters. After the death of General Birney, the project was abandoned and the command was assigned as infantry.

The 213th Regiment PV, or Seventh Union League Regiment, was recruited under the auspices of the Union League of Philadelphia. During its entire term of service, it was detailed on guard duty, stationed at Camp Parole, Annapolis, Maryland, and at Frederick, Maryland.

The 214th Regiment Infantry PV, or Eighth Union League Regiment, was recruited principally in Philadelphia under the auspices of the Union League of Philadelphia. Initially, the regiment performed guard and provost duty in the Shenandoah Valley. Then it was stationed at Washington. This was one of the last of the one-year Pennsylvania infantry regiments in the Federal service.[299]

The total of Philadelphia troops comprised approximately six thousand men.[300]

One-Hundred-Day Enlistment Regiments, 1864–1865

The alarm caused by the Confederate cavalry raid under General McCausland into Pennsylvania in June 1864—during which Chambersburg was burned in retaliation for the burning of Virginia Military Institute in

Lexington, Virginia—induced the government to issue a call on Pennsylvania for twelve thousand militia or volunteers to serve one hundred days "in the vicinity of Washington."

In regards to this third Confederate advance into the north, the *Richmond Whig* printed a communication on July 24, 1864, entitled "The Devoted Band," a part of which stated: "Fire and sword must be carried into the houses of those who are visiting these blessings on their neighbors. Philadelphia and even New York are not beyond the reach of a long and brave arm. The moral people of those cities cannot be better taught the virtues of invasion than by the blazing light of their own dwellings."

Among the Emergency Militia units responding from Philadelphia were the 192nd Regiment PV, or Revenue Guards. This regiment contained fifteen companies. It originated in the Revenue Guards formed by Colonel William B. Thomas, then collector of the Port of Philadelphia, from the force of the U.S. Custom House employees. Many of these troops had enlisted twice before as the 20th Regiment Pennsylvania Militia and had performed emergency service in September 1862 and again reenlisted as volunteers in June 1863. The 192nd performed guard duty at Baltimore and was then ordered to duty at the prison camp for Confederate officers at Johnson's Island, Lake Erie. They were then sent to the Ohio River for guard and patrol duty. After this tour of duty, some members of the unit reenlisted in the second iteration of the 192nd Regiment, which was mustered for a one-year term.

The 196th Regiment PV, or Fifth Union League Regiment, was organized with the cooperation of the Union League Military Committee. The unit was assigned to guard duty in the vicinity of Baltimore. It was then posted to Camp Douglas, Chicago, and employed in guard duty at the large prison camp for Confederates there.

The 197th Regiment PV, or Third Coal Exchange Regiment, was raised with the assistance of the Coal Exchange of Philadelphia, which had previously aided the 8th and 51st Regiments of Emergency Militia of 1862 and 1863. The regiment was assigned as replacements for combat troops to the tedious duty of guarding the prison camp for Confederates at Rock Island, Illinois, where it remained until its discharge.

The 215th Regiment PV was named the Ninth Union League Regiment, as it was recruited under the auspices of the Union League of Philadelphia and was the last of the regiments sent out from Philadelphia. It was ordered to duty in Delaware and on the Eastern Shore of Maryland. Following this service, it was stationed at Fort Delaware early in June 1865, remaining there until mustered out.

A few independent organizations that also served in the one-hundred-day militia included an infantry company of Colored Troops. This was an independent unit of black troops organized at Camp William Penn on July 20, 1864. It was commanded by Captain Converse Southard.

Stroud's Railroad Troop was an independent cavalry troop composed of railroad officials and employees, commanded by Captain G.D. Stroud, equipped and mounted by the Pennsylvania and the Northern Central Railroad Companies.

The Keystone Battery of Independent Artillery also was mustered and ordered to duty at Huntingdon, Bloomsburg, Chambersburg and Greencastle and in the Department of the Susquehanna on provost and guard duty.

The Philadelphia total comprised approximately four thousand troops.[301]

United States Colored Troops (USCT) and Camp William Penn

On July 17, 1862, Congress enacted a bill authorizing the president "to employ as many persons of African descent as he may deem necessary and proper for the suppression of the rebellion, and for this purpose he may organize and use them in such manner as he may judge best for the public welfare."

Massachusetts was first to enlist colored soldiers and formed the famed 54th Regiment Massachusetts Volunteer Infantry, Colored. One entire company of this regiment (B) was raised in Philadelphia by James Morris Walton, who became the major of the 54th. Lieutenants Frank M. Welsh and E.N. Hallowell were also active in securing Philadelphians for the ranks. Nearly every company of the 54th contained Philadelphia and Pennsylvania men. This was also true of the 55th Massachusetts Colored Regiment, of which Norwood Penrose Hallowell, of Philadelphia, became colonel.

Because the old prejudice against African Americans was generally so deeply rooted in Philadelphia, the recruits raised here for the two Massachusetts regiments were sent out at night in small squads by rail to camp in Massachusetts.

As a result of the legislation, and later included as part of the Emancipation Proclamation, the enlistment of African Americans into army service was authorized by the government. Previously, blacks had been barred from army service but had been able to enlist in the navy. General Order 143 was issued on May 22, 1863, establishing a Bureau of Colored Troops and authorizing their enlistment on a national scale.

Camp William Penn, the first training camp for black volunteers, then called Colored Troops, located at the northern border of the city along Cheltenham Avenue in historic La Mott, Montgomery County. Here, eleven regiments of Colored Troops were organized and trained. *GAR Museum Collection.*

At a meeting held in Philadelphia on March 25, 1863, the organization of a colored brigade was announced, to be commanded by Colonel William Angeroth. A committee reported that the secretary of war had promised immediate authority to proceed. At another gathering of citizens held in Sansom Street Hall on the evening of June 19, 1863, a committee was constituted to raise colored regiments. Thomas Webster of the Union League was named chairman. Many other members of the Union League and its Military Committee also were members of the committee. This committee was called the Supervisory Committee for the Recruitment of Colored Troops and was closely associated with the Union League.

On that same day, Lieutenant Colonel Charles C. Ruff notified the Citizens' Bounty Fund Committee that, as mustering officer at Philadelphia, he had "orders to authorize the formation of one regiment of ten companies of Colored Troops, each company to be eighty strong, which was to be mustered into the United States service and provided for, in all respects, the same as white troops." A week later, as a rendezvous for these troops, Camp William Penn was established just outside the city limits, in Cheltenham Township, Montgomery County. Lieutenant Colonel Louis Wagner of the 88th Regiment, Pennsylvania Volunteers, who had been badly wounded at the Second Battle of Bull Run, was appointed to command the camp.[302]

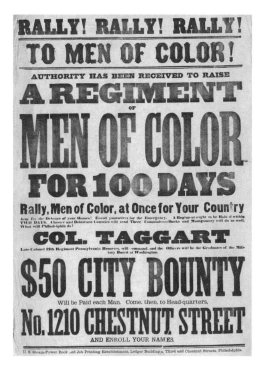

U.S. Colored Troops recruiting poster, 1864. *GAR Museum Collection.*

On June 17, 1863, in answer to a general call by the governor for all able-bodied men to defend the commonwealth from the Confederate invasion during the emergency leading to the Battle of Gettysburg, a company of African Americans was raised by Professor Octavius V. Catto from among his students at the Institute for Colored Youth (ICY). Under command of a veteran officer, Captain William Babe (Company K, 4th Pennsylvania Reserves), the men of the company appeared at the city armory and applied for uniforms and weapons. They were fitted out without question and sent to Harrisburg but were promptly returned to Philadelphia by order of General Couch, the department commander, due to a bureaucratic blunder and misinterpretation of the executive order. This company was promptly offered and quickly accepted by the government and mustered in on June 26, 1863, as Company A, 3rd Regiment, United States Colored Troops (USCT). It is now recognized to have been the first company of Colored Troops from Philadelphia enrolled in the United States Army.[303]

When the opportunity came to permit black men of the North to enlist under the flag of the Union, their community leaders were prompt to appeal to patriotism to enlist military service and in defense of their rights. In Philadelphia, thousands of copies of a circular were distributed, stating in part as follows:

> *This is our golden moment. The Government of the United States calls for every able-bodied colored man to enter the army for the three years' service, and join in fighting the battles of Liberty and the Union. A new era is open to us. For generations we have suffered under the horrors of slavery outrage and wrong!*

Our manhood has been denied, our citizenship blotted out, our souls seared and burned, our spirits cowed and crushed, and the hopes of the future of our race involved in doubt and darkness. But now the whole aspect of our relations with the white race is changed. If we love our country, if we love our families, our children, our homes, we must strike now while the country calls. More than a million of white men have left comfortable homes and joined the armies of the Union to save their country. Cannot we leave ours and swell the hosts of the Union, save our liberties, vindicate our manhood and deserve well of our country? Men of color! Brothers and fathers! We appeal to you! By all your concern for yourselves and your liberties, by all your regard for God and humanity, by all your desire for citizenship and equality before the law, by all your love of country, to stop at no subterfuges, listen to nothing that shall deter you from rallying for the army. Strike now and you are henceforth and forever Freemen! [304]

This appeal was signed by many prominent men of the black community, including Reverend William T. Catto and his son Octavius V. Catto. [305]

The famous lithograph copy of an original photo showing a company (Company G, 24th USCT Regiment) of Colored Troops at Camp William Penn. *GAR Museum Collection.*

142

Supervisory Committee HQ, 1210 Chestnut Street. A *Harper's Weekly* lithograph showing a scene in Chestnut Street proclaiming emancipation of the slaves. *GAR Museum Collection.*

White officers for the Colored Troops were selected with great care, generally from regiments of veteran troops who had combat experience in the field. The Supervisory Committee for the Recruitment of Colored Troops opened a school of instruction at 1210 Chestnut Street, where, under the direction of Major George A. Stearns and commissioner Colonel John H. Taggart (late of the 12th Regiment, PA Reserve Corps), applicants for commissions were instructed. Generally, these volunteer officers were well prepared and well suited to their new commands. On October 3, 1863, the 6th Regiment USCT and four companies of the 8th Regiment USCT paraded under arms in the city under command of Colonel John W. Ames and escorted by Lieutenant Colonel Louis Wagner and his staff.

These regiments were reviewed at the Union League House (at that time located at 1118 Chestnut Street) and provided with a dinner at the Union Volunteer Refreshment Saloon. The soldierly bearing of these troops won for them and their officers great praise from the newspapers and the public.[306]

Camp William Penn became the largest Federal facility to train black soldiers during the war. Eleven USCT regiments were eventually recruited and trained at Camp William Penn. The units were numbered the 3rd, 6th, 8th, 22nd, 24th, 25th, 32nd, 41st, 43rd, 45th and 127th Regiments of USCT. These units were rated as part of the regular force of the United States Army and were not credited to the quota of Philadelphia or the state of Pennsylvania. Most of the recruits came from Pennsylvania, Delaware and New Jersey.

The land used for Camp William Penn had been offered by the family of the abolitionist Lucretia Mott and her son-in-law, Edward Davis, a member of the Union League. The ground was located in the village of La Mott.

The area had functioned as a base for the Underground Railroad before the war and was inhabited by many Quakers and others sympathetic to the cause of equal rights for African Americans.

The site was situated in an ideal area near level ground and water, good roads and rail connections (the newly constructed North Penn Railroad). The location was distant from the predominately white areas of Philadelphia. During the camp's existence, many notable citizens came to visit and inspect the camp. Octavius V. Catto, Harriet Tubman, Lucretia Mott and Frederick Douglass, in addition to many politicians, addressed and encouraged the troops.

The camp commander, Lieutenant Colonel Wagner, was sympathetic to the black community and had been given command at his own request. He was a German immigrant who had already had much combat experience. He was then serving as a regimental commander but was badly wounded at the Second Battle of Bull Run. Wagner chose his staff well, as most came from experienced units.

Many of the regiments raised at Camp William Penn were destined to serve gallantly in the Richmond and Petersburg operations and were later assigned to the 25th Corps, which was composed of all the Colored Troops of the former 10th and 18th Corps in the Eastern Theater. Some of these troops would be distinguished by being awarded the Medal of Honor for bravery in combat. The 25th Corps was created on December 3, 1864, and after the surrender of Lee, the entire corps was transferred to Texas in May and June 1865 to guard the U.S.-Mexican border against French incursions. The corps was commanded by General Godfrey Weitzel, and the department commander was General Sheridan. The Colored Troops were stationed at the border along the Rio Grande. It was here that the black troops brought the first word of emancipation to the former slaves living there, which resulted in great celebration, now commonly known as "Juneteenth."[307]

The record for bravery under fire and efficiency in the campaigns in which they were engaged redounded to the credit of the African American soldiers in the Union army, and was shared by the white officers who commanded them. In a general order of October 11, 1864, General Benjamin F. Butler, referring to a charge made by these troops at the Battle of New Market Heights, Virginia, wrote: "Better men were never better led; better officers never led better men. A few more such charges and to command Colored Troops will be the post of honor in the American armies."

Since their honorable service in the Civil War, blacks have continued to be a vital part of the armed services of the nation.[308]

Another view of Camp William Penn, the training camp for U.S. Colored Troops. *GAR Museum Collection.*

Philadelphia's total number of Colored Troops comprises approximately two thousand men. The USCT units were recruited on a regional and even national basis, and it is difficult to determine the place of origin or birth for individual soldiers unless the regimental books are researched.[309]

TOTAL OF PHILADELPHIA TROOPS

An approximate grand total of 427,286 Pennsylvanians served in the Union forces during the Civil War, including approximately 8,600 African American volunteers. This number includes enlistees responding to President Lincoln's several calls for volunteers for the army, recruits, drafted men, substitutes and recruits for the regular U.S. Army, for a total of 362,284 men. Adding the 25,000 Pennsylvania militiamen who were called out for the Emergency Militia in September 1862 and the Gettysburg emergency of 1863, this brings the total to 387,284 men who served in over three hundred regiments, battalions, independent companies and artillery batteries of the volunteer force. One regiment of U.S. Army Regular Infantry, the 15th U.S. Infantry, was initially raised and trained in Philadelphia at Camp Roxborough before it was transferred to the West. Adding the over 40,000 Pennsylvanians who enlisted in the United States Navy and Marine Corps, this raises the grand total to over 427,286 (exclusive of Pennsylvanians who served in the U.S. regular army).

Philadelphia's total enlistment was approximately 100,000 men from all the various calls for volunteers; this also includes substantial enlistments in the U.S. Regular army, U.S. Navy and Marine Corps. The grand total of enlistments of all types by eligible Philadelphians is one of the highest percentages of any community in the nation. This fact alone should cause any citizen to swell with pride at the patriotism and selfless sacrifice of Philadelphians at every crisis of the nation's history, but especially during the Civil War.

Philadelphia Commanders

Major Generals

George B. McClellan—major general, commander of the United States Army, commander of the Army of the Potomac, November 5, 1861–November 7, 1862. He graduated from West Point in 1846. He served in the U.S. Corps of Engineers and in the Mexican War. Before the Civil War, he resigned from the army to pursue a successful career with the railroads. When the war broke out, he was promoted major general of Ohio militia. In May 1861, McClellan was promoted major general in the U.S. Army and made a department commander. After some small successes in his department, Lincoln promoted him to command of the Army of the Potomac. McClellan also served for a brief period as general in chief of the Union army. He commanded his army in several early campaigns in the East with mixed results. President Lincoln relieved McClellan in November 1862 for inaction. He eventually resigned from the army to run for president as a War Democrat in 1864 against Lincoln and was soundly defeated. He moved to Trenton, New Jersey, and became governor of that state after the war.

George G. Meade—major general, commander of the Army of the Potomac, June 28, 1863–July 1865 (the end of war). He graduated from West Point in 1835. He saw some limited service in the Second Seminole

Above: Old Baldy was the war horse of General George G. Meade. Baldy was severely wounded four times in battle but always managed to recover. He outlived his master by ten years. The head of Old Baldy became a sacred relic of Meade Post #1 of the Grand Army. He is now on display at the GAR Museum. *Author's collection.*

Left: A modern photo of the statue of General Meade on the south column of the Smith Memorial sculpted by Daniel Chester French. *Photo by Arlene Harris.*

War in Florida. Later, he became a noted engineer working for the U.S. Coastal Survey. He served in the Mexican War as a staff engineer to Generals Taylor and Scott. At the outbreak of the Civil War, Meade was promoted brigadier general and commanded a brigade in the Pennsylvania Reserve Corps. He was promoted major general in November 1862 and commanded successively the Division of Pennsylvania Reserves and the 5th Corps of the Army of the Potomac. Three days before the Battle of Gettysburg, he was ordered by President Lincoln to assume command of the Army of the Potomac and led it to victory at Gettysburg. He remained in command of the Army of the Potomac until the end of the war. As a gesture of gratitude to Meade for his stellar services before and during the war, the citizens of Philadelphia wished to present Meade a fine house for him and his family. Meade, when presented the house, declined such an honor due to his dutifulness and humility, explaining that he was "just performing his duty." The disappointed citizens thereafter offered the home to Mrs. Margaretta Meade, who gratefully accepted the honor for her family. She allowed her heroic husband to live with her in the house at 1836 Delancey Place. After the Civil War, General Meade was ranked third in seniority in the U.S. Army. At his request, he was placed in command of the military Department of the East with his headquarters in Philadelphia. He helped quell the Fenian Invasion of Canada and was sent for one year as military governor of the Department of the South with his base in Atlanta, Georgia. Meade was actively engaged in the civic life of Philadelphia, as well as in his military duties. He was named the first commissioner of Fairmount Park and served as vice-president and helped to design the layout of the park. He died in 1872 at the age of fifty-six as a result of a severe wound he had received in action in the Civil War. He was buried in a state funeral on November 11, 1872, attended by President Grant and many former officers of the armed services, political figures and citizens. He was laid to rest in Laurel Hill Cemetery.

Major Generals of the Volunteer Service

Robert Patterson—date of promotion, April 16, 1861. He was born in Ireland and immigrated to Philadelphia. He became a wealthy merchant. He served in the War of 1812 as a captain in the Pennsylvania militia. In the Mexican War, he served as a major general and commanded a division. At the outbreak of the Civil War, Patterson, though of advanced age, was appointed a major general of volunteers in command of the Army of the Shenandoah and the Department of Pennsylvania, although he was unsuccessful in holding the Confederate army in the Shenandoah Valley and was relieved of duty. He was laid to rest in Laurel Hill Cemetery.

David Bell Birney—(d. October 18, 1864) date of promotion, May 20, 1863. He was an abolitionist and colonel of the 23rd Pennsylvania Volunteers, Birney's Zouaves. He was promoted brigadier general and commanded a brigade in the 3rd Corps, Army of the Potomac. Later, he was promoted major general and commanded a division and the 10th Corps, Army of the James, but he died of fever in Philadelphia before he could assume his command. He is buried in Woodlands Cemetery.

GEORGE CADWALADER—date of promotion, April 25, 1862. He served in the Pennsylvania militia and as a brigadier general in the Mexican War. At the outbreak of the Civil War, he was appointed major general of Pennsylvania volunteers. He led a division in the Army of the Shenandoah and in the Western Theater. He was assigned to commands in Pennsylvania and Philadelphia.

GEORGE A. MCCALL—date of promotion, May 1861. McCall was a West Point graduate in 1822. He served honorably in the Second Seminole War and the Mexican War. In 1853, he was promoted to inspector general of the U.S. Army with the rank of colonel. At the outbreak of the Civil War, he was promoted major general of Pennsylvania troops and helped organize the state volunteers. He was named the commander of the famous Pennsylvania Reserves Division in the Army of the Potomac. He was engaged in the Peninsula Campaign. At the Battle of Glendale, he was wounded, captured and imprisoned at Libby Prison in Richmond. He was exchanged in August 1862 and resigned from the army due to debilitation as a result of his service. He is buried at Christ Church Burial Ground on Fifth and Arch Streets, Philadelphia.

CHARLES FERGUSON SMITH—(d. April 28, 1862) date of promotion, March 22, 1862. He graduated from West Point in 1825. He was appointed commandant of cadets at West Point from 1838 to 1843. He served in the Mexican War. At the outbreak of the Civil War, he was commissioned a brigadier general of volunteers and a colonel in the regular army, commanding the 3rd U.S. Infantry regiment. He served in the Western Theater as a division commander in Grant's army. For a time, he replaced Grant as commander of the Army of the Tennessee. He was injured by an accident and died of his injury just after the victory at Shiloh. His body was returned to Philadelphia, laid in state in Independence Hall and buried in a soldier's grave in Laurel Hill Cemetery.

BREVET PROMOTIONS TO GENERAL OF THE VOLUNTEER SERVICE

CHARLES H.T. COLLIS—date of promotion, March 13, 1865. He was born in Ireland and immigrated to Philadelphia. He served as colonel of the 114th Pennsylvania Volunteers, known as Collis's Zouaves for their colorful,

French-inspired uniforms. He received the Medal of Honor for bravery at Fredericksburg, Virginia. He was promoted to brigade command, and his unit served as the headquarters guard of General Meade for the Army of the Potomac. He was awarded brevet promotions to brigadier and major general.

ST. CLAIR A. MULHOLLAND—date of promotion, March 15, 1865. Mulholland was born in Ireland and immigrated to Philadelphia. He served as colonel of the 116th Pennsylvania Volunteers of the famed Irish Brigade. He received the Medal of Honor for bravery at Chancellorsville, Virginia, on May 3, 1863. He was promoted to general and commanded a brigade in the Army of the Potomac. After the war, he became police commissioner of Philadelphia, and was active in the Union League and veterans' groups. He is interred in Old Cathedral Cemetery.

GALUSHA PENNYPACKER—date of promotion, March 2, 1865. He served as colonel of the 97th Pennsylvania Volunteers. At the age of nineteen, he was promoted brigadier general and commanded a brigade in the 10th Corps, Army of the James, and received the Medal of Honor for bravery at Fort Fisher, North Carolina. He was laid to rest in the National Cemtery.

W. HENRY C. BOHLEN—date of promotion, April 28, 1862. He was colonel of the 75th PV and brigade commander in Carl Schurz's Division of Sigel's Corps. He was killed in action at Freeman's Ford on August 22, 1862. He now rests in Laurel Hill Cemetery.

HERMAN HAUPT—date of promotion, September 29, 1862. He commanded the Bureau of U.S. Military Railroads, where he was very effective in organizing the transportation of the military via the rail. He is buried in West Laurel Hill Cemetery.

Brigadier General Herman Haupt was a West Point classmate of General Meade. He served briefly in the army before pursuing a career in engineering railroads. He was named the director of the military railroads and accomplished miraculous feats of engineering. Haupt is buried in West Laurel Hill Cemetery. *GAR Museum Collection.*

JAMES ST. CLAIR MORTON—date of promotion, April 4, 1863. He graduated from West Point in 1851, placing second out of forty-two. He was assigned to the U.S. Corps of Engineers during his pre–Civil War career, being involved in the construction of fortifications in Charleston, South Carolina, Fort Jefferson in the Dry Tortugas, Florida, and Fort Delaware. In June 1862, he was promoted and assigned to be the chief engineer of General Don C. Buell's Army of the Ohio. He was promoted to brigadier general, U.S. volunteers, on April 4, 1863 and served as the Army of the Tennessee's chief engineer in the Nashville and Chattanooga area, as well as commanding an engineer "Pioneer" brigade. After participating in the Battles of Murfreesboro and Chickamauga, at his own request, he reverted from his generalship to his regular army rank of major of engineers (the only instance during the war of a general officer voluntarily reducing his rank). He served as chief of the Nashville defenses in the early part of 1864; he then was assigned as an assistant to the army chief engineer. In May 1864, he was assigned as the chief engineer of General Ambrose Burnside's independent 9th Corps in operations around Petersburg, Virginia. On June 17, he was killed in action while scouting the area in front of General Orlando B. Willcox's Division just before it was to attack. He is buried in Laurel Hill Cemetery.

ALFRED G. SULLY—date of promotion, September 6, 1862. He graduated from West Point in 1841. He became a noted Indian fighter on the western frontier. He was colonel of the 1st Minnesota Volunteers and was promoted brigadier general in command of a brigade in the 2nd Corps, Army of the Potomac. He is buried in Laurel Hill Cemetery.

THE PHILADELPHIA ELLETS—Charles Ellet Jr. was a civil engineer, born in Bucks County near Bristol, on January 1, 1810. He descended from a Quaker family. After study in Paris, he began work on engineering projects, including serving as chief engineer of the James River and Kanawha Canal. He concentrated his work on iron suspension bridges and constructed the wire suspension bridge across the Schuylkill River at Fairmont, the first of its kind in America. He prepared plans for many other similar bridges. After a period as chief engineer and president of the Schuylkill Navigation Co., he designed and built the first suspension bridge across the Niagara River below the falls, and later the longest single-span bridge in the world, over the Ohio River at Wheeling. He then continued his engineering work on surveys and hydrologic investigations, as well as railroad construction, becoming chief engineer of the Central Railroad of Virginia. In 1853, he built a railroad over the Blue Ridge at Rock Fish Gap, which was the most remarkable line then in existence.

Ellet then came up with a plan of using steamships as battering rams in time of war and brought his ideas to the naval service, but his plans were not accepted by the navy. It was not until the Confederate ironclad ram *Merrimac* (CSS *Virginia*), built according to suggestions contained in Ellet's memoranda to the Virginia legislature before the war, had demonstrated the efficiency of that means of defense that the secretary of war appointed him colonel of engineers in the army and commissioned him to buy vessels and convert them into rams. Accordingly, he purchased five steamboats at Pittsburgh and four side-wheel steamers at Cincinnati and, after strengthening them with heavy timbers and sheathing of iron bars and oak planks, took them down the river to join a naval squadron above Memphis. On June 6, 1862, a battle was fought in which Ellet, in command of the *Queen of the West*, rammed the Confederate *General Lovell*, cutting it nearly in two and causing it to sink in a few seconds. At the moment of the collision, Ellet, who was standing on deck in an exposed position, was struck in the knee by a pistol shot, which caused his death. As he was carried off the steamer, he called to his younger brother, Alfred W. Ellet, in command of the ram *Monarch*, "Stand to your post." Ellet was also a scientist of note and wrote a series of papers on a variety of subjects.

Charles Ellet was followed in command of the ram fleet by his son, twenty-year-old medical student Charles Rivers Ellet, who was then promoted colonel and assigned to the command. Young Ellet died in service on October 29, 1863, of sickness brought on by fever. He was twenty-one. Both Charles Ellet and his son are buried in Laurel Hill Cemetery.[310]

Philadelphia and the Navy

Since its founding in 1683, Philadelphia has been a major seaport and boasted the oldest U.S. Navy Yard in the nation. The navy yard was relocated after the Civil War to League Island near the airport and is now under private management.

The first U.S. Navy Yard was established in the First Ward, just south of Washington Avenue, and fronted on the Delaware River. The entrance was on Federal Street. It included, in an irregular quadrangle, eighteen acres, which were enclosed on the land sides by a high brick wall. The principal buildings were two immense ship houses, molding lofts, machine shops and barracks. A sectional floating dry dock was also a part of the equipment. Before the Civil War, the average number of men employed at the yard was about eight hundred. These civilian employees generally lived, with their families, in the local neighborhood of Southwark, which surrounded the area.

The navy yard occupied the site of the pre–Revolutionary Association Battery, where, at a later period, Joshua Humphreys had managed his shipyard. This leading naval architect built the frigate *United States* here in 1797 and, in 1799, launched the famous frigate *Philadelphia*, which was presented to the government by Pennsylvania. This ship was forever associated with the brilliant exploits of Stephen Decatur in the Tripoli War.

The government established the navy yard in 1800, and it became the chief building and outfitting yard of the navy. The ship of the line *North Carolina* was launched here in 1820, and in 1837 the frigate *Pennsylvania*, the largest ship ever constructed up to that date, was completed. Many other ships of the line were

Navy yard in 1861. This sketch is from Taylor's *Philadelphia in the Civil War* and shows the navy yard at Delaware Avenue and Federal Street. *GAR Museum Collection.*

built at this yard by Philadelphia workmen. The *Princeton*, fastest ship of its time, famous in the annals of the Kane Arctic Expedition, was launched here.

The Civil War gave employment at the navy yard to a force of workers numbering, at times, over three thousand. A remarkable achievement was the building of the sloop of war *Tuscarora*, which was constructed in fifty-eight days and launched on August 24, 1861. This feat had never been equaled in naval history. Constant repair and outfitting work throughout the war kept the navy yard busy. In February 1861, workmen were busy outfitting the *Water Witch*, *Jamestown*, *Pawnee* and *St. Lawrence*.[311]

A notable innovation in naval warfare was the design and construction of a workable submarine, the USS *Alligator*. It was designed by a French immigrant, Brutus DeVilleroi, who supervised its construction at the Neafie & Levy private yard. It was launched on May 1, 1862, and went into service in June. The *Alligator* served in the James River area but had a mixed record of success. Its first commander was Samuel Eakins, and later it was commanded by Thomas Selfridge. Improvements that increased its effectiveness were made on the *Alligator* at the Washington Navy Yard, and Lincoln observed the submarine in operation on March 18, 1863. It was slated for duty in the effort to capture Charleston, South Carolina, and was to be transferred to that sector. While being towed to its new base, it foundered in a storm off Cape Hatteras, North Carolina, and was lost on April 2, 1863.[312]

In the course of the war, a number of notable warships were built "of good Delaware white oak" at the Philadelphia Navy Yard. There were forty United States warships on the seas at the beginning of the war, and the remainder were on station in distant parts of the world. As they gradually reported back, they were assigned to the various navy yards for refitting and recruiting, including at the Philadelphia Navy Yard and at private yards nearby.[313]

On June 18, 1862, the city councils tried to induce the government to establish a new navy yard at League Island at the confluence of the Schuylkill and Delaware Rivers. Eventually, in 1871, the city presented the site to the navy. After removal to that location, the old navy yard was sold at auction on December 2, 1875. The new site became the modern navy yard, in use from 1875 until 1995.

One of the most remarkable figures in Philadelphia's long history of naval service was Captain Charles Stewart. He was born in Philadelphia in 1778 during the American Revolution and lived past the Civil War, dying in 1869. He commanded ships in several wars and was commandant of the Philadelphia Navy Yard twice. His last term coincided with the outbreak of the Civil War. In 1862, at the end of his long career of noble service, he was promoted to the rank of rear admiral. He was the senior retired officer of the navy and was retired after seventy-one years of service. He died at ninety-one in 1869. He is buried at Woodlands Cemetery, Philadelphia.[314]

Arguably the most effective Philadelphia naval officer of the Civil War was Rear Admiral John A. Dahlgren. He was born in the city, the son of the Swedish consul, in 1809. Dahlgren entered the U.S. Navy in 1826 as a midshipman. He served at various times for the U.S. Coastal Survey, as an ordnance officer and as a weapons specialist. While assigned to the Washington Navy Yard in 1847, Dahlgren organized the navy's Ordnance Department. He became an expert in cannon and ordnance and developed a number of innovative guns and ammunition (including the boat howitzer) and improved shell guns and the large-caliber iron naval cannon known as the Dahlgren gun, a bottle-shaped gun that became the ancestor of modern naval ordnance. He was named commander of the Washington Naval Yard and chief of the Naval Ordnance Bureau with the rank of captain. In February 1863, Dahlgren was promoted rear admiral and placed in command of the South Atlantic Blockading Squadron, the fleet in charge of the South Atlantic Coast. He worked closely with General Sherman in securing Savannah as a base for army operations. After the war, he returned as commander of the Washington Navy Yard until his death in 1870.[315]

Admiral Dahlgren's son, Ulric, was an army colonel serving in the Army of the Potomac. He lost a leg in the Gettysburg Campaign at Hagerstown, Maryland. Colonel Dahlgren was killed in action in the controversial Kilpatrick-Dahlgren Cavalry Raid on Richmond, Virginia, in late February 1864. Secret papers were found on his body by the Confederates detailing a plot to burn the capital and assassinate Jefferson Davis and other leaders. This discovery outraged the South and reinforced the bitterness of the Southerners. The real reason for the raid was to free Union prisoners of war held in Richmond. Both Admiral Dahlgren and his heroic son Ulric are buried in historic Laurel Hill Cemetery in Philadelphia. To demonstrate the true tragedy of divided loyalties in civil war, Admiral Dahlgren's younger brother, Charles Dahlgren, was an ardent Secessionist and slaveholder and served as a brigadier general in the Confederate army.[316]

Percival Drayton was born in Charleston, South Carolina, scion of a prominent South Carolina family. A relative had served in the Continental Congress. Drayton's father, William, moved the family to Philadelphia when he served as president of the Bank of the United States. Drayton entered the navy as a midshipman in 1827. His older brother Thomas was a West Point graduate in 1828. At the outbreak of war, Drayton was in command of the gunboat USS *Pocahontas* and was engaged at the Battle of Port Royal Sound on November 7, 1861, and the capture of Hilton Head, South Carolina, at which battle the shore forts were commanded by his brother Thomas, a brigadier general in the Confederate service. Later, he commanded the sloop of war *Pawnee* and the ironclad monitor *Passaic* in the Charleston area of operations. He was promoted captain. He was assigned as superintendent of ordnance at the New York Navy Yard. As fleet captain, he was assigned to the command of the West Gulf Blockading Squadron under Rear Admiral David Glasgow Farragut. He commanded the squadron flagship the sloop of war *Hartford* and took part in the August 1864 Battle of Mobile Bay. Appointed chief of the Bureau of Navigation in late April 1865, Drayton took ill and died at Washington, D.C., on August 4, 1865. He is also buried among the pantheon of war heroes at Laurel Hill Cemetery.[317]

U.S. Marine Corps

Philadelphia is the birthplace of the U.S. Marine Corps. On November 10, 1775, the first marines were recruited for naval service at the Tun Tavern on the corner of Water Street, near Spruce. (The Tun Tavern was also the birthplace of the Grand Lodge of the Masonic Temple.) Since that time, Philadelphia has enjoyed a close relationship with the U.S. Marine Corps. During the Civil War, there was an active recruiting service for U.S. Marines in the city, and hundreds of marines were enlisted and trained here. A recruiting station was operated at 311 South Front Street by Captain William Stokes Boyd of the USMC.

The best-known marine officer of the Civil War was Philadelphia-born Jacob Zeilin. He attended West Point but did not graduate. He entered the U.S. Marine Corps as a second lieutenant in October 1831 and began a distinguished career in that service. Zeilin served onboard ships and ashore at the Philadelphia Navy Yard. He served onboard the USS *Congress* as commander of the marine detachment in the Mexican War and was involved in the capture of Los Angeles and California under Commodore Robert F. Stockton in 1846–1847.

In June 1852, while stationed at the New York Navy Yard, he was selected to accompany Commodore Perry as fleet marine officer in the famous expedition to Japan and served with the marine detachment on the USS *Mississippi*, in which he cruised to Japan with Commodore Perry's expedition. In fact, Zeilin was the second American to set foot on Japanese soil on July 14, 1853.

Brigadier General Jacob Zeilin was commandant of the Marine Corps in the Civil War and its first general. Zeilin was a Philadelphian and is buried in Laurel Hill Cemetery. *Laurel Hill Cemetery Collection.*

At the outbreak of the Civil War, Zeilin was in command of the Washington Marine Barracks with the rank of major. On July 21, 1861, Zeilin commanded a small battalion of marines at the First Battle of Bull Run and was slightly wounded. On June 10, 1864, he was promoted to commandant of the marine corps with the rank of colonel. In 1874, Zeilin was named the first marine corps general officer when he was promoted brigadier general.

After the war, Zeilin was instrumental in saving the marine corps from elimination by Congress when he testified to its effectiveness and necessity. As commandant of the marine corps, he officially approved of the design of the "Eagle, Globe and Anchor" as its emblem.

Brigadier General Zeilin retired from the Marine Corps on November 1, 1876, after serving over forty-five years as a marine officer. He died in Washington, D.C., in 1880, perhaps of a broken heart due to the tragic, accidental death of his beloved son, an officer in the marines. Both the Zeilins are buried in Laurel Hill Cemetery. Every November 10, the anniversary of the founding of the Marine Corps, appropriate honor ceremonies are held at General Zeilin's grave by marines who honor the Philadelphian who saved the Corps.[318]

SHIPS BUILT AT THE PHILADELPHIA NAVY YARD FOR THE CIVIL WAR

The following ships were constructed at the Philadelphia Navy Yard and were outfitted by city war manufacturers. Most saw active service with the fleets and on blockading service. They included the sloops of war *Tuscarora*, *Juniata*, *Swatara*, *Yantic*, *Monongahela* and *Shenandoah*; the double-ender gunboat *Miami*; gunboat *Kansas*; steam frigate *Neshaminy*; steamer *Tacony*; ironclad double turret monitor *Tonawanda*; and many others.[319]

A number of warships were also constructed at private shipyards along the Delaware River under contract to the navy. By far the most important vessel built at Philadelphia for war service and the most formidable ship of the navy was the *New Ironsides*, the contract for which was awarded to William Cramp & Sons. This fighting monster was launched, armed and in service eleven months after the work was commenced. It was of a distinctly new type, having a displacement of 5,080 tons, ship-rigged, 1,800 horsepower engines and carrying sixteen 2,200-pounder Dahlgren guns and two Parrott rifled guns on pivots. The broadside weight was 1,100 pounds. Its wooden framing was the heaviest ever placed in a ship. It was sheathed with four-inch iron plates backed with fourteen inches of oak. The plating covered the ship from the spar deck to a line four feet below the water level. Its length was 232 feet; beam, 57 feet, 6 inches; and draught, 15 feet. The *New Ironsides* was intended for coastal service when it was "bark" rigged with fewer sails. The plates for the ship were made by Bailey, Brown & Co., of Pittsburgh and at the Bristol, Pennsylvania Iron Works. The engines were built by S.V. Merrick & Sons of Philadelphia. This new type of warship was launched on May 10, 1862, and christened by the venerable Commodore Charles Stewart. Soon afterward, it became the flagship of Admiral S.F. Du Pont.

In the course of the war, the *New Ironsides* participated in twenty battles, including that of Fort Fisher, where it engaged the heavy Confederate batteries at short range and through it all sustained only slight damage. While in dock at League Island in 1866, it was destroyed by fire.

In other private shipyards, hundreds of skilled mechanics were busy on government ship construction and repair throughout the war. At the Neafie & Levy works, many of the engines were built for naval use. This firm built the boilers for the revolutionary submarine USS *Alligator*, which was constructed at Bordentown, New Jersey, by E.A. Stevens. A gunboat was also launched at Bordentown on March 15, 1862, that is said to have been the first warship ever built in New Jersey. In the summer of 1862, two monitors, the *Sangamon* and *Lehigh*, were completed at Chester, Pennsylvania, by the firm of Reaney, Son & Archbold.[320]

THE NAVAL HOSPITAL AND HOME AT GRAY'S FERRY

The Naval Home and Hospital, later called the Naval Asylum, was maintained in Philadelphia by the United States government at Gray's Ferry Avenue and Bainbridge Street. It was established in 1826. It occupied ground that was once the homestead of a noted Tory of the Revolution, James Pemberton. For seven years, dating from 1838, the United States Naval Academy was located at the Naval Home in Philadelphia before it was relocated to Annapolis. The Naval Home was financed by an assessment of twenty cents per capita upon all the sailors of the U.S. Navy and Marine Corps. The beautiful grounds included twenty-five acres. The main building, Biddle Hall, was constructed in 1832 and designed by the noted architect William Strickland. It is of marble, three stories high and 380 feet long. It was formerly flanked by the governor's and surgeon's residences and a number of lesser structures. This attractive "snug harbor" was crowded throughout the Civil War with wounded, sick and retired officers and sailors from the war fleets of the navy.

Even fifty years after the Civil War, naval veterans who fought under Farragut, Porter, Du Pont and other great admirals of that period were still living at the Naval Home. The Naval Asylum at Philadelphia was closed in 1976 and removed to Gulfport, Mississippi. Today, the Naval Home has been converted into a condominium complex, called Naval Square. But at least the main building and the grounds have been preserved for posterity to admire.[321]

Principal Civil War–Era Cemeteries

LAUREL HILL CEMETERY

A large number of well-known nineteenth-century civic and military figures are interred at Laurel Hill Cemetery. The army is represented by forty-two Civil War–era generals, including General George G. Meade, victorious commander of the Union army at Gettysburg; Charles Ferguson Smith, commander of the western army before Shiloh; Robert Patterson of the Shenandoah Valley Campaign of 1861 and his two general sons, Francis of the New Jersey Brigade and Robert Emmet of the 115th Pennsylvania Regiment; and John C. Pemberton, commander of the Southern forces at the siege of Vicksburg. Pemberton is one of several Confederate veterans at Laurel Hill.

The navy boasts of a number of admirals, commodores and captains interred here, including Admiral John Dahlgren, famed for his work with naval ordnance. Marine corps veterans include General Jacob Zeilin, commandant of the marine corps during the Civil War and the first general. There are six Medal of Honor recipients who rest here: Robert Kelly, master's mate USN; Frank Furness, captain of the 6th Pennsylvania Cavalry; George Pitman, sergeant of the 1st New York Cavalry; John Story, sergeant of the 109th Pennsylvania Infantry; Pinkerton Vaughn, sergeant in the USMC; and Henry Bingham, brevet brigadier general, 140th PV. Other military notables buried here include Colonel Ulric Dahlgren, killed in the Richmond cavalry raid; Colonel Charles Ellet of the Mississippi ram fleet; George Alfred

Townsend, known as "GATH," the most famous war correspondent of the period; and the battlefield nurse Mary Morris Husband.

Also found here are volunteer soldiers, sailors and marines who served gallantly when called to war. Some of the Union veterans—including Lieutenant William Tyrrell, a hero of Gettysburg—are interred in the Meade Post #1 GAR burial plot. Most are scattered throughout the cemetery resting in honored glory; some are yet to be identified.

The first official Memorial Day service in Philadelphia was held at Laurel Hill on May 30, 1868. The services were sponsored by the newly formed organization of Union veterans of the Civil War, the Grand Army of the Republic (GAR). The Meade Post #1, GAR, was responsible for the veterans' graves and for holding the annual Memorial Day services every May 30 for many years. They also adopted the tradition of placing markers on the graves of veterans. Recently, this tradition was revived, and the project was begun to return the traditional grave marker of the Meade Post to every veteran's grave.[322]

WOODLANDS CEMETERY

Similar to Laurel Hill, the Woodlands was opened in 1840 as a rural Victorian garden cemetery on the former estate of William Hamilton. During the Civil War, soldiers who died in the hospitals in Philadelphia were interred there, but they were removed to the National Cemetery in 1884. Notable burials at Woodlands include Union generals John Joseph Abercrombie, Hartman Bache, David Bell Birney and George Crossman; Admiral Charles Stewart; Medal of Honor recipients Sylvester Bonnaffon and navy veteran Thomas Cripps; army surgeons Jacob DaCosta, W.W. Keen and Silas Weir Mitchell; wartime railroad supervisors J. Edgar Thompson and Thomas A. Scott, who served as assistant secretary of war; Gettysburg volunteer nurse Emily Bliss Souder; and many other military and civilian leaders of the time.[323]

THE PHILADELPHIA NATIONAL CEMETERY

More than four thousand veterans who served in the armed services of the United States rest in the National Cemetery at Limekiln Pike and Haines Street. It is the largest national cemetery north of Arlington National Cemetery.

Yet, few Philadelphians know anything about the National Cemetery. It is situated on the eastern limits of Germantown off the main roads, making the site little known. There is no sign visible from the highways to identify the spot. But visitors are always impressed with the beauty of the grounds and the evidence of careful attention to the graves. The cemetery is under the care of the Veterans Administration, and the United States flag flies every day from the flagstaff. Many bodies interred here were removed from other private cemeteries.

The government established this National Cemetery in 1884, buying a twelve-acre tract that had long been an attractive country estate. The large house on the property was retained as the cemetery office and the dwelling of the superintendent. When the cemetery was opened, the region around the cemetery was known as Pittsville. In recent years, Germantown, on the west, and Oak Lane, on the east, have expanded and virtually absorbed Pittsville.

Some of the oldest markers are for men who died at Fort Mifflin, on the Delaware River, and were originally buried there. Several died in America's oldest conflicts. The great majority of the graves are those of men who served in the Civil War. Both the Union and Confederate army are represented. Confederates who died in Philadelphia while prisoners of war were interred here. A monument that the United States government erected in 1911 commemorates 184 soldiers of the Confederacy who died in area hospitals. For many years, the Confederate monument was the largest memorial in the National Cemetery.

One stone constitutes one of the largest memorials at an individual grave. This marks the resting place of Major General Galusha Pennypacker, who died in 1917. He was a Medal of Honor recipient in the Civil War, 97th Pennsylvania Infantry. He received his distinction for bravery at Fort Fisher, North Carolina, on January 15, 1865. At the age of twenty, Pennypacker was the youngest man ever promoted brigadier general. His monument stands today on Logan Circle.

The equality of the veteran dead is illustrated by the fact that not far from the grave of General Pennypacker is a small stone inscribed: "George Washington, USA, 926." This is the section for black soldiers. At the time of the Civil War, there was a military hospital at Bristol, Bucks County, called China Hall Hospital, which served Colored Troops. In 1888, all the bodies were removed from the Bristol cemetery to the Germantown National Cemetery.[324]

MONUMENTS AND MEMORIALS
IN THE NATIONAL CEMETERY

A Confederate memorial originally to be placed by the Daughters of the Confederacy to the Confederate soldiers buried there is now located at Hollywood Cemetery, Richmond, Virginia, where it was taken after a protest came from Grand Army Ellis Post 6 of Germantown against its erection.[325]

At the time of the Civil War, there were also a number of private cemeteries in Philadelphia that were contracted to accept and bury servicemen who died in Philadelphia during the war while under treatment at the various military hospitals. The graves of these veterans were removed starting in 1884 to the new National Cemetery. Some of these cemeteries were eliminated in the early twentieth century, and the graves were removed to new locations.[326]

MOUNT MORIAH CEMETERY

Mount Moriah Cemetery is situated in both Philadelphia and Yeadon, Delaware County, along Cobb's Creek Parkway, near Darby. The soldiers' hospital plot contains over four hundred graves marked with government stones with names inscribed. Most of the interments came from deaths in the hospitals of the city. The soldiers' plot remains well maintained by Beverly National Cemetery. There are several other military burial plots in the cemetery, including the Naval Home Plot on the Yeadon side, the Soldiers' Home Plot, the Keystone Artillery Plot, the Methodist Chaplains Plot, the Old Guard Plot, Grand Army Post #5 Plot on the Philadelphia side and Post #56 Plot on the Yeadon side. The rest of Mount Moriah is in an unfortunate deep decline.

These Civil War–era cemeteries once contained the graves of many veterans, but in the course of time they were removed to make way for "progress." The bodies were disinterred and transferred to other local grounds. Among these were Monument Cemetery on Broad and Berks; Lafayette on Ninth and Federal; the three cemeteries along Ridge Avenue at Twenty-second Street, located during the war across from Camp Cadwalader; and Lebanon Cemetery for African Americans near Passayunk Avenue and Penrose Ferry Road in South Philadelphia.

Prominent Civil War–Era Philadelphians

Alexander Henry, War Mayor of Philadelphia

Alexander Henry was born on April 14, 1823, and served effectively as mayor during the tumultuous period of the Civil War. He was prominent in the efforts to suppress Confederate sympathizers within the city and helped organize civilians to assist in constructing earthworks to defend the city during the 1863 Gettysburg Campaign.

Henry was born and raised in Philadelphia and was educated in local schools. He was a son of John and Elizabeth (Bayard) Henry and a grandson of Reverend Alexander Henry. He graduated with high honors from Princeton University in 1840. He studied law, passed his bar exam in 1844 and established a prosperous legal firm. He became active in local politics and represented the Seventh Ward on the city council.

In 1858, Henry ran for the office of mayor as a member of the People's Party, a fusion of political parties opposed to the extension of slavery, among which was the emerging Republican Party. He was elected mayor, defeating incumbent Democrat Richard Vaux. Among his policies was strong support for the city's proposed system of public transportation, including streetcars. He also dramatically strengthened the police force and had direct control over its operations.

On the arrival of President-elect Lincoln in Philadelphia on February 21, 1861, on his way to Washington to be inaugurated, Mayor Henry gave him a grand welcome and tendered him the hospitality of the city. President Lincoln returned again to visit the Great Central Fair in June 1864 when, once again, Mayor Henry served as host. After the assassination of Lincoln in April 1865, the president's body was ceremoniously transported through the North to his final resting place in Springfield, Illinois. At Philadelphia, Mayor Henry served as the representative of the city at that sad and tragic time.

After the Civil War began in 1861 with the Confederates firing upon the U.S. Fort Sumter and on the flag, Philadelphia's Southern leanings changed, and hostility moved from abolitionists to Southern sympathizers. Mobs threatened a Secessionist newspaper and the homes of suspected sympathizers. Henry responded to the growing crisis and led efforts, along with the city police, to turn away the rioters and quell all unrest, which he was to do successfully throughout the war. Henry aligned himself with the Republican Party and was reelected to successive terms.

During the Gettysburg Campaign in June 1863, he called out the Home Guard under Brigadier General A.J. Pleasonton to help defend the city and encouraged citizens to help strengthen the line of earthworks and small forts ringing the main approaches to Philadelphia. Henry, along with city commander Major General Napoleon J.T. Dana, organized a work party of seven hundred men for this effort. The Union victory at Gettysburg under Philadelphian General Meade prevented the threat to the city.

In late 1865, Henry chose not to run for another term and left office on January 1, 1866. He became a trustee of the University of Pennsylvania, a bank director, commissioner of Fairmount Park and an inspector of Eastern State Penitentiary. He also was a leading member of the board of directors that planned the 1876 Centennial Exposition. He retired to a stately home in the Germantown region. Henry died in Philadelphia on December 6, 1883, at age sixty from pneumonia after returning from a prolonged visit to Europe after the untimely death of his only child, his son. He was buried in Laurel Hill Cemetery. Henry Avenue in the Andorra neighborhood was named for the illustrious mayor.

Mayor Henry was in large part responsible for the maintenance of law and order in Philadelphia that contributed to making Philadelphia the "Arsenal of the Union" during hostilities, a center of military recruitment, training and war production. He managed the affairs of Philadelphia during the war with great ability.[327]

OCTAVIUS V. CATTO

Octavius V. Catto was born in Charleston, South Carolina, on February 22, 1839. His father was a Presbyterian minister who brought his family to Philadelphia when Octavius was a child. Catto grew up in Philadelphia and was afforded an excellent education in the city grammar schools and at the academy in Allentown, New Jersey, to where his family had briefly moved, and finally at the Institute for Colored Youth at 715 Lombard Street in South Philadelphia.

The Institute for Colored Youth was one of the finest institutions of its kind in existence, providing a college-level education free of charge to colored youth to prepare them as teachers in black schools and as professionals. Catto graduated from the institute in 1858 as valedictorian. He was immediately added to the teaching staff as assistant to the principal, Professor E.D. Bassett, who was probably the best-known black scholar in the country. Catto taught classes in English literature, higher mathematics and classical languages. His reputation for scholarship and excellence in teaching was so great that he was offered the position of principal of colored schools in New York and the superintendency of the colored schools of Washington, D.C. Catto

A rare lithograph of Octavius V. Catto, the great Civil War and civil rights champion. Catto was a respected professor who led his own students to volunteer for service in the Gettysburg Emergency. *GAR Museum Collection.*

declined these honors, however, to remain in Philadelphia at the institute. In May 1864, Catto, as a distinguished graduate of the institute, was invited to deliver the commencement address and history of the institute in the classical style. This was a great and appropriate honor accorded only to the finest and most esteemed of the educational elite of the community.

Catto became more active in intellectual pursuits, founding the Banneker Literary Institute, and with an increasing interest in politics, he founded the Equal Rights League in October 1864. He was actively involved in sports as the founder and captain of one of the finest baseball teams in the city, the Pythian Baseball Club, for which he played an outstanding shortstop position, as well as serving as player-coach. He was a member of a number of other civic, literary, patriotic and political groups, including the Franklin Institute, Philadelphia Library Company, Fourth Ward Black Political Club and the Union League Association. Catto's facile mind was active in expanding intellectual horizons and saw political activity as a means to foster betterment for his people. He was largely responsible for the adoption of the Bill of Rights for equal access to the streetcars in the city, as was legislated in Pennsylvania in 1867.

During the Civil War, while still a young man, he was a staunch supporter of the Union, the Lincoln administration, the efforts of the Republican Party to improve civil rights for blacks and to assist in the war effort and the struggle to end the scourge of slavery. When the Confederates invaded Pennsylvania in 1863, culminating in the Battle of Gettysburg, a call for Emergency Militia went out to spur volunteering to repel the invader. One of the first units to volunteer was a company of black men raised by Octavius Catto, many of whom were Catto's own students. The company was commanded by Captain William Babe, a veteran of previous service with the Pennsylvania Reserve Corps. Answering the urgent call for volunteers as announced by the governor, the eager volunteers reported to the city arsenal for duty. They were uniformed and equipped and sent by train to Harrisburg to join the army. But the authorities there under General Couch ingloriously rejected the unit with the excuse that black troops were not authorized. Catto, undaunted by the rejection, returned to Philadelphia and under recent War Department authority threw himself into the effort to raise black troops to fight for their own emancipation. He joined with Frederick Douglass and other prominent black leaders to form a Recruitment Committee and was tireless in his efforts to convince young black men to rally to the colors. With the assistance of the Union League, with which Catto worked closely, and with his considerable influence, eleven regiments of Colored Troops were raised in the area, organized at Camp William Penn, trained, equipped and sent to the warfront.

Working in concert with the nascent Republican Party, which he wholeheartedly embraced, and with the support of the Union League, Catto unceasingly pursued the coveted goal of full and equal rights for blacks. In fact, the Union League presented Catto, Frederick Douglass and James Purvis with a magnificent banner for the April 26, 1870 city celebration organized to proclaim Pennsylvania's adoption of the Fifteenth Amendment assuring black males the vote. Catto was an eloquent, persuasive and powerful speaker with an upright, intelligent and charismatic bearing, possessed of impeccable academic credentials. He had a deep and abiding belief in the power of education to improve the status of blacks and as a goal for all citizens. In a January 1865 speech before the Union League Association, which he had founded to cooperate with the Union League of Philadelphia, Catto said: "It is the duty of every man, to the extent of his interest and means to provide for the immediate improvement of the four or five millions of ignorant and previously dependent laborers, who will be thrown upon society by the reorganization of the Union. It is for the good of the nation that every element of its people, mingled as they are, shall have a true and intelligent conception of the allegiance due to the established powers."

Catto's equal rights crusade was capped in October 1870 when Pennsylvania ratified the Fifteenth Amendment, guaranteeing voting rights for black men. But it was a long and harrowing path to acceptance by the majority. In the next election of 1871, under threats and actual violent attacks on black voters, Catto was placed on active duty with the National Guard and ordered by his commanding officer, General Louis Wagner, to call out his regiment for service in quelling the disturbances. While engaged in his duties, Catto was cruelly murdered by political rivals.

Almost the entire city praised Catto as a martyr to the cause of civil rights. A backlash against the violence turned out a large majority for the Republican ticket that year, which swept to victory due to the ultimate sacrifice of one dedicated to his principles, thereby validating his cause.

Several days after the fatal attack, a large and impassioned meeting of Catto's friends was held at National Hall on Twelfth and Market Streets. Numerous prominent speakers extolled the virtues of Catto's life and denounced the treacherous murder in stark terms. At this time, a large public funeral was planned and paid for at city expense.

The largest public funeral in the city since that of Abraham Lincoln was held for Octavius Catto on October 16, 1871. Because Catto was at the time serving in the Pennsylvania National Guard as a major and inspector general of the 5th Brigade and, in fact, was on duty at the time of his murder, a full military funeral was authorized. Catto was laid in state in the city armory at Broad and Race Streets. His bier was guarded by troops of the 5th Brigade of the National Guard. Thousands thronged the streets to gain access and a view of the martyred hero.

Catto's body was conducted to a final resting place in Lebanon Cemetery in South Philadelphia (later removed to Eden Cemetery, Upper

Darby, Pennsylvania). Soon thereafter, the National Guard authorized the "Catto" medal for guardsmen who served gallantly and were worthy of distinction.

The death of Octavius Catto generated sympathy and acceptance of the voting rights of blacks and moved the black community solidly behind the rising Republican Party. Later, Catto would be honored by the city by having a public school named for him. A number of fraternal and civic organizations would also name themselves after Catto.[328]

GEORGE H. BOKER

George Henry Boker was born on October 6, 1823, the son of a prominent Philadelphia banker. In 1842, he graduated from Princeton University and engaged in literary pursuits. He wrote poetry and a blank verse tragedy set in medieval Spain that was published and became quite popular, even being staged successfully in London and later mounted at the Walnut Street Theatre in Philadelphia.

During the Civil War, Boker supported the cause of Union and freedom both by writing patriotic poems and by helping to found the Union Club (later organized as the Union League of Philadelphia) in November 1862. The goals of the organization were to lend support to the government, raise funds for the war effort and encourage enlistments in the army. Boker served as the secretary of the Union League until he was appointed ambassador to Turkey in November 1871 by President Grant.

Boker was a distinguished diplomat whose tact and dignity helped re-establish diplomatic relations with the Ottoman government and proved instrumental in the negotiation of several important treaties. Boker even assisted the eminent archaeologist Heinrich Schliemann to obtain the permits necessary for excavations in the ancient city of Troy from the Turkish government.

Boker later accepted a new appointment as envoy extraordinary and minister plenipotentiary to Russia. Despite some success in Russia and his personal friendship with the czar, Boker was recalled in 1878. He was welcomed home and was elected the president of the Union League and received an appointment to the Fairmont Park Commission. He remained active in the beautification of Philadelphia's city parks until his death in 1890. He is buried in Laurel Hill Cemetery.[329]

MORTON MCMICHAEL

Morton McMichael was a prominent journalist born in Burlington, New Jersey, on October 2, 1807. He graduated from the University of Pennsylvania and became a lawyer, and in 1827 he was admitted to the Philadelphia bar. He became editor of the *Saturday Evening Post* in 1826 and later was editor in chief of the *Saturday Courier* and began the publication of the *Saturday News*. In 1844, he assisted in the editorship of the *Saturday Gazette*, and in 1847 he acquired an interest in the *North American*, which was, during that year, consolidated with the *United States Gazette* and became known as the *North American and United States Gazette*. He was sole proprietor of this journal from 1854 until his death, and under his management and editorship it grew to be one of the best-known newspapers in the country.

He also served as an alderman of Philadelphia and as sheriff of Philadelphia County. During the Civil War, he was a staunch advocate for the Union and the Lincoln administration. He was a founder of the Union League of Philadelphia and served as president. His three sons served the nation in the army during the war.

He was elected in 1866 as the first Republican mayor of the city. In 1867, at the organization of the Fairmount Park Commission, he was chosen president. He held this position until his death. He was also appointed a delegate to the fourth Constitutional convention of Pennsylvania.

He was frequently invited to address public audiences on great occasions, and he achieved note as an orator. The city erected a bronze statue of him in East Fairmount Park that bears the inscription, "An honored and beloved citizen of Philadelphia." McMichael died in Philadelphia on January 6, 1879, and was laid to rest in Laurel Hill Cemetery.[330]

Notable Women of Philadelphia

MRS. ELLEN ORBISON HARRIS

For many women, the Civil War offered an opportunity to use their unique skills as organizers and caregivers. Mrs. Harris first left her home at 1106 Pine Street to join others to form the Ladies' Aid Society of Philadelphia. Not satisfied with raising money and supplies for the soldiers, Mrs. Harris decided to go to the field and distribute them.

Her good sense and fair-mindedness did not go unnoticed. She soon became the representative for many other organizations, including Penn Relief, the Patriotic Daughters of Lancaster and aid societies from the interior of Pennsylvania, as well as the Christian and Sanitary Commissions. Large quantities of goods were distributed by this good woman.

Mrs. Harris visited over one hundred hospitals of the Army of the Potomac in and around Washington. She not only served as a nurse, washing and feeding the men, but also offered them religious instruction and consolation to many of them and their families.

At the invasion of Pennsylvania, she went forward to Harrisburg, which was under threat. After three days, she returned to Philadelphia and arrived at Washington on June 30, 1863. The next three days were spent forwarding hospital stores and obtaining transportation. On July 3, she left Washington with a few supplies and reached the Gettysburg Battlefield in the ambulance that had carried wounded General Hancock to Westminster. The next week was spent amid the horrors of blood and torment, alleviating a vast number of suffering men.

At the close of the war, Mrs. Harris returned to Philadelphia after suffering from the effects of sunstroke received while assisting in field hospitals in Virginia.[331]

"French" Mary Tepe,
Vivandiere of Collis's Zouaves

At the outset of the war, both the Union and Confederate armies forbade the enlistment of women in combat roles. A small number of women served openly and in a semi-official role, uniformed as soldiers and known to have seen combat with their units. These women were designated "vivandieres," sometimes also known as "cantinieres," and were recruited into European-flavored regiments known as Zouaves. These troops sported a French-inspired uniform originating during the Napoleonic Wars. The vivandiere gradually achieved an official status. Each regiment had fixed regulations for cantinieres.

A tiny number of Philadelphian women followed the soldiers as vivandieres. These included Virginia Hall of the 72nd Pennsylvania Fire Zouaves[332] and Mary Tepe of the 27th and 114th Pennsylvania. Only the members of one Pennsylvania unit wore the full French Zouave uniform, were trained in Zouave drill and adhered to French military custom: Collis's Zouaves, 114th Pennsylvania Volunteers. At the end of his three-month enlistment, Collis returned to Philadelphia to form a company known as the Zouaves

Mary Tepe, vivandiere of the 114th PV, Collis's Zouaves. Known as "French Mary," Tepe wore the unit uniform, marched and fought with the men and was wounded at Fredericksburg. She was decorated with the Kearney Cross in May 1863. *GAR Museum Collection.*

D'Afrique, modeled after the elite Algerian troops of the French army. Many of the men in this company were veterans of European service.[333]

One custom Collis employed was the recruitment of a vivandiere. Marie, or Mary, was that woman. Born in France in 1834, she was raised by her father and immigrated to the large French community in Philadelphia after his death. Mary married Bernardo Tepe when she was twenty and was determined to join him when he enlisted in the 27th PV. Sometime during 1861, she left her husband. One veteran gave this reason: "One night some soldiers, among whom was her husband, broke into the vivandiere's tent and stole $1,600.00. The men were afterwards punished, but the Vivandiere decided to quit the Regiment. She refused to have anything to do with her husband…[she was] requested to continue with the regiment, but her indignation was so great that she left."[334]

The following year, she joined the 114th PVI at the request of Colonel Collis:

Her uniform was similar to that of the women who followed the Eagles of France. She wore a blue Zouave jacket, a short skirt, trimmed with red braid, which reached to just below the knees and red trousers over a pair of boots. She wore a man's sailor hat turned down. She purchased a store of tobacco; cigars; hams; and other things not issued by the government and carried the whiskey in a small oval keg strapped to her shoulder. When the Regiment was not in action, she cooked, washed and mended for the men. She drew the pay of a soldier and was allowed 25 cents per day extra for hospital and headquarters services. After two years, some friction in the Paymaster's Department about the enlistment of women stopped her pay, but did not dampen her patriotism. She continued to sell goods to the soldiers and $5 per pint for whiskey was not an unusual price.[335]

Marie is better known as "French Mary," the vivandiere of the 114th Pennsylvania. She participated in most of the operation of the regiment, including combat at the Battle of Fredericksburg on December 13, 1862, where she received a bullet wound to the ankle. She received a letter (dated December 21, 1862) from Colonel Collis thanking her for her bravery.

After the Battle of Chancellorsville, Marie received the Kearny Cross for helping to organize one of the field hospitals. A member of the 114th said about the event:

We were pleased to find that quite a number of the valiant comrades of our Regiment had received medals for meritorious conduct in battle…even Marie, the vivandiere received one, but she would not wear it remarking that General

Birney, her division commander, *could keep it, as she did not want the present…she was a courageous woman and often got within range of the enemy's fire while parting with the contents of her canteen among our wounded men. Her skirts were riddled by bullets during the Battle of Chancellorsville.*[336]

Marie was also awarded a silver cup by the regimental commander, Lieutenant Colonel Cavada, that was inscribed: "To Marie, for noble conduct on the field of battle."[337]

It was believed that Mary Tepe was still with the 114th in Washington, D.C., for the grand review held on May 23, 1865, followed by the mustering out of the regiment a few days later.

In later life, Marie, aged and an invalid, suffered from rheumatism and a Rebel bullet that she still carried in her left ankle. Widowed and living alone outside of Pittsburgh, the vivandiere of her youth took her own life in May 1901 by drinking poison.[338]

Marie was laid to rest un-mourned and forgotten, buried in an unmarked grave. Sometime ago, members of the Pittsburgh Camp #3 of the Sons of Union Veterans found her final resting place, obtained a military stone and dedicated it in a fitting ceremony. Finally, Marie received the recognition she justly deserved.[339]

Miss Harriet "Hetty" A. Jones

Among the many noble women who devoted their time and service to the Union cause, and of relieving the suffering of soldiers during the Civil War, there were few who sacrificed more than Miss Hetty Jones. She was the daughter of the Reverend Horatio Gates Jones, former pastor of the Lower Merion Baptist Church, and a sister of the Judge J. Richter Jones, who was the colonel of the 58th Regiment, Pennsylvania volunteers, who was killed at the battle near Newbern, North Carolina, in May 1863.

At the beginning of the war Miss Jones helped to equip companies of troops from her own neighborhood. When she received the news of the death of her brother, she at once devoted herself to the relief of the sick and wounded. At first she spent her time at the Filbert Street Hospital in Philadelphia, caring for those brought back from the field. Her kindness was appreciated, and as a soldier once observed, "I have often seen her sit and talk away the pain and make glad the heart of the wounded."[340]

Although delicate and prone to illness herself, she travelled to Fort Monroe, Virginia, to help with the care of those in need. Although she was urged by her friends to return home and regain her strength, she considered it her duty to continue on. On November 2, 1964, she started on her way to City Point, Virginia, the headquarters of the army. She attached herself to the Third Division, Second Corps Hospital, and at once secured the warm affection of the soldiers.

In her journal, she spoke about her duty, saying, "Another battle is expected; and then our poor crippled boys will need all the care that we can give. God grant that we may do something for them!"

Two days after writing this, in a chilly, leaking tent, she fell ill again. She did not want to alert her family at first, but soon, they had to be sent for. On December 21, 1864, she passed away in her leaky tent at City Point. Like the faithful soldier, she died at her post.

Her remains were laid beside those of her father and brother, Colonel John R. Jones, in Leverington Cemetery in Roxborough. A number of the convalescent soldiers from the Filbert Street Hospital in the city attended her funeral.[341]

MRS. SARAH JOSEPHA HALE

Sarah Josepha Hale was born in Newport, New Hampshire, on October 24, 1788. Her intelligence and desire for education were apparent from a young age. With the help of her brother, she received a college-level education in spite of the fact she never enrolled in school. Her career as a teacher lasted only until she met a young lawyer named David Hale. They soon fell in love and married. With her husband's support, she wrote stories for her family and then for the local newspapers. Sarah was pregnant with her fifth child when her husband died. Sarah returned to teaching and continued to write to help support her family.

In 1827, with the help of her husband's friends, she published a book, *Northwood: A Tale of New England*. Although it was fiction, it was the first such book to weave the issue of slavery into the plot. John Blake of Boston planned to publish a new women's magazine, the *Ladies' Magazine*. After reading Sarah's book, he offered her the position of editor. Sarah wanted to have a magazine that would promote the American woman. Most publications were just translated from French. Mrs. Hale wanted to use

American writers with fresh ideas and to educate women on health and how to create a happy environment for their families. As her magazine progressed, she was approached by Louis Godey, a Philadelphia publisher. After the merger, Godey and Mrs. Hale forged a highly successful partnership that turned *Godey's Lady's Book* into one of the most successful enterprises of its day, with upward of 150,000 subscribers. During the Civil War, there was very little drop-off of subscribers. Mrs. Hale was aware that American women included both the North and the South. The magazine remained uncontroversial for the extent of the war. This continued a thread of continuity to the community of women. As an arbiter of taste and fashion, she influenced generations of American women throughout the country. Her success was reflected in the longevity of her role as editor. Mrs. Hale retired at eighty-nine years old.

Her contributions include being a founder of Vassar College; promoting the Women's Medical Hospital in Philadelphia; and raising funds to preserve Bunker Hill and Mount Vernon. She is most famous for lobbying to make Thanksgiving a national holiday. This was accomplished when Lincoln announced the holiday in the middle of the Civil War. Finally, she is known as the author of "Mary Had a Little Lamb."[342]

Lucretia Mott

Lucretia Mott was born and raised in a Quaker community in Massachusetts, "thoroughly imbued with women's rights" (in her words). After the death of her first child, she became more involved in her religion. By 1818, she was serving as a minister. She and her husband, James Mott, followed Elias Hicks in the "Great Separation" of 1827, opposing the more evangelical and orthodox branch of the Society of Friends.

Like many "Hicksite" Quakers, Lucretia Mott considered slavery an evil to be opposed. The Hicksites refused to wear cotton cloth, cane sugar and other goods produced by slaves. While living in Philadelphia, she became more active and, with the support of her husband, delivered speeches in favor of the abolition of slavery. In 1840, she was selected as a delegate to the World Anti-Slavery Convention in London, which she found controlled by factions opposed to the membership of women. While sitting outside of the convention, Mott met a young bride by the name of Elizabeth Cady Stanton.

In 1848, Lucretia Mott and Elizabeth Cady Stanton, along with others, held the Women's Rights Convention in Seneca Falls, New York. The "Declaration of Sentiments," written primarily by Stanton and Mott, was a deliberate parallel to the "Declaration of Independence": "We hold these truths to be self-evident, that all men and women are created equal."

During the Civil War, Mott continued to advocate emancipation and equal rights. It was on her family's land that Camp William Penn was located to organize and train black troops for service in the army. Lucretia Mott often spoke to the Colored Troops in camp to encourage them in their service.

After the war, she continued her involvement in causes for peace and equality through her later life. Lucretia Mott died in 1880 and was buried next to her husband in Fair Hill Quaker Burial Ground.[343]

MARY MORRIS HUSBAND

Mrs. Mary Morris Husband was the granddaughter of Robert Morris, the financier of the Revolutionary War and signer of the Declaration of Independence. Her husband was a highly respected member of the Philadelphia bar. She had two sons who enlisted in the army at the beginning of the war. Although not in the best of health, she followed her desire to render aid to the suffering. She served both as a nurse and a skilled cook, first at the hospital on Twenty-second and Woods Streets, Philadelphia.

Her fear for her sons induced her to travel to the front to minister to the sick and wounded. While on the Virginia Peninsula in the summer of 1862, she received word that one of her sons was gravely ill. She hastened to nurse, and after a great struggle and frequent relapses, he rallied and began to recover.

When her son recovered, she resolved to devote herself to care for the sick and wounded in the army. She began her work on the hospital transport off Harrison's Landing, even coming under fire from the enemy. Later, she was assigned by the Sanitary Commission to the position of superintendent of one of the transports that bore the wounded to New York.

As the war moved from the Peninsula, Mrs. Husband went to Washington and tried to obtain a pass and transportation for supplies for the army, but to no avail. Dorothea Dix, director of the Army Nurse Corps, requested her to take charge of the Camden Street Hospital in Baltimore, Maryland.

A period sketch of Mary Morris Husband, the famed volunteer nurse known as "Pockets" to the soldiers. *GAR Museum Collection.*

Afterward, she traveled to Antietam, where the battle was still in progress. Here, at the Smoketown Hospital, she went to work nursing the wounded. She was constantly at her post in the hospital and dispensed to those who needed the delicacies and medicines they required. She made a flag for her tent by sewing on a section of calico a figure of a bottle cut out of red flannel, and the bottle flag flew, telling of the medicines dispensed there.

The men saw her as she came out of her tent, a large figure with a benevolent and motherly face. She perpetually wore an apron full of pockets, all stored full of something to benefit or amuse her "boys": an apple, orange or perhaps a magazine or set of checkers and dominoes.

After the Battle of Chancellorsville, she went to a hospital on the north side of the Rappahannock River, where she dressed wounds all day and slept in an ambulance. Here she remained until forced north with the army by Lee's invasion of Pennsylvania in June and July 1863.

Mrs. Husband passed a few anxious days in Philadelphia trying to obtain permission to travel to Gettysburg. Determined to go to the front to aid her soldier boys, she reached the battlefield on the morning of July 4 by way of Westminster in General Meade's mail wagon. She labored there until she was attacked by fever and carried back home to Philadelphia.

Mrs. Husband continued her service until the end of the war. Whether as matron at Camp Parole in Annapolis or taking charge of a diet kitchen at City Point, her duties remained arduous, but she made no complaint.

At the end of the war, Mrs. Husband was gratified by the sight of the army marching through Richmond. As they passed, they recognized her, and hundreds of voices rang out "Hurrah for Mother Husband!"

She passed away in 1894 and was laid to rest in Laurel Hill Cemetery. Her monument reads, "Here lies all that was mortal of one whom all delighted to honor."[344]

ANNA M. ROSS

Anna Maria Ross was a native of Philadelphia. She spent her entire adult life engaged in earnest activity in works of benevolence and Christian kindness on behalf of the needy and suffering. Her many good works during the Civil War have given her claim to the title of the "Soldier's Friend."

Her work for the soldiers was chiefly performed in connection with the Cooper Shop Hospital and the famous Cooper Shop Refreshment Saloon. Miss Ross was appointed principal of the hospital and devoted

herself to it with an energy that never wavered. She was always concerned with the well-being of those committed to her charge. And if the donation box at the entrance of the hospital chanced to be empty, she made up the difference from her own purse.

The spring of 1863 found Miss Ross still occupied with her labors at the hospital. In addition, she was promoting a large fair for the purpose of

A contemporary photo of the beloved volunteer nurse Anna M. Ross, who worked for the relief of the soldiers and sacrificed her health in their cause, dying of exhaustion on the day the Soldiers' Home was opened. *GAR Museum Collection.*

aiding in the establishment of a permanent home for discharged soldiers who were unable to do active labor. She traveled throughout Pennsylvania and New Jersey to obtain assistance in this important undertaking. In June, the fair was held and was a great success, and a large sum was added to the fund previously obtained.

Her work bore fruit, and soon a suitable building had been obtained, and many busy days were occupied finishing the task. But as her friends assembled at the dedication of the Soldiers' Home, Miss Ross passed away the very same day. Her funeral was attended by a large and sorrowful crowd. She was laid to rest in the American Mechanics Cemetery. The tomb of white marble with a relief represents a female figure ministering to a soldier. Her grave was later removed to Lawnview Cemetery.

She was so esteemed by the soldiers that the veterans of Grand Army Post #94 named their post after her: Anna M. Ross Post.[345]

MARY LEE

Mrs. Mary Lee was born in the north of Ireland of Scotch parentage but came with her parents to the United States.

At the outset of the Civil War, one of her sons enlisted in the Pennsylvania Reserve Corps, and afterward in the 72nd Pennsylvania Volunteers, which served throughout the war. Her daughter Amanda served with her as a volunteer nurse.

Mrs. Lee wanted to do something for the soldiers when they were traveling to the front in April 1861. She was one of the first to help with the organization of the Union Volunteer Refreshment Saloon. At the firing of the signal gun, called "Fort Brown," that announced that troops were on their way to Philadelphia, Mrs. Lee and her co-workers rushed to the Union Refreshment Saloon, near the navy yard, and prepared an ample meal for the soldiers, caring at the same time for any sick or wounded among them.

She had heard of the sufferings endured by the soldiers at the front and in hospitals remote from the cities, and she desired to go and minister to them. As a skilled cook, admirable nurse and excellent manager, she traveled on a hospital transport, the *Spaulding*, one of the steamers assigned to the United States Sanitary Commission. She arrived at Harrison Landing on the Peninsula with stores of supplies from the Union Volunteer Refreshment Committee and her personal friends. Here, she joined others in caring for the afflicted.

After a brief visit home, she started back to Washington on September 5, 1862. Finding that the army was just then moving west to Maryland and learning that a battle was impending, she decided to rejoin the troops at the front. It was almost impossible to obtain transportation, but through the intercession of Captain Gleason of the 71st Pennsylvania Volunteers, she was permitted to follow with her stores in a forage wagon and arrived at the rear of the army the night before the Battle of Antietam. The battle commenced at dawn on September 17, and during the progress, she was stationed on the Sharpsburg Road, where she had her supplies and large tubs of water, one to bathe and bind the wounds and the other to refresh anyone suffering from thirst. During the fighting, she was famed for having made hot apple dumplings to give to the men. Mrs. Lee stayed at the area hospitals for nearly three months.

In December, Mrs. Lee was present for the Battle of Fredericksburg. She then returned home for a short time before traveling back to the front to the hospital of the Second Corps, where she remained until spring. Here she cared for the wounded after the Battle of Chancellorsville. In July, she arrived at Gettysburg four days after the battle, remaining there for two months.

Mrs. Lee continued to devote her time for the duration of the war. She returned home in the middle of May 1865 and worked ceaselessly to the last final work of the Union Volunteer Refreshment Saloon, where she had begun her labors for the soldiers.

She died in 1893 and was buried at the Ebenezer Methodist Churchyard. The burial ground was removed to Arlington Cemetery, Delaware County, Pennsylvania, and a proper marker was placed in 1998.[346]

ELIZABETH E. SCHINDEL HUTTER

Mrs. Hutter was the wife of Reverend Dr. E.W. Hutter the minister of St. Matthew's Lutheran Church, Philadelphia. She was born in Lebanon, Pennsylvania.

During the war, Mrs. Hutter frequently went to the front, rendering valuable service to the suffering as a nurse. She was the first woman to arrive at the battlefield of Bull Run and to go to Gettysburg, receiving permission from President Lincoln and going in a special railroad car.

She took a conspicuous role in the Great Sanitary Fair held in Philadelphia in 1864 and is credited with having collected a great amount of money for that purpose. Among her many friends were Presidents Lincoln and Grant, Secretary Stanton, Governor Curtin, General Meade and many others.

In 1867, she was appointed inspector of the Soldier's Orphan Schools by Governor Geary; she was the only woman up to that time to receive such a commission. She was buried at Laurel Hill Cemetery.[347]

CHARLOTTE FORTEN-GRIMKE

Charlotte Forten-Grimke was born in Philadelphia and belonged to the prominent African American Forten-Purvis family. Her family members were activists for Black causes, and Charlotte also proved to be an active leader of the early civil rights movement. Her parents were Robert Bridges Forten and Mary Woods Forten. Her father and his brother-in-law, Robert Purvis, were key members of the Philadelphia Vigilance Committee, an antislavery assistance network for runaway slaves. Her mother worked in the Philadelphia Female Anti-Slavery Society. Charlotte's grandfather was James Forten Sr., a successful abolitionist and wealthy sail-maker in Philadelphia.

Charlotte was sent in 1854 to Higginson Grammar School in Salem, Massachusetts, where she was the first nonwhite student. After Higginson, she attended the Normal School in Salem. She became a noted advocate for emancipation, a poet, educator and abolitionist. After graduation, Charlotte turned to teaching. She returned home to Philadelphia due to a case of tuberculosis.

During the Civil War, she was the first black teacher to serve in the Sea Islands mission at St. Helena, South Carolina, to teach freed slaves. She worked for the Philadelphia-based Port Royal Relief Association, a movement inspired by the Quakers. While in South Carolina, she touched many lives, chronicling this period in a series of essays, *Life on the Sea Islands*, which was published in *Atlantic Monthly* in the May and June issues of 1864.[348]

She wed Francis Grimke, nephew of the crusading abolitionist Grimke sisters, in December 1878 at the age of forty-one. Charlotte aided her husband in his ministry at the Fifteenth Street Presbyterian Church in Washington, D.C., and organized a women's missionary group. She died in 1914.[349]

ANNA E. DICKINSON

Anna E. Dickinson was born in Philadelphia in 1842. Her father was a Philadelphia merchant, and her mother belonged to an aristocratic Philadelphia family. Both parents were devout Quakers. Her father, an abolitionist, died from a heart attack after delivering a passionate antislavery speech in 1844 when Anna was two years old. As a result of his death, the family lost their property and found itself in reduced financial circumstances.

Anna grew into a restless, willful, yet imaginative child who caused her ·family much anxiety. Her childhood was not an easy one. Some of her schoolmates made fun of her poor clothes, and this drove her to strive even harder to better herself. Anna's ambition and stubbornness were traits that fueled her determination. She had a talent for rhetoric and on one occasion even scrubbed sidewalks for twenty-five cents so she could hear Wendell Phillips lecture on the "Lost Arts."

In 1860, she gave her first speech on "Woman's Rights and Wrongs" before the Association of Progressive Friends. After this she turned to the lecture circuit. She focused her attention to abolition and shared the stage with many notables such as Frederick Douglass.

Anna was a staunch supporter of the Colored Troops during the Civil War and delivered an address to the black community at the time of Gettysburg to inspire enlistments. On that day, she shared the podium with Frederick Douglass and Republican congressman Judge William Kelley. She also visited Camp William Penn and spoke to the troops there, praising their efforts in the cause of Union and emancipation.

Certainly the greatest honor of her life was an invitation to address Congress in the House of Representatives on January 16, 1864. Assembled to hear her was one of the most illustrious audiences that ever met in Washington. President Lincoln, members of Congress, foreign diplomats and much of Washington society attended to hear the twenty-year-old. The proceeds of this lecture were over $1,000, which were donated to the National Freedmen's Relief Society.[350]

Dickinson continued to work unceasingly for social justice and reform during her long lifetime. She died in 1932, her impact on abolition, the women's rights movement and the ultimate success of the Union in the Civil War assured to history. Unfortunately, her role has now been largely forgotten.[351]

"Three Sundays in April"

Triumph to Tragedy

At 11:00 a.m. on April 3, 1865, the *Philadelphia Inquirer* posted a bulletin proclaiming the fall of Richmond on the previous day. Further dispatches informed about the occupation of the city by Union troops.

Summoned by the ringing of the bell of Independence Hall, people thronged to the heart of the city. Within an hour jubilant citizens, led by the fire companies, were parading the streets. From the navy yard came thousands of workmen, headed by the marine band, who paraded to the business district. When passing the newspaper offices and the mayor's office, at Fifth and Chestnut Streets, there was great jubilation and joyous cheers. The public schools were dismissed, and the children, with songs and flags, marched through their neighborhoods. A joyful mass meeting was held in front of the Customs House (Chestnut Street above Fourth). The Union League hung out every flag in its house on Chestnut Street. In fact, the entire city was soon awash in red, white and blue.

Until late at night, the streets were brightly illuminated and crowded with scores of military bands leading impromptu parades of visitors and city residents. The excitement of that day of rejoicing only ended with utter exhaustion of the people. They knew that soon, Johnnie would "come marching home."[352]

General Robert E. Lee surrendered to General Grant and the Union forces at Appomattox Court House on Palm Sunday, April 9, 1865. The news reached Philadelphia the same day about 9.40 p.m. From the mayor's office, it was telegraphed to various parts of the city, and within an hour the streets downtown, usually dark and deserted at that time on Sundays, were crowded with rejoicing citizens. The windows of the newspaper offices were illuminated. Over the door of the Union League flashed the word "Victory." Bells rang everywhere. The fire companies brought their hose carriages to Independence Hall and added to the din of the hour. Great crowds, mad with joy, surged around the Cradle of Liberty. In thousands of homes, thanks were offered up to heaven that long absent fathers, husbands and sons would soon be home from the war and back at the firesides they had left so long ago to fight for their country's flag. Down on Washington Avenue, the historic little cannon, "Fort Brown," the watchdog of the Union Volunteer Refreshment Committee, stirred up all of Southwark by thundering out thirty-six rounds of powder, one blast for every state. On Monday, no one thought of business or work. At sunrise, the bells were ringing again and bands were playing patriotic airs in the tower of Independence Hall. Flags were flying from thousands of windows. At 9:00 a.m., schoolchildren marched down Chestnut Street, unmindful of the rain. At noon, the Union League Artillery Battery fired two hundred rounds at Center Square (now city hall) at Broad and Market Streets, and at sunset, by order of Mayor Henry, one hundred rounds were fired at Nineteenth and Hamilton Streets by the city battery.

That Monday, April 10, was the beginning of a week of joy all over the North. Never did a people know a greater swing of emotion from gladness to sorrow and despair.[353]

Never were two successive Sundays the scene of more diverse emotions. The world knew on the morning of Sunday, April 16, that Abraham Lincoln had been assassinated at Ford's Theatre in Washington and died on the morning of Saturday, April 15, 1865, the day before. Shocked people picked up and opened their newspapers that day and blanched at the black words they saw there. Again the people crowded to the heart of the old town.

There was immediate and genuine sorrow at the tragic loss of the martyred president, seemingly at the very moment of his triumphal victory. But there were also those in Philadelphia who were staunch critics of the president and the cause for which the war had been fought, and these opponents of Lincoln tended to stay indoors, for many of his supporters and the discharged soldiers sought vengeance for his loss.

On that memorable Sunday and early on Monday, most of the black crepe and mourning goods in the stores of Philadelphia and in many homes were brought out and draped outside to demonstrate the inhabitants' sorrow. Most of the residents in Philadelphia saw only somber streets or the frozen stare on the silent faces of the people who crowded around the newspaper offices as one bulletin from Washington followed another concerning Lincoln's death. Thousands of soldiers, freshly discharged, crowded around their comrades and officers and sought to be led back to the South for a new campaign of revenge.

But the honorable people of the South repudiated the Lincoln assassination conspirators and their deadly deed, and the war, although not officially ended by President Johnson's proclamation until nearly a year later, was not conducted for reprisal.

The 214th Pennsylvania Volunteers, 8th Union League Regiment, one of the last Philadelphia units to leave for service, arrived in Washington on the very day of the murder. It was as late as April 26 when the last regiment, the 215th Regiment (9th Union League), departed to relieve the returning combat veterans. This was the last body of soldiery to leave Philadelphia in the course of the war.[354]

The funeral services for the president were held in Washington at noon on April 19, four years to the hour from the fateful riot at Baltimore, where the first soldiers from Philadelphia and Massachusetts had been killed. At the same hour, in churches in every loyal city and state, the people gathered in testimony of their love for the martyred president.[355]

The body of the president reached Philadelphia on Saturday, April 22, and was followed by a large escort of soldiers and citizens from the Broad and Prime Street Station to Independence Hall. All that night and into the following Sunday, April 23, people processed reverently through the silent, mournful chamber of Independence Hall to gaze upon Lincoln's peaceful though careworn face.[356]

On three successive Sundays in April 1865, the populace had been subjected to the glorious news of the surrender of the Confederate army at Appomattox; then experienced the tragedy of the assassination of Abraham Lincoln; followed closely by the arrival of Lincoln's remains for a final visit to one of his favorite cities in the North.

At three o'clock on Monday morning, April 24, the First City Troop and the 187th PA Regiment, with muffled drums and arms reversed, the military salute to the fallen, escorted Lincoln's body to the Kensington Station at Front and Montgomery to board the funeral train to New York City. The train was waiting there to take Lincoln on to other cities and mourners on the long journey back to his final resting place at his former home in Springfield, Illinois.[357]

"Johnny Comes Marching Home" and Welcome Back

B eginning with May 21, 1865, when the 114ᵗʰ Regiment, Pennsylvania Volunteers (Collis's Zouaves), arrived home, the Philadelphia regiments and companies returned at frequent intervals and generally without advance information necessary for the arrangement of suitable receptions. It was, therefore, decided by the city authorities, with the concurrence of the higher military officers, to organize a grand review and thus afford the public a glimpse of the veterans and give expression to the soldiers of the honor in which they were held. The review took place June 10, 1865, in the midst of a heavy rainstorm. The reviewing stand was erected on the west side of Broad Street, between Market and Filbert Streets. Here were assembled a great throng of officials, officers and distinguished guests.[358]

Another stand, situated on the east side of Broad Street below Market Street, contained sick and wounded veterans and their families. On a third stand, north of Filbert Street, five hundred young ladies were placed to sing patriotic songs. Many other private stands bordered the route. For this event, every effort was made to secure the return of as many of the local regiments as possible. The route of the parade extended from Camp Cadwalader, far out Ridge Avenue, to the Volunteer Refreshment Saloons at the foot of Washington Avenue, where a much-appreciated dinner awaited every soldier. At the head of the review rode Major General George Gordon Meade and a brilliant staff, accompanied by the First Troop Philadelphia City Cavalry. The veterans were escorted by delegations from the city fire companies. The military division included detachments of the many Philadelphia regiments and batteries that had been discharged from service. In the rear of the army units came the sailors and marines from the United States ships in port.[359]

"Return of the Colors" Honor Ceremony, July 4, 1866—Final Act of the War

Never before was Philadelphia so beautifully decorated with the red, white and blue as on July Fourth 1866, for on that memorable day the soldiers of Pennsylvania were to return to the loving care of their state the battle flags that they had carried and fought under in so many battles. Broad, Market and Chestnut Streets were ablaze with streamers and flowers. With the onset of the day, the call of fife and drum pulsed in the air. With every new train, fresh thousands of soldiers and civilian onlookers poured into the crowded streets. At Independence Hall, on the spot facing Independence Square where the Declaration had been read to rally the people in defiance of Great Britain, a great stage had been erected, large enough to seat five thousand people. The first to arrive were the children of the Soldiers' Orphan Schools, for whom seats to the right and left of the "Court of Honor" had been provided. Behind them, still somber in mourning garb, were gathered the "invited guests," nearly all from the families of fallen soldiers. High up in the shadow of the old tower were placed the singers and the military band. A little lower in front stood the speakers' platform, flanked by tables for the press. Long before the coming of the parade of veterans, every foot of ground was filled with waiting citizens. From every window gazed groups of onlookers.

Promptly at ten o'clock in the morning, the march stepped off. The head of the column was formed on Broad Street above Arch Street. The route of the parade was down Broad Street to Market Street, to Twelfth Street, to Chestnut Street, to Second Street, to Walnut Street and to the rear of Independence Square.

First came Major General Winfield S. Hancock, his staff and escort, followed by the "First Defenders." Closely behind these came a host of banners, each war-worn flag carried by a color sergeant and escorted by six color corporals forming the color guard. The crowds cheered wildly as they caught sight of the glorious old battle flags waving in the breeze.

Return of the Pennsylvania Battle Flags. A sketch from Taylor's *Philadelphia in the Civil War* showing the final act of the Civil War in Philadelphia. On July 4, 1866, the battle flags of Pennsylvania regiments were returned to the state in a massive parade and ceremony at Independence Hall. The flags were then stored in quiet glory in Harrisburg, where they may still be viewed. *GAR Museum Collection.*

This brought tears to many filled with pent-up emotions of patriotic joy. In sequential order the colors, were borne to the waiting war governor of the commonwealth, Andrew G. Curtin, who was to receive them from the hands of General Meade as revered objects to be honored and preserved for future generations to view and ponder.[360]

Upon the massing of the veteran troops on Independence Square, the color guards were gathered in the Court of Honor, and with impressive speeches highlighting their individual service, the flags were presented by Major General Meade to Governor Curtin, who accepted them on behalf of the state of Pennsylvania.

The program included music provided by the Philadelphia military Birgfield's Band; prayers by Reverend Thomas Brainerd; the presentation of the regimental colors to Governor Curtin by Major General Meade; and addresses by the prominent figures of the war effort from Philadelphia. At the close of these exercises, cannons stationed in Washington Square fired a salute.

Few scenes in the history of Philadelphia were attended with so much pomp and drama as that seen when each war-worn guard of veterans parted from its beloved faded flags, which cost the lives of so many comrades in their defense.

During the day, the Keystone Battery, at the request of the Union League, fired one hundred guns on Penn Square. The celebration ended with fireworks at Penn Square. In charge of the Henry Guards, composed of Philadelphia police, the battle flags were stored in Sansom Street Hall under guard until the next day, when they were taken to Harrisburg for careful storage. These flags numbered over 330 standards. They were exhibited for many years in glass cases at the capitol, but they have now been removed to a proper facility for preservation.

Later that evening, Generals Meade, Humphreys and other Pennsylvania commanders were fêted at the new Union League House on Broad Street. General Meade was honored with the gold medal of the Union League, and General Humphreys was presented with the silver medal.[361]

Independence Hall during the Civil War

O n May 10, 1861, the *Philadelphia Inquirer* reported that Major Robert Anderson, the hero of Fort Sumter, arrived in Philadelphia while accompanying Mrs. Lincoln to Boston. His reception in the city was extraordinary. From the railroad station he was escorted in an open coach surrounded by a military guard and drawn by white horses through streets crowded with cheering throngs to Independence Hall, where Mayor Henry and city councils held a reception for him. Councils previously had voted to present the major with a sword in recognition of his defense of Fort Sumter.

On June 11, 1861, Lieutenant Adam Slemmer, who had held Fort Pickens until it was reinforced, received friends and congratulations in Independence Hall and, in the same manner as Major Anderson, was escorted through the streets and addressed by the mayor.

Many other prominent heroes of war service, as well as noted civic and political leaders, were hosted at Independence Hall for lavish receptions by the city. These included General Meade, General Hancock, President Lincoln, Vice President Hamlin, congressmen and many others.

However, all the heroes who came to Philadelphia were not received so joyfully. Many prominent casualties of the city were often afforded funeral services in the city, lying in state in Independence Hall, a powerful symbol and icon of America's past struggles. One of the first such casualties was Colonel Elmer Ellsworth, commander of Ellsworth's Zouaves (11th New York Volunteers). This leader had been shot down while attempting to remove

Parade of the Philadelphia Zouaves Corps in front of Independence Hall—1862. *Courtesy of the Historical Society of Pennsylvania.*

from the Marshall House Tavern in Alexandria a Southern flag that President Lincoln could see from the White House windows. Colonel Ellsworth's body was returned to the city on May 25. Included in the guard of honor was a Zouave, Francis E. Brownell, who had shot Ellsworth's murderer and who brought along the Secession flag that the colonel had cut down.

On June 12, the body of Lieutenant John Greble (1st U.S. Artillery), the first Pennsylvania officer killed in action at Big Bethel, arrived in the city and was escorted by a number of militia units to Independence Hall, where a funeral service was conducted.

Throughout the war, fallen heroes who had sacrificed their lives for the nation were brought back to Philadelphia via train, paraded to Independence Hall, laid in state and visited by mournful admirers before they were either laid to rest in a local cemetery or transported on to their hometowns for final interment. There were dozens of such sorrowful and tragic ceremonials held similarly during the course of the conflict. These victims of the conflict were mourned publicly and were buried with impressive ceremonies, but in a short time, thousands of their comrades fell and most lay where they had fallen, mourned only by their families. Other fallen heroes included:

The reception of the remains of Colonel Edward Baker, killed at the Battle of Ball's Bluff on November 7, 1861, was marked by a great demonstration. The remains of Colonel John S. Slocum, Major Solomon Ballou and Captain Levi Towers of the 2nd Rhode Island Regiment, killed at the First Battle of Bull Run, were received on March 26, 1862, by Colonel Staunton's 67th PV Regiment and escorted to Independence Hall.

The body of Major General Charles F. Smith, who was in command of the troops that captured Fort Donelson, was escorted to Independence Hall by a company of the Home Guard on May 3, 1862, and interred in Laurel Hill on May 6 with full military honors.

The funeral of Colonel John P. Van Lear, of the 6th New Jersey Regiment and killed at Williamsburg, took place on May 22, 1862, with military honors, and that of Colonel Charles Ellet Jr., of the ram fleet, took place on June 27, 1862. Both bodies lay in state in Independence Hall. General Bohlen of the 75th PV, who fell at Rappahannock Station in Virginia, was also afforded a military funeral at the shrine of Liberty in August 1862.

Colonel John A. Koltes was buried on September 5, 1862. Brigadier General Frank E. Patterson, son of Major General Robert Patterson, died at Fairfax Court House on November 26, 1862, and was honored with an imposing military display.

One of the most noteworthy funerals was that of Colonel John Richter Jones of the 58th PV on June 3, 1863. He was killed at Gum Swamp, North Carolina, on May 22. Among the commanding officers of regiments associated with Philadelphia, who were killed in action, were Colonels O.H. Rippey, Fair Oaks; John M. Gosline, Gaines' Mill; Henry J. Stainrook, Chancellorsville; and Francis Mahler at Gettysburg, all of whom were honored by funeral services at Independence Hall.

Camp Independence at Independence Hall, 1862, a wartime photograph of the army recruiting camp established on Independence Square. *GAR Museum Collection.*

Captain Thomas Elliott of the 28th PV, a trusted staff officer of General John W. Geary, was killed in action at Peach Tree Creek on July 20, 1864. Several days later, his remains were returned home and lay in honor at Independence Hall before taken to Laurel Hill for final interment.

On April 14, 1865, regimental colors were presented to the final unit of Colored Troops to leave the city for duty, the 24th USCT. They were reviewed at Independence Hall, and in a solemn ceremony attended by large crowds, the flags were entrusted to the care of the unit to guard unto death, if needed. The dedicatory address was delivered by Professor Octavius V. Catto, who had raised one of the first black companies for service in the Gettysburg emergency of 1863.[362]

The body of Abraham Lincoln was received on April 22, 1865, and escorted to Independence Hall by a large military and civic procession. It was estimated that tens of thousands passed through the hall in the eighteen hours it was open to the public to view Lincoln's remains and pay their final tribute before the cortege moved on to the next stop on the lonely way to his final resting place in Springfield.[363]

Civil War–Era Veterans' Organizations

A t the very conclusion of hostilities, the discharged veterans of the conflict began to establish fraternal societies and organized posts to maintain comradeship gained during their service, to promote patriotism and love of country and to provide material assistance to the widows and orphans of their comrades who had fallen and to their incapacitated fellow veterans. They also sought to commemorate their brave service to the nation and memorialize their deeds. A number of groups were organized to meet these goals, and Philadelphia became a center for the movement. In the post–Civil War period and into the twentieth century while still they lived, they created monuments to preserve their memory in towns and cities and on battlefields where they and their units had struggled. The monuments are still evident and visible in Philadelphia, though nowadays they are somewhat forlorn and forgotten.

MILITARY ORDER OF THE LOYAL LEGION

The Military Order of the Loyal Legion of the United States (MOLLUS) had its inception on the day the nation learned that President Abraham Lincoln had died at the hand of an assassin.

In honor of that illustrious leader and of the great cause for which we had fought; in recognition of the affectionate friendship which had been inspired among the officers of the Army and Navy; in historic recollection of role of the Society of the Cincinnati, which had embraced the officers of the Revolutionary Army, it was determined to form a similar Order; and at a meeting of a few officers in the city of Philadelphia the initial steps were taken for its organization. It was the first of the military societies which followed after the close of the War.[364]

On April 15, 1865, a meeting was held at the office of Lieutenant Colonel Thomas Ellwood Zell, in Philadelphia, to propose that the officers and ex-officers of the army and navy act as a guard of honor to the remains of the president. It was determined by those present to call a meeting of those who had served in the war on April 20, 1865, when Colonel Zell presented a proposal that a society should be formed to commemorate the events and principles of the War for the Union, and that resolutions should be adopted to found such an organization. Following this, additional meetings of those interested were held, and a provisional organization was created at a meeting held May 31 in Congress Hall on Independence Square.

Brevet Lieutenant Colonel Samuel Brown Wylie Mitchell, Lieutenant Colonel Thomas Ellwood Zell and Captain Peter Dirck Keyser were there designated as the founders of the order, with Colonel Mitchell's insignia and diploma bearing No. 1.

The plan for a permanent organization having been adopted, the Commandery of the State of Pennsylvania was organized November 4, 1865, to date from April 15, commemorating the day of the first meeting.[365]

GRAND ARMY OF THE REPUBLIC

Beside the campfires of the veterans of the Union armed forces, the men had dreamed and talked of the preservation of the comradeship they had enjoyed under adversity in service to their country. It was an army surgeon in Springfield, Illinois, the home city of the martyred war president, who took the first step to create an organization. Dr. Benjamin F. Stephenson organized the first post of the Grand Army of the Republic (GAR) at Decatur, Illinois, on April 6, 1866, thus becoming the founder of the order. He called together veterans from throughout the nation to gather to build the greatest association of military veterans ever known.

Ellis' Post #6, Grand Army of the Republic Monument on Market Square, Germantown. A lithograph of the soldiers' memorial commemorating the service of local veterans. *GAR Museum Collection.*

The first meeting was held in Springfield on July 12, 1866. With Dr. Stephenson as provisional commander in chief, he called the first National Encampment to convene at Indianapolis, Indiana, on November 20, 1866. Prior to this, many states had organized departments that began to accept individual posts into the order.

The Second National Encampment was held in Philadelphia on January 15, 16 and 17, 1868, and hosted by the posts of the city. Major General John A. Logan was elected commander in chief. Logan instituted the annual Memorial Day for May 30 each year at this convention. The principles of the order were exemplified in the motto "Friendship, Charity and Loyalty." Former military rank was not officially recognized in the order. All honorably discharged veterans were eligible for membership, regardless of whether a major general or a private soldier; all were equal in the post hall, including colored (African American) veterans.

Membership in the order reached its zenith at circa 500,000 members in 1890, organized into over eight thousand posts nationwide and in several foreign countries. The last member of the Grand Army, Albert Woolson of Duluth, Minnesota, died at age 109 in 1956, and with him the order ceased to exist. The Grand Army of the Republic did, however, create a descendant organization that carries on its principles and mission: the Sons of Union Veterans of the Civil War. This organization was inaugurated by a Philadelphia post—Anna M. Ross Post #94—when it created a cadet corps in 1879 to assist the post with its ceremonials and carry on its work.[366]

Three National Encampments (reunions) of the Grand Army of the Republic were held in Philadelphia: January 15, 1868, Second Encampment; June 30, 1876, Tenth Encampment; and the September 6, 1899 Thirty-third Encampment, which was attended by seventeen thousand veterans, making it the largest in the history of the Grand Army.

Five Philadelphians served as commander in chief of the order, the highest office in the Grand Army. Philadelphia boasted thirty-six posts of the Grand Army of the Republic at the heyday of the order in 1892. The two largest in membership and considered elite posts were Post #1, General George G. Meade at 1221 Chestnut Street (formerly Concert Hall); and Post #2 (no name) at 667 North Twelfth Street. There were also several specialty posts appealing to certain groups of veterans. Examples were the German-speaking Koltes Post #228 at Keystone Hall, corner of Second and Poplar Streets; the Cavalry Post #35 at Broad and Wood Streets; and Post #77, which had no name, but members were also members of the Patriotic Order Sons of America at POS of A Hall 524 North Sixth Street. Post

#191 Pennsylvania Reserves at the southwest corner of Fifth and Chestnut Streets (Old City Hall at Independence Hall), later at Industrial Hall, 318 North Broad Street, attracted former veterans of that famous corps. Navy and marine veterans joined Post #400, the Naval Post, at the northwest corner of Eighth and Vine Streets, later 132 South Eighth Street. Two posts were named after beloved volunteer nurses: Post #12, Hetty Jones, on Ridge Avenue in Roxborough; and Anna M. Ross Post #94 at the southeast corner of Girard Avenue and Hutchinson Street. Colored veterans had three posts for African American veterans: Post #27, John W. Jackson at Magnolia Hall, Sixteenth and Lombard Streets; Post #80, Robert Bryan, on the southeast corner Eleventh and Bainbridge Streets; and Post #103, Charles Sumner, at 909 North Ninth Street.[367]

MEMORIAL DAY IN PHILADELPHIA

The veterans of Civil War service sought to venerate the memory of their comrades who had fallen during the war and commemorate their deeds. They also mourned those who followed afterward in death until the last

Memorial Day services at Laurel Hill Cemetery conducted by the Meade Post #1, Grand Army of the Republic on May 30, 1901. *Abraham Lincoln Foundation of the Union League Archive.*

Grand Army veteran died. A ceremony of remembrance was observed annually from 1868 down to the present Memorial Day. On Memorial Day (sometimes called Decoration Day), May 30, appropriate services and ceremonies were held at the burial places of departed comrades and veterans of all wars, and their graves were marked with flowers and wreaths. Armed escorts of the veterans discharged traditional rifle volleys over the dead in salute, and families and friends joined in the solemn proceedings to honor those who had served.

The duties for Memorial Day were divided among the different GAR posts, with each taking charge of the ceremonies year after year at the same cemetery. Often, the post dedicated a burial plot for its comrades at this same cemetery. An example was the Meade Post #1 plot at Laurel Hill Cemetery.[368]

Over the years, Post #1 hosted impressive ceremonies on Memorial Day that included many famous visitors and guests, including: Generals Grant and Sherman; President Benjamin Harrison, who attended in 1891 and was the guest of honor; and many noted Civil War heroes, such as Joshua L. Chamberlin, a member of the post, Dr. Russell Conwell and many others.

REGIMENTAL ASSOCIATIONS

The spirit of fraternity and loyalty to traditions among the veterans in civil life prompted the organization of regimental associations for the perpetuation of friendships and for mutual aid in the years to come for members of the same commands.

Some of the activities of the regimental associations have been excursions to the scenes of their campaigns and battles as soldiers and the publication of regimental histories of the unit. One of the most important of the many things accomplished by the associations was the placement of beautiful memorials and monuments, often erected with state assistance, and dedicated on the site of their positions on the battle line, marking for all time the scenes where they fought. This has conspicuously been done at the sites of victories such as Antietam, Gettysburg and around Chattanooga, but also at former prison camps.

These memorials have been turned over to the care of the federal and state governments.[369]

ORGANIZATION OF NAVAL VETERANS

The first organization of Union veterans of the navy was the Farragut Naval Veteran Association No. 1, formed in Philadelphia within two years of the close of the war. The order included, as eligible, any officer or enlisted man who served in the United States Navy, Marine Corps or Revenue Marine (Coast Guard) during any portion of the Civil War. The Second National Convention met at Philadelphia in the hall of Naval Post 400 in September 1888. Generally, the annual conventions were held at the same places and coincident with the National Encampments of the Grand Army of the Republic, with which the majority of the navy veterans were also identified. This included GAR posts composed exclusively of seamen, one of which, Post 400, was organized in 1883 in Philadelphia.

An independent association that existed in Philadelphia was the Naval Veteran Legion, which was closely allied to Naval Post 400. The legion originated in a reunion of the survivors of the crew of the sloop of war *Jamestown* who were shipwrecked during a voyage around the world in the course of the Civil War.[370]

WOMEN'S RELIEF CORPS

The Grand Army of the Republic conferred official standing upon this organization of patriotic women as a national auxiliary to the GAR. The Women's Relief Corps was formed from a large number of local and state corps, generally composed of the female relatives of soldiers and informally attached to various posts. All loyal women were eligible for membership. The officers and delegates were accorded every courtesy by the Grand Army of the Republic and were invited to witness ceremonies and post activities.

The mission of the Women's Relief Corps was to specially aid and assist the members of the Grand Army of the Republic and to perpetuate the memory of the heroic dead, as well as to inculcate lessons of patriotism and love of country not only the membership but also among children.[371]

Medal-of-Honor Legion of the United States

An act was passed by the Congress of the United States and approved by the president on July 12, 1862, authorizing the War Department "to cause Medals of Honor to be prepared, with suitable emblematic devices, and to direct that the same be presented in the name of Congress to such non-commissioned officers and privates as shall most distinguish themselves by their gallantry in action and other soldier-like qualities during the present insurrection."

By a further act approved March 3, 1863, commissioned officers were included among those eligible for heroism in action for the distinction of the Medal of Honor.

Under an act approved December 21, 1861, the secretary of the navy was authorized "to cause Medals of Honor to be prepared, with suitable emblematic devices, for presentation to such petty officers, seamen, landsmen and marines as shall most distinguish themselves by their gallantry in action and other seaman-like qualities during the present war." Under a further act approved July 16, 1862, seamen "distinguishing themselves in battle or by extraordinary heroism in the line of their profession" were eligible to promotion, "as they were best qualified, upon recommendation of their commanding officer, approved by the commander and the Department." Such promotion carried with it the right to the Medal of Honor.

By virtue of these acts, Medals of Honor were presented to those found to be worthy of them in the armed services during the Civil War. By later enactment, Congress provided for awarding Medals of Honor to soldiers, sailors and marines who distinguished themselves "conspicuously by gallantry and intrepidity at the risk of his or her life above and beyond the call of duty while engaged in an action against an enemy of the United States" down to the present time.

At Washington, D.C, on April 23, 1890, veterans of the army and navy holding Medals of Honor met and organized a military and naval order named the Medal-of-Honor Legion of the United States of America. Gatherings of this order were often held in Philadelphia at the Union League.[372]

Medal of Honor Recipients

O ver seventy-five Civil War veterans associated with Philadelphia were recipients of the Medal of Honor for their war service. They include men from all branches of the armed services, regular army, volunteers, navy and marines. Most of them received the award years after the war, even into the early twentieth century. Many were prominent members of Philadelphia society, and others were ordinary citizens who had demonstrated extraordinary service in combat. Among the better-known recipients was Henry H. Bingham, who was a ten-term congressman and leader of the Republican Party. At the Battle of the Wilderness, Virginia, on May 6, 1864, he rallied and led into action troops that had given way under the fierce assaults. Bingham was promoted a brigadier general by brevet. Bingham is buried in Laurel Hill Cemetery.

Another recipient was Thomas Cripps, a quartermaster in the navy. He served aboard USS *Richmond*. As captain of a gun during action against Rebel forts and gunboats and with the ram *Tennessee* in Mobile Bay on August 5, 1864, Cripps fought his gun with skill and courage throughout a furious two-hour battle that resulted in the surrender of the ram *Tennessee* and in the damaging and destruction of batteries at Fort Morgan. He is buried in Woodlands Cemetery.

Michael Dougherty was born in Ireland and immigrated to Philadelphia. He served in the 13th Pennsylvania Cavalry. At the head of his company, he dashed across an open field, exposed to a deadly fire from the enemy, and succeeded in dislodging the enemy from a house, which he and his comrades defended for several hours against repeated attacks, thus preventing the enemy from flanking the position of the Union forces. Dougherty was captured and sent to Andersonville Prison, which he survived. On his return home, he was aboard the USS *Sultana* when it blew up in the Mississippi, but again he survived. After the war, he moved to Bristol, Pennsylvania, where he worked and lived. He was active in the Grand Army Post #73 and the Ancient Order of Hibernians. He is buried in St. Mark's Catholic Churchyard, Bristol.

Frank Furness served as captain and commander of Company F, 6th Pennsylvania Cavalry (Rush's Lancers). He was awarded the Medal of Honor for his bravery at the Battle of Trevilian Station, Virginia, on June 12, 1864, for bravery in carrying ammunition while running to an outpost across an open space that was swept by fire of the enemy. After the war, he became the best-known architect in Philadelphia. He is buried in Laurel Hill Cemetery.

John F. Mackie served as a sergeant in the United States Marine Corps. When his award was issued to him on July 10, 1863, he became the first member of the Marine Corps to receive the Medal of Honor. However, since he was on active duty at the time, his medal came to him later via the mail.

St. Clair Mulholland was born in Ireland. While serving as major of the 116th Pennsylvania Volunteers at Chancellorsville, Virginia, on May 4, 1863, he commanded the picket line, holding the enemy in check all night to cover the retreat of the army. After the war, he served as commissioner of police and was a member of the Union League. He is buried in Old Cathedral Cemetery, Philadelphia.

George C. Platt was awarded the Medal of Honor as a private in Troop H, 6th U.S. Cavalry, for action on July 3, 1863, at Fairfield, Pennsylvania, in the Gettysburg Campaign. He seized his regiment's flag when the color-bearer fell in a hand-to-hand fight and prevented it from falling into the hands of the enemy. The Platt Bridge over the Schuylkill River was named for him. He is buried in Holy Cross Cemetery, Yeadon, Pennsylvania.

Alfred Sellers received the Medal of Honor for action at Gettysburg, Pennsylvania, on July 1, 1863. In command of his 90th Pennsylvania Regiment, he held his position under a withering fire, from which position the enemy was repulsed. He is buried in Mount Vernon Cemetery, Philadelphia.

Finally, John M. Vanderslice was a private in the 8th Pennsylvania Cavalry. At Hatchers Run, Virginia, on February 6, 1865, he was the first man to storm the enemy's rifle pits, which were captured. After the war, Vanderslice was active in the leadership of the Grand Army of the Republic veterans' organization.[373]

Philadelphia's Civil War Memorials, Monuments and Parks

Among the monuments and memorials erected in the city by veterans and citizens to commemorate the honorable service of Philadelphians in the Civil War are the equestrian statue of General John F. Reynolds at the North Plaza of city hall; the equestrian statue of General George B. McClellan at the North Plaza of city hall; the monument of the Artillery Corps, Washington Grays in front of the Union League; the monument of the First Regiment Infantry (Gray Reserves), known as the *Spirit of '61*, in front of the Union League; the bronze memorial tablet of the Union League regiments in the main corridor of the Union League House; the monument for the alumni and cadets of Girard College who served during the Civil War on the campus of Girard College; the soldiers and sailors of the Civil War monument on Market Square, Germantown; the monument, *Silent Sentinel*, for the soldiers' home (formerly at Mount Moriah Cemetery); the monument for Abraham Lincoln, the Emancipator, along Kelly Drive at Lemon Hill; the equestrian statue of General U.S. Grant on Kelly Drive; the equestrian statue of General George G. Meade behind Memorial Hall, West Fairmount Park; the statue of the soldier of the Civil War (Courtland Saunders Post #21, GAR) near George's Hill, West Fairmount Park; the Civil War soldiers and sailors memorial pylons monument dedicated to the army and navy near Twentieth Street and Benjamin Franklin Parkway; the Garfield Memorial (president and general in the Civil War) along Kelly Drive, East Fairmount Park; the General Galusha Pennypacker Memorial at Nineteenth Street and Benjamin Franklin Parkway on Logan Circle; the all wars memorial to colored

Above: A contemporary lithograph of the principal Philadelphia Civil War Memorial, also known as the Smith Memorial. *GAR Museum Collection.*

Below left: Abraham Lincoln Monument. A lithograph of Lincoln's the Emancipator monument, dedicated in 1871, one of the first Lincoln memorials in the country. It stands in silent glory along Kelly Drive. *GAR Museum Collection.*

Below right: A picture of the notable equestrian monument of General Meade dedicated in 1887 and placed in West Fairmount Park behind Memorial Hall. The sculptor was Alexander M. Calder, and the monument was produced from captured Confederate cannon. *GAR Museum Collection.*

Above: Dr. Russell Conwell's grave. Russell Conwell was the founder of Temple University. He was a Union officer in the Civil War and dedicated his life to the ministry and education based on incidents he experienced during the war. *Author's collection.*

Right: An early Civil War monument erected in Cedar Hill Cemetery in Frankford honoring local veterans who fell during the war. *Author's collection.*

A modern view of the Philadelphia Civil War Memorial—popularly known as the Smith Memorial after its benefactor—located in West Fairmount Park on the Centennial Concourse grounds next to Memorial Hall. *Photo by Arlene Harris.*

soldiers and sailors on Logan Circle; the Frankford Civil War Monument in Cedar Hill Cemetery; the soldiers monument; Hetty Jones Tomb, Leverington Cemetery; the Scott Legion Monument in Philadelphia National Cemetery; the Civil War memorial tablet to students of the university who fell in the Civil War, University of Pennsylvania; the Corporal Johnny Ring Statue, Corporal Johnny Ring Garden, Mitten Hall, main campus, Temple University; Lincoln the Lawyer, in front of Temple Law School on Broad Street; Captain John Ericsson Fountain (who designed the USS *Monitor*) on the west side of Eakins Oval in front of the art museum; Clark Park Civil War Memorial (a boulder from Devil's Den at Gettysburg) on the north side of Clark Park; and the Philadelphia Civil War Memorial, also known as the Smith Memorial, from a bequest of Richard Smith on Centennial Concourse in West Fairmount Park. The military and naval figures featured on this last memorial are the equestrian statue of General Winfield S. Hancock, the equestrian statue of General George B. McClellan, the statue of General Meade, the statue of General Reynolds, and the busts of Admiral David D. Porter, General John F. Hartranft, Admiral Dahlgren, General S. Wylie Crawford, General James A. Beaver and war governor Andrew G. Curtin, executed by Moses Ezekiel, a noted sculptor who had served in the Confederate army. In addition, there are other memorials, plaques and monuments scattered throughout the area, in churches, cemeteries and institutions. Like a treasure hunt of history, the dedicated can seek out these vestiges of the Civil War and ponder their meaning and significance.[374]

PUBLIC SQUARES AND PARKS NAMED FOR CIVIL WAR NOTABLES

These sites were dedicated to heroes of the war by the Grand Army of the Republic veterans and their posts or were honored by the city. They include the Greble Park, Third Street near Moyamensing Avenue, named in honor of Lieutenant John Greble, 1st U.S. Artillery, who was the first Union officer killed in action in the Civil War; the Birney Park, Sixth Street and Germantown Avenue, named for General David Bell Birney; Thomas J. Powers Park, Ann, Mercer and Almond Streets in Port Richmond, named for a navy veteran and politician; Anna M. Ross Park, Tenth Street and Glenwood Avenue, named for the beloved volunteer nurse; Baker Park, Rising Sun Avenue and York Road, named for General Edward Baker, one

The stately equestrian monument dedicated to General Meade by the citizens of Philadelphia. *GAR Museum Collection.*

of the first major casualties in the war; Reynolds Park, Snyder and Passyunk Avenues and Twenty-third Street, named for General John F. Reynolds, who was killed at Gettysburg; and George C. Platt Memorial Bridge, located over the Schuylkill River, named for an Irish immigrant cavalry trooper who enlisted in the 6th United States Cavalry. He was awarded the Medal of Honor for bravery at the Battle of Fairfield, Pennsylvania, in the Gettysburg Campaign.[375]

Philadelphia-Based Civil War Museums, Institutions and Organizations

Abraham Lincoln Foundation of the Union League of Philadelphia; Sir John
    Templeton Center for Civil War History Research at the Union League
African American Museum in Philadelphia
Athenaeum on Washington Square
Atwater-Kent Museum of the City of Philadelphia
City of Philadelphia—Department of Records
Civil War Museum of Philadelphia (in transition)
College of Physicians of Philadelphia
First Troop Philadelphia City Cavalry Museum
Fort Mifflin on the Delaware
Free Library of Philadelphia
General Meade Society of Philadelphia
Grand Army of the Republic (GAR) Civil War Museum & Library
Historical Society of Pennsylvania
Laurel Hill Cemetery
Lest We Forget Museum of African American Slavery
Library Company of Philadelphia
Masonic Library & Museum of Pennsylvania
Military Order of the Loyal Legion of the United States, Pennsylvania
    Commandery
Mother Bethel AME Church and Richard Allen Museum
National Archives & Records Administration, Mid-Atlantic Region
103rd Engineer Battalion Museum

Philadelphia Civil War History Consortium at the Union League of Philadelphia

Philadelphia History Museum at the Atwater Kent

Rosenbach Museum & Library

Temple University—Civil War and Emancipation Studies Urban Archives—Special Collections at Paley Library; Blockson Collection of African American History

Underground Railroad Museum at Belmont Mansion

University of Pennsylvania Rare Book and Manuscript Library

Woodlands Cemetery

Notes

Philadelphia at the Outbreak of Rebellion

1. Taylor, *Philadelphia in the Civil War*, 9; Gallman, *Mastering Wartime*, 1–3.
2. Scharf, and Westcott, *History of Philadelphia.*
3. Gallman, Mastering Wartime, 2; Weigley, *Philadelphia*, 363.
4. Scharf and Westcott, *History of Philadelphia*, 2171.
5. Ibid., 1703.
6. Dusinberre, *Civil War Issues in Philadelphia.*
7. Wainwright, "The Loyal Opposition," 294; Weigley, *Philadelphia*, 375.
8. Mackay, "Philadelphia During the Civil War."
9. Dusinberre, *Civil War Issues in Philadelphia*, 27–33.
10. Ibid., 76–79.
11. Weigley, *Philadelphia*, 391–92.
12. Dusinberre, *Civil War Issues in Philadelphia*, 102–3.
13. *Philadelphia Inquirer*, November 8, 1860.
14. Dusinberre, *Civil War Issues in Philadelphia*, 95.
15. Ibid., 111.
16. Ibid., 108.
17. Ibid., 109.
18. *Philadelphia Inquirer*, December 17, 1860.
19. Ibid., December 20, 1860.
20. Dusinberre, *Civil War Issues in Philadelphia*, 116–17.
21. *Philadelphia Inquirer*, April 13 and 15, 1861.

22. Ibid., April 13, 1861.
23. Taylor, *Philadelphia in the Civil War*, 29.
24. *Public Ledger*, April 15, 1861; Mackay, "Philadelphia During the Civil War"; Weigley, *Philadelphia*, 394–95; Taylor, *Philadelphia in the Civil War*, 27–28.
25. Gallman, *Mastering Wartime*, 11–12; Weigley, *Philadelphia*, 395–96.
26. Mackay, "Philadelphia During the Civil War," 4–5.
27. Ibid., 5.
28. Ibid.
29. *Philadelphia Inquirer*, April 15, 1861.
30. Mackay, "Philadelphia During the Civil War," 5–6.
31. *Philadelphia Inquirer*, April 15, 1861.
32. Ibid.
33. Mackay, "Philadelphia During the Civil War," 6.
34. Ibid., 6.
35. *Philadelphia Inquirer*, April 20, 1861.
36. Mackay, "Philadelphia During the Civil War," 8.
37. Taylor, *Philadelphia in the Civil War*, 265.

ETHNIC MAKE-UP OF PHILADELPHIA, IMMIGRATION AND MILITARY PARTICIPATION

38. Gallman, *Mastering Wartime*, 1; Davis and Haller, *Peoples of Philadelphia*, 136–37.
39. Davis and Haller, *Peoples of Philadelphia*, 137: Clark, *Irish in Philadelphia*; *Leaving the Emerald Isle*.
40. Clark, *Irish in Philadelphia*.
41. Miller, *Philadelphia: Immigrant City*.
42. Ibid.

The Irish were initially poorer than the Germans, who were often skilled laborers or craftsmen. In 1850, nearly half of the Irish worked in day labor, handloom weaving or carting, and less than a third of them were in skilled trades. The construction laborers, especially, lived in alleys and side streets all over the city. There were some Irish concentrations in the Southwark, Moyamensing and Gray's Ferry districts along the southern border of the city. Two-thirds of the Germans, by contrast, were employed in trades such as tailoring, shoemaking and baking, and they had settled heavily in the Northern Liberties, Kensington, Fishtown and other newer manufacturing districts to the northeast of the old city.

43. Ibid., 138.
44. Weigley, *Philadelphia*, 385.
45. Wolf, "The American Jew as Patriot, Soldier and Citizen."
46. Taylor, *Philadelphia in the Civil War*, 187–95.
47. Rolph, *Two Hispanic Brothers.*
48. Kowalewski, *Captain Mlotkowski*; Bolek, *Who's Who in Polish America.*
49. Pivany, *Hungarians in the American Civil War*; Vida, "True Cause of Freedom." Other immigrants from Philadelphia included General Joshua T. Owen from Wales; Colonel Max Einstein, a German Jew; General Alexander Schimmelfennig, a Prussian German; and General Henry Bohlen, born in Germany. Those from Ireland were Michael Kerwin of the 13th Pennsylvania Cavalry, the Irish Dragoons; Dennis O'Kane of the Philadelphia Brigade; St. Clair Mulholland of the Irish Brigade and Medal of Honor recipient; Charles Collis of the 114th Pennsylvania Volunteers, another Medal of Honor recipient; Dennis Heenan of the 116th Pennsylvania Volunteers; James Gwyn of the 118th Pennsylvania Volunteers, the Corn Exchange Regiment; John Flynn of the 28th Pennsylvania Volunteers; and a number more. Canada was represented by William H. Boyd of the 21st Pennsylvania Cavalry.
50. Lonn, *Foreigners in the Union Army*; Bates, *Martial Deeds of Pennsylvania.*

FIRST PHILADELPHIA VOLUNTEERS TO THE WARFRONT AND THE BALTIMORE RIOT

51. *Public Ledger*, April 16, 1861; *Philadelphia Inquirer*, April 16, 1861.
52. *Philadelphia Inquirer*, April 20, 1861–April 23, 1861; Taylor, *Philadelphia in the Civil War*, 28–29; Weigley, *Philadelphia*, 395: Mackay, "Philadelphia During the Civil War," 9. Private George Leisenring, 2nd Regiment, Washington Brigade, died of his wounds suffered in the Baltimore Riot at Pennsylvania Hospital and was buried in Union Wesleyan and Harmony Burial Ground in Fishtown (then Kensington).
53. Mackay, "Philadelphia During the Civil War," 9; Oberholtzer, *Philadelphia*, 11, 362.
54. Scharf and Westcott, *History of Philadelphia*, 790; Weigley, *Philadelphia*, 398; *Philadelphia Inquirer*, April 24, 1861.

55. Bates, *History of Pennsylvania Volunteers*; Taylor, *Philadelphia in the Civil War*, 31; Weigley, *Philadelphia*, 396.

56. Gallman, *Mastering Wartime*, 254; Bacon, *Sinews of War.*

57. Mackay, "Philadelphia During the Civil War," 10–11; *North American*, April 29, 1861.

58. *North American*, April 25, 1861; Mackay, "Philadelphia During the Civil War," 11–12.

59. Ibid., 12.

60. Ibid., 12–13; *North American*, April 26, 1861.

61. *North American*, April 22, 1861.

62. Mackay, "Philadelphia During the Civil War," 13; approved by an ordinance of City Councils, May 23, 1861, under an act of the Pennsylvania General Assembly, May 16, 1861. See "Report of General Pleasonton to Mayor Henry" (1861).

63. *North American*, April 26, 1861; Mackay, "Philadelphia During the Civil War," 13.

64. Mackay, "Philadelphia During the Civil War," 13–14.

65. Ibid., 14.

POLITICAL OPPOSITION TO THE WAR

66. Wainwright, "Loyal Opposition," 294–314; *The Age*, July 14, 1864; Mackay, "Philadelphia During the Civil War," 15–16.

67. Wainwright, "Loyal Opposition," 297; Mackay, "Philadelphia During the Civil War," 26.

68. Scharf and Westcott, *History of Philadelphia*, 770.

69. Wainwright, "Loyal Opposition," 299.

70. Mackay, "Philadelphia During the Civil War," 35.

71. Wainwright, "Loyal Opposition," 312; Mackay, "Philadelphia During the Civil War," 35–36.

72. Wainwright, "Loyal Opposition," 295–96.

73. Ibid., 295.

74. Ibid.; Weigley, *Philadelphia*, 403.

75. Weigley, *Philadelphia*, 407.

76. Ibid., 402–4.

77. Wainwright, "Loyal Opposition," 300.

78. Sprogle, *Philadelphia Police*; Gallman, *Mastering Wartime*, 183–85.

79. Wainwright, "Loyal Opposition," 308; Oberholtzer, *Philadelphia*, 379.
80. Weigley, *Philadelphia*, 405.
81. Greenberg, *Charles Ingersoll*, 190–217.
82. Dusinberre, *Civil War Issues in Philadephia*, 174.

ABRAHAM LINCOLN IN PHILADELPHIA

83. Hoch, *Lincoln Trail*, 8–11, 44.
84. Basler, *Collected Works.*
85. Mires, *Independence Hall*, 6–8.
86. Weigley, *Philadelphia*, 393.
87. Hoch, *Lincoln Trail*, 8–9.
88. Basler, *Collected Works*, vol. 4, 240–41.
89. This narration was approved by William B. Spittall, a surviving Pinkerton agent who was one of the guards in Lincoln's car. Allan Pinkerton was delegated by General McClellan to organize the Secret Service of the army. He held a military commission as "Major E.J. Allen" (the maiden name of Pinkerton's wife). Taylor, *Philadelphia in the Civil War*, 16.
90. Taylor, *Philadelphia in the Civil War*, 16.
91. Hoch, *Lincoln Trail*, 135.
92. *Philadelphia Inquirer*, April 24, 1865.
93. Basler, *Collected Works*. Local newspapers noted that in the very same room in which Lincoln lay in state, he had pledged his life to the promise of liberty found in the Declaration, and they reprinted the text of his February 22, 1861 speech with its stunning conclusion: "If this country cannot be saved without giving up that principle…I would rather be assassinated!"

PHILADELPHIA CIVIL WAR MILITARY HOSPITALS

94. Mackay, "Philadelphia During the Civil War," 25–26; Taylor, *Philadelphia in the Civil War*, 224–27.
95. Mackay, "Philadelphia During the Civil War," 25.
96. Weigley, *Philadelphia*, 402.
97. Taylor, *Philadelphia in the Civil War*, 228.

98. Weigley, *Philadelphia*, 395; Taylor, *Philadelphia in the Civil War*, 29; *Philadelphia Inquirer*, April 23, 1861.

99. Weigley, *Philadelphia*, 402; Taylor, *Philadelphia in the Civil War*, 231–34.

100. Weigley, *Philadelphia*, 399–400; Taylor, *Philadelphia in the Civil War*, 231–34.

101. *Medical and Surgical History of the War of the Rebellion*, 906–8.

102. Ibid., 906.

103. Weigley, *Philadelphia*, 399; Taylor, *Philadelphia in the Civil War*, 231–34; *Satterlee Hospital*.

104. Vieira, *West Philadelphia Illustrated*, 178–79; Taylor, *Philadelphia in the Civil War*, 234–35; Mackay, "Philadelphia During the Civil War," 25; *Notes on Satterlee Hospital*, from collection at the GAR Museum.

105. Taylor, *Philadelphia in the Civil War*, 227.

106. Ibid.

107. Weigley, *Philadelphia*, 399; Taylor, *Philadelphia in the Civil War*, 227; *Philadelphia Inquirer*, November 11, 1862.

108. Rev. S. Hotchkins, *Ancient and Modern Germantown, Mt. Airy and Chestnut Hill, 1889*. The information was furnished by Dr. James Darrach of Germantown, Germantown Historical Society.

109. Taylor, *Philadelphia in the Civil War*, 228; Mackay, "Philadelphia During the Civil War," 25.

110. Taylor, *Philadelphia in the Civil War*, 228, 230; Mackay, "Philadelphia During the Civil War," 25.

111. Taylor, *Philadelphia in the Civil War*, 229; Mackay, "Philadelphia During the Civil War," 25.

112. Miller, *History of the German Hospital*; Mills, *Military History of the Falls of Schuylkill*; Taylor, *Philadelphia in the Civil War*, 228.

113. Taylor, *Philadelphia in the Civil War*, 224–37. A Pennsylvania State Historical marker for Mower Hospital was placed at the Wyndmoor Station in 2000 by a committee headed by Dr. Sandford Sher, a local historian and specialist in Mower Hospital.

BENEVOLENT AND VOLUNTEER SERVICE ORGANIZATIONS OF PHILADELPHIA

114. Taylor, *Philadelphia in the Civil War*, 262; Gallman, *Mastering Wartime*, 126.

115. Maxwell, *Lincoln's Fifth Wheel*; Brockett and Vaughn, *Women's Work in the*

Civil War, 596–606; Mackay, "Philadelphia During the Civil War," 27–28. In 1862, much-prized certificates were given to children for picking lint for bandages. So great was the zeal of the boys and girls in the schools that the secretary of the Sanitary Commission sent out word late in the year that no more lint could be accepted.

116. Taylor, *Philadelphia in the Civil War*, 263.
117. Stille, *Memorial of the Great Central Fair. Our Daily Fair* was the daily newspaper of the fair.
118. Taylor, *Philadelphia in the Civil War*, 263; Gallman, *Mastering Wartime*, 126.
119. Meade, *Life and Letters of General Meade*, 209.
120. Stille, *Memorial of the Great Central Fair*; *Public Ledger*, July 1, 1864.
121. Gallman, *Mastering Wartime*, 126; Taylor, *Philadelphia in the Civil War*, 262–64; Mackay, "Philadelphia During the Civil War," 27–28.
122. Taylor, *Philadelphia in the Civil War*, 265.
123. Ibid., 264.
124. Brockett and Vaughn, *Women's Work in the Civil War*, 293–94; Taylor, *Philadelphia in the Civil War*, 306.
125. Taylor, *Philadelphia in the Civil War*, 307.
126. Ibid.; Brockett and Vaughn, *Women's Work in the Civil War*, 647–49.
127. Taylor, *Philadelphia in the Civil War*, 307.
128. Ibid.
129. Ibid.
130. Ibid., 308.
131. Ibid., 309.
132. *Philadelphia Inquirer*, February 10, 1863; May 12, 1863; February 17, 1864; May 26, 1864; November 17, 1864; Gallman, *Mastering Wartime*, 136.

Many Confederate prisoners and refugees were brought into Philadelphia. Public meetings were held to help organize relief. The prisoners were fed, clothed and given work. Philadelphia's charity toward the late enemy was as generous as its patriotism.

Soldiers' relief efforts by the city: The final report of the Commission for the Relief of Families of Philadelphia Volunteers indicates that financial assistance was given in the course of the war to 48,707 families. In addition, money was repaid to the Philadelphia Gas Works for sums disbursed to dependents of employees who had enlisted. The commission met the funeral expenses of 780 soldiers or members of soldiers' families. The members of the commission were citizens of the city, including the mayor, Alexander Henry, as president and Charles P. Trego as vice-president; Theodore Cuyler, MD, Charles E. Lex, Matthew W. Baldwin, Caleb Cope and other civic leaders. Taylor, *Philadelphia in the Civil War*; Mitchell, *In Wartime*.

Southwark Refreshment Saloon Movement

133. Taylor, *Philadelphia in the Civil War*, 206; Mackay, "Philadelphia During the Civil War," 21; Weigley, *Philadelphia*, 399; Gallman, *Mastering Wartime*, 135.
134. Mackay, "Philadelphia During the Civil War," 22.
135. Gallman, *Mastering Wartime*, 129; Taylor, *Philadelphia in the Civil War*, 207; Mackay, "Philadelphia During the Civil War," 20.
136. Mackay, "Philadelphia During the Civil War," 20; Taylor, *Philadelphia in the Civil War*, 207.
137. Mackay, Philadelphia During the Civil War," 21; Taylor, *Philadelphia in the Civil War*, 209.
138. Mackay, "Philadelphia During the Civil War," 21.
139. Taylor, *Philadelphia in the Civil War*, 207. The Confederate ram *Atlanta* was an ironclad converted from an English blockade runner, the *Fingal*. The *Atlanta* was captured with but five shots by the monitor USS *Weehawken* in the Savannah River on June 17, 1863. This ship was repaired at the Philadelphia Navy Yard and used as a U.S. Navy warship.
140. Mackay, "Philadelphia During the Civil War," 22; Taylor, *Philadelphia in the Civil War*, 209.
141. Taylor, *Philadelphia in the Civil War*, 208.
142. Mackay, "Philadelphia During the Civil War," 22.
143. Ibid.; Taylor, *Philadelphia in the Civil War*, 211: Gallman, *Mastering Wartime*, 138.
144. Mackay, "Philadelphia During the Civil War," 23.
145. Ibid.; Taylor, *Philadelphia in the Civil War*, 212.
146. Mackay, "Philadelphia During the Civil War," 23; Taylor, *Philadelphia in the Civil War*, 211.
147. Weigley, *Philadelphia*, 399: Gallman, *Mastering Wartime*, 129; Taylor, *Philadelphia in the Civil War*, 212.
148. Taylor, *Philadelphia in the Civil War*, 212.
149. Rosenblatt, *Anti-Rebel*, 56.
150. Moore, *History of the Cooper Shop Refreshment Saloon*. The death of the devoted creator of this home, Miss Anna M. Ross, due to her efforts at the

refreshment saloon is a sad incident in the story of Civil War benevolence in Philadelphia. Post #94, GAR, Department of Pennsylvania (now represented by the Anna M. Ross Camp #1 of the Sons of Union Veterans), took its name from this martyr to duty, and a city park at Tenth Street and Glenwood Avenue perpetuates her memory. Her grave was located in the American Mechanics Cemetery but was transferred to Lawnview Cemetery when the area was developed for housing.

151. Mackay, "Philadelphia During the Civil War," 24; *Report of the Managers, Soldiers' Home, Sixteenth and Filbert Streets, Philadelphia*, 3. Among the occupations adopted by discharged soldiers after the war was that of messenger. The men employed by the Soldiers' City Messenger Company wore red military caps and charged one cent per message.

152. Taylor, *Philadelphia in the Civil War*, 211.

BENEVOLENCE OF VOLUNTEER FIREMEN

153. Ibid., 237.

154. Ibid., 238.

155. Mackay, "Philadelphia During the Civil War," 11; Taylor, *Philadelphia in the Civil War*, 238.

156. Taylor, *Philadelphia in the Civil War*, 238; Bates, *History of Pennsylvania Volunteers*.

157. Taylor, *Philadelphia in the Civil War*, 238–39.

158. Ibid., 239.

THE UNION LEAGUE OF PHILADELPHIA

159. Weigley, Philadelphia, 405–7; Gallman, Mastering Wartime, 95–96; Mackay, "Philadelphia During the Civil War," 26; Whiteman, *Gentlemen in Crisis*.

160. Mackay, "Philadelphia During the Civil War," 26; Taylor, *Philadelphia in the Civil War*, 240.

161. Mackay, "Philadelphia During the Civil War," 27; Taylor, *Philadelphia in the Civil War*, 240. Lieutenant James Hamilton Kuhn was a son of Hartman, who was killed in action while serving as aide-de-camp to General Meade.

162. Taylor, *Philadelphia in the Civil War*, 240.
163. Ibid.
164. Ibid., 240–41.
165. Whiteman, *Gentlemen in Crisis—The First Century of the Union League of Philadelphia*, 45.
166. Ibid.
167. Gallman, *Mastering Wartime*, 115–16.
168. Taylor, *Philadelphia in the Civil War*, 241. On the evening of April 10, 1865, the news of the surrender of General Lee's Confederate force was brought to the Union League by Miss Louise Claghorn and Mrs. John W. Forney, who had followed a telegraph worker to the press office and obtained the dispatch after it had been copied for publication. The original, attested by Mr. J. Gillingham Fell, is preserved in the archives.

The continued interest of the Union League in the events of the Civil War was also evidenced by a group of its members composing "The Pilgrims to the Battlefields of the Rebellion." This organization consisted of over thirty members, of whom many were veterans. The "Pilgrims" held an annual banquet on Lincoln's Birthday and undertook a visit, each year, to some of the scenes of battles and campaigns of the Civil War. This object is continued to this day by the Civil War Round Table of the Union League and Post #1 Society.

*On his visit to Philadelphia on June 16, 1864, to visit the Great Central Sanitary Fair and attend a reception by the Union League, Abraham Lincoln was entertained at the League House and spoke to the league members to answer words of welcome: "I believe of the Union League— an organization free from political prejudices, and promoted in its formation by motives of the highest patriotism, I have many a time heard of its doing great good work." Taylor, *Philadelphia in the Civil War*, 242.

CIVIL WAR PHILADELPHIA RAILROAD TRANSPORTATION

169. Gallman, *Mastering Wartime*, 279; Taylor, *Philadelphia in the Civil War*, 44.
170. Abdill, *Civil War Railroads*; Burgess and Kennedy, *Centennial History of the Pennsylvania Railroad Company*.
171. Mackay, "Philadelphia During the Civil War," 14–15.
172. Taylor, *Philadelphia in the Civil War*, 44–45.

173. Ibid., 45.

174. Ibid., 44.

175. Haupt, *Reminiscences of General Herman Haupt*.

176. Abdill, *Civil War Railroads*; McPherson, *Battle Cry of Freedom*.

177. *Official Records, War of the Rebellion* (1880); Bates, *History of Pennsylvania Volunteers*; Taylor, *Philadelphia in the Civil War*, 46.

178. Taylor, *Philadelphia in the Civil War*, 45. Major General George B. McClellan was a native of Philadelphia. He was assigned to the U.S. Corps of Engineers after graduation from West Point in 1846. He resigned from the army in 1857 to pursue a career in railroads. He was a son of Dr. George McClellan of Philadelphia (president of Jefferson Medical College). He was born near the southwest corner of Ninth and Walnut Streets on December 3, 1826. McClellan entered politics after his resignation from army service and ran as Democratic Party opponent to Lincoln in the presidential election of 1864. Later, he served several terms as governor of New Jersey.

179. Ibid., 45.

180. Ibid.

181. *Soldiers Guide in Philadelphia*, 1865. The Pennsylvania Central Railroad occupied the building on the south side of Market Street east of Eleventh in 1852, when the Philadelphia, Wilmington and Baltimore Railroad Company vacated it upon completion of its new terminal building at Broad and Prime Streets. It was here that the Pennsylvania Railroad was organized, and it was its main point of arrival and departure, the cars being hauled to and from West Philadelphia by horses or mules. In the Civil War, the hotel on the site was the New Mansion House.

In later years, a large proportion of the men who occupied important positions with the railroad companies located in Philadelphia were veterans of military service. In the summer of 1864, the demonstrations of disloyalty in the Pennsylvania coal region, manifested by strikes and riots, induced the government to take military control of the Philadelphia and Reading Railroad in order to secure the necessary supply of coal for the war effort. During the course of the war, there were troops stationed at Pottsville, Schuylkill County, including the 10th New Jersey Infantry, the 1st NY Artillery and the Veteran Reserve Corps. During the Gettysburg Campaign, some Pennsylvania Emergency Militia units were assigned to duty in this region.

WAR INDUSTRIES AND MANUFACTURING

182. *Lorin Blodget's Manufactures of Philadelphia*; Weigley, *Philadelphia*, 397–98.

183. Gallman, *Mastering Wartime*, 267.

184. Mackay, "Philadelphia During the Civil War," 16; Gallman, *Mastering Wartime*, 243; *Public Ledger*, November. 27, 29; December 3, 1860; Scharf and Westcott, *History of Philadelphia*, 378.

185. Gallman, *Mastering Wartime*, 282.

186. Ibid., 288.

187. *Philadelphia Inquirer*, March 31, 1862.

188. Gallman, *Mastering Wartime*, 254; *Edwin T. Freedley's Philadelphia and Its Manufactures*.

189. Gallman, *Mastering Wartime*, 255.

190. Scranton, Proprietary Capitalism, 304–9.

FINANCING THE WAR

191. Gallman, *Mastering Wartime*, 267, 277; Mackay, "Philadelphia During the Civil War," 18.

192. Taylor, *Philadelphia in the Civil War*, 220–23: Mackay, "Philadelphia During the Civil War," 19; Oberholtzer, *Jay Cooke*, 128–32.

193. Taylor, *Philadelphia in the Civil War*, 223; Gallman, *Mastering Wartime*, 278; Mackay, "Philadelphia During the Civil War," 20.

TRAINING CAMPS

194. U.S. Army Regulations, 1861, 74–78.

195. Ibid., 76.

196. McPherson, *Battle Cry of Freedom*.

197. Bates, *History of Pennsylvania Volunteers*.

198. Civil War Society, *Encyclopedia of the Civil War*.

199. Taylor, *Philadelphia in the Civil War*, 270; Mills, *Military History of the Falls of Schuylkill*, 28–44; Bates, *History of Pennsylvania Volunteers*.

200. Weigley, *Philadelphia*, 395; Taylor, *Philadelphia in the Civil War*, 270.

201. *Philadelphia Inquirer*, January 22, 1862.

202. Ibid., November 23, 1861.

PHILADELPHIA DURING THE GETTYSBURG CAMPAIGN

203. Weigley, *Philadelphia*, 409; Taylor, *Philadelphia in the Civil War*, 245; Scharf and Westcott, *History of Philadelphia*, 1029–033.

"During the Civil War fear was felt for the safety of the assets of the banks, including the Germantown National Bank. When Pennsylvania was invaded by Lee's army, a special meeting of the Bank directors was held June 29, 1863. They decided to burn all the bank notes in possession of the bank. Paper money was burned, and coins were stored in the vaults. Most of this was gold, which was packed in a strong box and shipped by express to New York City and was consigned to the Bank of New York. The success of the Union forces at Gettysburg enabled the officers to bring the assets back." Germantown National Bank, from *The Beehive*, vol. 7, no. 2, 13.

204. Taylor, *Philadelphia in the Civil War*, 245.

205. Mills, *Military History of the Falls of Schuylkill*; Bates, *History of Pennsylvania Volunteers*.

206. Mackay, "Philadelphia During the Civil War," 33.

207. Mills, *Military History of the Falls of Schuylkill*.

208. Mackay, "Philadelphia During the Civil War," 10.

209. Ibid.

210. Taylor, *Philadelphia in the Civil War*, 26.

211. Ibid., 27.

212. Mackay, "Philadelphia During the Civil War," 10.

213. Scharf and Westcott, *History of Philadelphia*, 1016–22.

214. Ibid. 1016–22.

215. Taylor, *Philadelphia in the Civil War*, 196; Alotta, *Stop the Evil*; Scharf and Westcott, *History of Philadelphia*.

PHILADELPHIA-BASED MILITARY UNITS

216. Taylor, *Philadelphia in the Civil War*, 33–34; Gallman, *Mastering Wartime*, 11–12; Weigley, *Philadelphia*, 395; Mackay, "Philadelphia During the Civil War," 8.

217. Mackay, "Philadelphia During the Civil War," 10–11; Weigley, *Philadelphia*, 395; Taylor, *Philadelphia in the Civil War*, 39.

218. Gallman, *Mastering Wartime*, 12; *Public Ledger*, April 17, 1861.

219. Taylor, *Philadelphia in the Civil War*, 35.

220. Ibid., 35–36.

221. Ibid., 36.

222. Ibid.

223. Ibid.

224. Weigley, *Philadelphia*, 396.

225. Taylor, *Philadelphia in the Civil War*, 37.

226. Ibid., 25.

227. *History of the Twenty Third Pennsylvania.*

228. Taylor, *Philadelphia in the Civil War*, 38.

229. *Army and Navy Journal*, November 19, 1864, 196.

230. Taylor, *Philadelphia in the Civil War*, 38.

231. First Troop Philadelphia City Cavalry, *History of the First Troop.*

232. Taylor, *Philadelphia in the Civil War*, 39.

233. Ibid.

234. General Order No. 191.

235. Gallman, *Mastering Wartime*, 23.

236. Godcharles, *Pennsylvania Political*; Wray, *Birney's Zouaves.*

237. Gallman, *Mastering Wartime*, 17.

238. General Order 33.

239. *Official Records, War of the Rebellion*; Shannon, *Organization and Administration of the Union Army*; 28th Regiment, Reunion of the 28th & 147th Regiments, Pennsylvania Volunteers, Philadelphia, November 24, 1871.

240. Bates, *History of the Pennsylvania Volunteers*; Sypher, *History of the Pennsylvania Reserve Corps.*

241. Bates, *History of the Pennsylvania Volunteers.*

242. Sypher, *History of the Pennsylvania Reserve Corps.*

243. Ibid.; Bates, *History of the Pennsylvania Volunteers.*

244. The staff of General McCall, commander of the Pennsylvania Reserves, included Lieutenant Colonel Henry J. Biddle, AAG, Captain Henry Sheetz and Captain Henry Coppee, all of Philadelphia.
Major General Samuel Wylie Crawford, of Philadelphia, was a surgeon in the garrison at Fort Sumter in 1861 who later accepted a combat command.

245. Taylor, *Philadelphia in the Civil War*, 67.

246. Ibid., 81; Banes, *History of the Philadelphia Brigade.*
On April 21, 1861, a meeting of citizens of California was held at the Metropolitan Hotel in New York City, Senator Edward D. Baker being one of the vice-presidents. Resolutions were adopted "to raise a regiment composed of men from the Pacific coast and others who might choose to join."

247. Taylor, *Philadelphia in the Civil War*, 81.

248. Ibid., 83–84.

249. Ibid., 85.

250. Ibid., 93.

251. Ibid., 96.

252. Ibid., 99–101; Nachtigall, *Geschichte des 75sten Regiments*.

253. Taylor, *Philadelphia in the Civil War*, 104–5.

254. Ibid., 106–8; Vautier, *History of the 88th Pennsylvania Volunteers*.

255. Durkin, *The Last Man and The Last Life*.

256. Taylor, *Philadelphia in the Civil War*, 111–12.

257. Galloway, "Ninety-fifth Pennsylvania Volunteers."

258. Taylor, *Philadelphia in the Civil War*, 116–17.

259. Ibid., 118–19.

260. Veale, *"The 109th Regiment Penna. Veteran Volunteers."*

261. Taylor, *Philadelphia in the Civil War*, 124.

262. Hagerty, *Collis' Zouaves*; Rauscher, *Music on the March*; Bates, *History of Pennsylvania Volunteers*, 1185.

263. Taylor, *Philadelphia in the Civil War*, 126–27.

264. Mulholland, *Story of the 116th Regiment*.

265. Smith, *History of the Corn Exchange Regiment*.

266. Maier, *Rough and Regular*.

267. Survivor's Association, *History of the 121st Regiment*.
Lieutenant Joseph Rosengarten (later brevet major) was detailed to the staff of Major General John F. Reynolds and was with Reynolds at Gettysburg when he was killed in action.
Captain William W. Dorr, of Company K, killed at Spotsylvania on May 10, 1864, was a son of the Reverend Dr. Dorr of Christ Church, on the walls of which his comrades placed a memorial tablet.

268. Taylor, *Philadelphia in the Civil War*, 141–42.

269. Ibid., 143.

270. Gibbs, *History of the 187th Regiment*.

271. Taylor, *Philadelphia in the Civil War*, 145–46.

272. Ibid., 147–49.

273. Ibid., 147–54.

274. Ibid.

275. Ward, *History of the Second Pennsylvania*.

276. Taylor, *Philadelphia in the Civil War*, 152.

277. Ibid., 152.

278. Ibid., 153.

279. Ibid., 152–53.

280. Ibid., 155–56.

281. Rawle, *History of the Third Pennsylvania Cavalry.*

282. Taylor, *Philadelphia in the Civil War*, 160–62.

283. Gracey, *Annals of the Sixth Pennsylvania Cavalry.*

284. Carpenter, *A List of the Battles.*

285. Kirk, *History of the Fifteenth Pennsylvania Volunteer Cavalry.*

286. Taylor, *Philadelphia in the Civil War*, 181–82.

287 Ibid., 155–84.

288. Ibid., 146.

289. Ibid., 215–18.

290. Ibid., 218–20; Gallman, *Mastering Wartime*, 19–20.

291. Gallman, *Mastering Wartime*, 22–23; Weigley, *Philadelphia*, 409–10.

292. *Life of Rev. Thomas Brainerd.*

293. Taylor, *Philadelphia in the Civil War*, 242–44.

294. Ibid., 244.

295. First Troop Philadelphia City Cavalry, *History of the First Troop.*

296. Taylor, *Philadelphia in the Civil War*, 247–49.

297. Ibid., 247–51.

298. Ibid., 275.

299. Ibid., 271–75.

300. Ibid., 272–75.

301. Ibid., 276–79.

302. Ibid., 186–89.

303. Ibid., 188.

304. Ibid.

305. Ibid.; Gallman, *Mastering Wartime*, 49; Biddle and Dubin, *Tasting Freedom.*

306. Taylor, *Philadelphia in the Civil War*, 190. Reverend Jeremiah Asher was an abolitionist who took a leave of absence from his church (Shiloh Baptist) to serve as a chaplain of the 6th Regiment United States Colored Troops and died in service during the war.

307. Hart, *Slavery and Abolition.*

The first recorded suggestion for the employment of Colored Troops in the Federal army is found in a letter written to Simon Cameron, secretary of war, on April 16, 1861, by Burr Porter, late major in the Ottoman army. Official Records.

President Lincoln, writing to Horace Greeley on August 22, 1861, said: "If there be those who would not save the Union unless at the same time they could save slavery, I do not agree with them. If there be those who would not save the Union unless they could at the same time destroy slavery, I do not agree with them."

General Order No. 143, May 22, 1863, provided for a bureau to be attached to the office of the adjutant general at Washington to record all matters relating to the organization of Colored Troops.

For the assistance of these volunteers, the Colored Women's Sanitary Commission was formed, with headquarters at 404 Walnut Street, Philadelphia.

308. Taylor, *Philadelphia in the Civil War*, 186–95.

309. Ibid.; Gallman, *Mastering Wartime*, 35–53; Bates, *History of the Pennsylvania Volunteers*.

PHILADELPHIA COMMANDERS

310. *National Cyclopaedia of American Biography*; Taylor, *Philadelphia in the Civil War*, 293–94, 259–60.

PHILADELPHIA AND THE NAVY

311. Taylor, *Philadelphia in the Civil War*, 200.

312. Veit, "The Innovative, Mysterious Alligator," 26–29.

313. Weigley, *Philadelphia*, 398; Mackay, "Philadelphia During the Civil War," 15.

314. Taylor, *Philadelphia in the Civil War*, 200.

315. Ibid., 320–21.

316. Ibid., 321.

317. Drayton, Naval Letters, 1861–1865.

U.S. MARINE CORPS

318. Taylor, *Philadelphia in the Civil War*, 200; Simmons, *United States Marines*.

319. Taylor, *Philadelphia in the Civil War*, 203.

320. Ibid., 202. The Delaware River wards of Southwark furnished a large percentage of the men who formed the crews of the Philadelphia-built warships, and later, when drafts threatened, the employment of thousands of men in the shipyards and machine shops along the Delaware River was used as a valid reason for the deficiency found in filling quotas of volunteers for the army.

Numerous prize ships were brought to Philadelphia during the course of the war. But many commercial ship owners lost their merchant vessels to Confederate privateers. The packet ship *Tonawanda* of the Cope Line, Captain Theodore Julius, was captured on October 9, 1862, by the famous CSS *Alabama*.

At the close of the war, the navy had in service over 51,500 seamen and 7,500 officers. The approximate total number killed during the war was 4,647 officers and men. The sailors and marines enlisted from Pennsylvania during the war numbered over 14,000.

While the English-built Confederate privateers, largely manned by British crews, were capturing and burning American merchant ships, Philadelphia filled a ship—the bark *Achilles*—with food to the value of $30,000 for the relief of the starving workers of British mills. Taylor, *Philadelphia in the Civil War*.

321. Ibid., 206.

PRINCIPAL CIVIL WAR–ERA CEMETERIES

322. Brooks and Waskie, *History and Guide to Laurel Hill Cemetery*.
323. Scharf and Westcott, *History of Philadelphia*.
324. Articles by the "Man on the Corner," Naaman K. Ployd, 1927, Germantown newspaper.
325. *Germantown Independent-Gazette*, 1912.
326. *Official Records, War of the Rebellion*, 229–38.

PROMINENT CIVIL WAR–ERA PHILADELPHIANS

327. *Appleton's Cyclopedia*.
328. Lane, *Roots of Violence*; Silcox, "Nineteenth Century Philadelphia Black Militant."

329. *Appleton's Cyclopedia*.
330. Ibid.

NOTABLE WOMEN OF PHILADELPHIA

331. Brockett and Vaughan, *Woman's Work in the Civil War*, 149–60.
332. Bauer, "Viva la Vivandieres," 20–24.
333. Collis, *A Woman's War Record*.
334. Conklin, *Women at Gettysburg*.
335. Rauscher, *Music on the March*.
336. Conklin, *Women at Gettysburg*; *Evening Bulletin*, May 14, 1863.
337. Hagerty, *Collis' Zouaves*.
338. *Pittsburgh Dispatch*, "Death of French Mary," May 15, 1901.
339. Melchiori, "The Death of French Mary," 14–15.
340. Brockett and Vaughan, *Woman's Work in the Civil War*, 779–82.
341. Gillespie, *A Book of Remembrance*.
342. Dubois, *To My Countrywomen*.
343. Cromwell, *Lucretia Mott*.
344. Brockett and Vaughan, *Woman's Work in the Civil War*.
345. Ibid.; Waskie, "Brief History of the Philadelphia Refreshment Saloons."
346. Conklin, *Women at Gettysburg*.
347. *Philadelphia Inquirer*, "Elizabeth E. Hutter—Obituary," June 20, 1895.
348. Gallman, *The North Fights the Civil War*, 136.
349. Forten, *Journal, 1953*.
350. Gallman, *America's Joan of Arc*.
351. Ibid., 36–37.

"THREE SUNDAYS IN APRIL"

352. Taylor, *Philadelphia in the Civil War*, 310; Mackay, "Philadelphia During the Civil War," 42–43.
353. Taylor, *Philadelphia in the Civil War*, 311; Mackay, "Philadelphia During the Civil War," 45–46.
354. Weigley, *Philadelphia*, 417–18; Taylor, *Philadelphia in the Civil War*, 311–12; Mackay, "Philadelphia During the Civil War," 47–48.

355. Donald, *The Civil War and Reconstruction.*
356. Weigley, *Philadelphia*, 417; Mackay, "Philadelphia During the Civil War," 47–51.
357. *Philadelphia Inquirer*, April 25, 1865. Mayor Henry, the city officials and police wore mourning crepe on their sleeves thirty days following the date of the ceremonies incident to the departure of the Lincoln funeral train.

"Johnny Comes Marching Home" and Welcome Back

358. Taylor, *Philadelphia in the Civil War*, 313.
359. *Philadelphia Inquirer*, June 12, 1865.
360. Weigley, *Philadelphia*, 418.
361. *Philadelphia Inquirer*, July 5, 1866; Taylor, *Philadelphia in the Civil War*, 315–19.

Independence Hall during the Civil War

362. *Philadelphia Inquirer*, April 15, 1865.
363. Mires, *Independence Hall in American Memory*; *Philadelphia Inquirer.*

Civil War–Era Veterans' Organizations

364. Taylor, *Philadelphia in the Civil War*, 324.
365. Zell, "The Organization of the Loyal Legion"; Taylor, *Philadelphia in the Civil War*, 322–24; Devens, "Twenty-fifth Anniversary Oration at the MOLLUS Reunion."
366. Taylor, *Philadelphia in the Civil War*, 324–25; Beath, *History of the Grand Army of the Republic.* Discharged veterans of the army and navy residing in Philadelphia held a meeting in 1865, the presiding officer being Lieutenant Colonel Henry A. Cook, of Baxter's Fire Zouaves (72nd PV), and proposed to secure a charter for a society of veterans and to establish branch organizations throughout Pennsylvania. *Army and Navy Journal,*

May 1865. This was one of the many now forgotten organizations that were absorbed into the Grand Army of the Republic.

367. Taylor, *Philadelphia in the Civil War*, 326–27; *Grand Army Scout & Soldiers Mail*; *National Tribune*, GAR newspaper.

368. Taylor, *Philadelphia in the Civil War*, 328–29.

369. Ibid., 330–31. The State of Pennsylvania awarded to each regiment the sum of $1,500 to pay the cost of battlefield monuments. Nearly all of those erected were far more expensive; the additional outlay was paid by the regimental associations.

370. Ibid., 331–32. The Philadelphia Naval Veteran Association No. 32 once counted hundreds of members.

371. Ibid., 332–33.

372. Ibid., 333.

MEDAL OF HONOR RECIPIENTS

373. Ibid., 335–36; Mulholland, *Military Order Congress Medal of the Honor Legion of the United States*.

PHILADELPHIA'S CIVIL WAR MEMORIALS, MONUMENTS AND PARKS

374. Taylor, *Philadelphia in the Civil War*, 338–39.

375. Ibid., 339; Mulholland, *Military Order Congress Medal of Honor Legion of the United States*.

Bibliography

PHILADELPHIA AND THE CIVIL WAR

Appleton's Cyclopaedia of American Biography. New York: D. Appleton and Company, 1889.

Basler, Roy P., et al., eds. *The Collected Works of Abraham Lincoln*. 9 vols. New Brunswick, NJ: Rutgers University, 1953.

Biddle, Daniel, and Murray Dubin. *Tasting Freedom—Octavius Catto and the Battle for Equality in Civil War America*. Philadelphia: Temple Press, 2010.

Blockson, Charles L. *Philadelphia, 1639–2000*. Charleston, SC: Arcadia Publishing, 2000.

Bollet, Alfred Jay, MD. *Civil War Medicine*. Galen Press, 2002.

Brainerd, Mary. *Life of Rev. Thomas Brainerd, Pastor of Od Pine Presbyterian Church*. Philadelphia: Lippincotta,1870.

Brockett, L.P., MD, and Mrs. Mary C. Vaughn. *Women's Work in the Civil War: A Record of Heroism, Patriots and Patience*. Philadelphia, 1867.

Brown, George William. *Baltimore and the 19th of April 1861*. Baltimore, MD: Johns Hopkins University, 1887.

Civil War Society. *Encyclopedia of the Civil War*. Civil War Society, 1997.

Davis, Susan G. *Parades and Power: Street Theater in Nineteenth-Century Philadelphia*. Philadelphia, 1986.

Dorwart, Jeffery M. *Fort Mifflin of Philadelphia*. Philadelphia: University of Pennsylvania Press, 1998.

Dusinberre, William. *Civil War Issues in Philadelphia, 1856–1865*. Philadelphia, 1965.

Feldberg, Michael Jay. "The Philadelphia Riots of 1844: A Social History." PhD diss., University of Rochester, 1970.

———. *The Turbulent Era: Riot and Disorder in Jacksonian America.* New York, 1980.

Fite, Emerson, David. *Social and Economic Conditions in the North.* New York, 1910.

Gallman, J. Matthew. *Mastering Wartime: A Social History of Philadelphia during the Civil War.* Cambridge, UK: Cambridge University Press, 1990.

Geary, James W. *We Need Men: The Union Draft in the Civil War.* DeKalb: Northern Illinois University Press, 1991.

Glassberg, Eudice. "Philadelphians in Need: Client Experiences with Two Benevolent Societies, 1830–1880." PhD diss., University of Pennsylvania, 1979.

Godcharles, Frederic A. *Pennsylvania Political, Governmental, Military and Civil: Military Volume.* New York: American Historical Society, Inc., 1933.

Hart, Albert Bushnell. *Slavery and Abolition.* New York: Harper Brothers, 1906.

Hay, John, and John G. Nicolay. *Letters and State Papers of Abraham Lincoln.* New York: Century, 1894.

Hoch, Bradley R. *The Lincoln Trail in Pennsylvania.* University Park: Pennsylvania State University Press, 2001.

Hunt, Roger D., and Jack Brown. *Brevet Brigadier Generals in Blue.* N.p.: Stan Clark Military Books, 1990.

Laurie, Bruce. *Working People of Philadelphia, 1800–1860.* Philadelphia, 1980.

Lindstrom, Diane. *Economic Development in the Philadelphia Region, 1810–1850.* New York, 1978.

MacKay, Winnifred K. "Philadelphia During the Civil War, 1861–1865." *Pennsylvania Magazine of History and Biography* 98 (April 1972): 3–49.

Maxwell, William Q. *Lincoln's Fifth Wheel: The Sanitary Commission.* New York, 1956.

McPherson, James M. *Battle Cry of Freedom.* New York: Ballantine Books, 1989.

———. *Ordeal by Fire: The Civil War and Reconstruction.* 2nd ed. New York: McGraw Hill, 1992.

Meade, George G., III, ed. *Life and Letters of General Meade.* New York, Charles Scribner's Sons, 1913.

Miller, Albert G. *History of the German Hospital of Philadelphia.* Philadelphia: Lippincott, 1905.

Mires, Charlene. *Independence Hall in American Memory.* Philadelphia: University of Pennsylvania Press, 2002.

Mitchell, S. Weir. *In Wartime.* Boston: Houghton Mifflin, 1884.

Monkkonen, Eric H. *Police in Urban America, 1860.* N.p.: Cambridge University Press, 1981.

Moore, James. *History of the Cooper Shop Refreshment Saloon*. Philadelphia, 1866.

Murdock, Eugene C. *The Civil War in the North: A Selective Annotated Bibliography*. New York, 1987.

———, ed. *One Million Men: The Civil War Draft in the North*. Champaign: University of Illinois, 1971.

———. *Patriotism Limited 1862–1865: The Civil War Draft & Bounty System*. Kent, OH: Kent State University Press, 1967.

Nash, Gary B. *First City: Philadelphia and the Forging of Historical Memory*. Philadelphia: University of Pennsylvania Press, 2002.

Nevins, Allan. *The War for the Union*. 4 vols. New York, 1959 to 1971.

Oberholtzer, Ellis Paxson. *Jay Cooke: Financier of the Civil War*. N.p.: George W. Jacobs, 1907.

———. *Philadelphia: A History of the City and Its People*. Philadelphia, n.d.

Paludan, Philip Shaw. *A People's Contest: The Union and Civil War, 1861–1865*. New York, 1988.

Rosenblatt, Emil, ed. *Anti-Rebel: The Civil War Letters of Wilbur Fisk*. Croton-on-Hudson, NY, 1983.

Sauers, Richard. *A Guide to Civil War Philadelphia*. Cambridge, MA: DaCapo Press, 2003.

Scharf, Thomas, and Thompson Westcott. *History of Philadelphia, 1609–1884*. Philadelphia, 1884.

Scott, Donald. *Camp William Penn*. Charleston, SC: Arcadia Publishing, 2008.

Scranton, Philip. *Proprietary Capitalism: The Textile Manufacture at Philadelphia, 1800–1885*. Philadelphia, 1983.

Shannon, Fred Albert. *The Organization and Administration of the Union Army, 1861–65*. Cleveland, OH: Arthur H. Clark Co., 1928.

Sher, Sanford P. "Mower Civil War Hospital." *Germantown Crier* 50 (2000): 74–77.

Simmons, Edwin H. *The United States Marines: A History*. 4th ed. Annapolis, MD: Naval Institute Press, 2003.

Stille, Charles J. *Memorial of the Great Central Fair for the U.S. Sanitary Commission Held at Philadelphia, June 1864*. Philadelphia, 1864.

Taylor, Frank H. *Philadelphia in the Civil War, 1861–1865*. Philadelphia, 1913.

Toklish, Michael J. *Jefferson Square Park*. Published by Friends of Jefferson Square Park, April 2007.

Varon, Elizabeth R. *Disunion! The Coming of the American Civil War, 1789–1859*. Chapel Hill: University of North Carolina Press, 2008.

Vieira, M. Lafitte. *West Philadelphia Illustrated*. Philadelphia: Arden Press, 1903.

Warner, Sam Bass, Jr. *The Private City: Philadelphia in Three Periods of Its Growth*. Philadelphia, 1968.

War of the Rebellion: A Compilation of the Official Records of the Union and Confederate Armies. Series III, vols. 2 and 3. Government Printing Office. Washington, D.C., 1880.

Weigley, Russell F., ed. *Philadelphia: A 300-Year History.* New York, 1982.

Whiteman, Maxwell. *Gentlemen in Crisis: The First Century of the Union League in Philadelphia, 1862–1962.* N.p.: Union League Publication, 1975.

Wilson, W. Emerson. *Fort Delaware in the Civil War.* N.p.: Fort Delaware Society, 1986.

CIVIL WAR RAILROADS

Abdill, George B. *Civil War Railroads.* N.p.: Superior Pub. Co., 1961.

Burgess, George H., and Miles C. Kennedy. *Centennial History of the Pennsylvania Railroad Company.* Philadelphia: Pennsylvania Railroad Co., 1949.

Haupt, Herman. *Reminiscences of General Herman Haupt: Limited Autograph Edition.* N.p.: Wright and Joys Co., 1901.

Wilson, William Bender. *History of the Pennsylvania Railroad Company with Plan of Organization, Portraits of Officials, and Biographical Sketches.* Vol. 1. N.p.: Henry T. Coates & Company, 1895.

ETHNIC PHILADELPHIA

Bates, Samuel P. *Martial Deeds of Pennsylvania.* Philadelphia: T.H. Davis & Co., 1876.

Bolek, Rev. Francis, ed. *Who's Who in Polish America.* New York: Harbinger House, 1943.

Clark, Dennis. *The Irish in Philadelphia: Ten Generations of Urban Experience.* Philadelphia: Temple University Press, 1973.

Davis, Allen F., and Mark H. Haller. *The Peoples of Philadelphia: A History of Ethnic Groups and Lower-Class Life 1790–1940.* Philadelphia: Temple University Press, 1973.

Donald, David H., et al. *The Civil War and Reconstruction.* New York: Norton, 2001.

Kowalewski, John A. *Captain Mlotkowski of Fort Delaware.* Fort Delaware, PA: Memorial Brigade Society, 1976.

Leaving the Emerald Isle: Irish Immigration to Philadelphia. N.p.: Historical Society of Pennsylvania, Balch Institute, n.d.

Lonn, Ella. *Foreigners in the Union Army and Navy*. Baton Rouge: Louisiana State University Press, 1951.

Miller, Fredric M. *Philadelphia: Immigrant City*. N.p.: Balch On-Line Resources, n.d.

Pivany, Eugene. *Hungarians in the American Civil War*. Cleveland, OH: Dongo, 1913.

Rolph, Daniel. *Two Hispanic Brothers and Soldiers: History Hits*. N.p.: Historical Society of Pennsylvania, 2010.

Vida, Istvan K. "The True Cause of Freedom: The Kossuth Emigration and the Hungarians in the Civil War." Diss., University of Debrecen, Hungary, 2006.

Wilson, W.E. *Fort Delaware*. Newark, DE, 1957.

Wolf, Simon. "The American Jew as Patriot, Soldier and Citizen." *North American Review* (June 1895). N.p.: Jewish-American History Documentation Foundation, 2011.

Enlisting the Troops

Alotta, Robert I. *Stop the Evil: A Civil War History of Desertion and Murder*. San Rafael, CA: Presidio Press, 1978.

Banes, Charles H. *A History of the Philadelphia Brigade: 69th, 71st, 72nd, and the 106th Pennsylvania Volunteers*. Philadelphia, 1876.

Bates, Samuel P. *History of the Pennsylvania Volunteers, 1861–65*. Harrisburg, PA, 1868–1871.

Carpenter, J. Edward. *A List of the Battles, Engagements, Actions and Important Skirmishes in Which the Eighth Pennsylvania Cavalry Participated During the War of 1861–1865*. Philadelphia: Allen, Lane & Scott's Printing House, 1866.

Chamberlin, Thomas, Lt. Col. *History of the One Hundred and Fiftieth Regiment, Pennsylvania Volunteers, Second Regiment, Bucktail Brigade*. Revised and enlarged edition, with complete roster. Philadelphia: T. McManus Jr. & Co., 1905.

Durkin, James. *The Last Man and the Last Life, History of the 90th Pennsylvania*. Glenside, PA: Santorelli Publisher, 2000.

Ernsberger, Donald. *Paddy Owen's Regulars: A History of the 69th Penna "Irish Volunteers."* Vols. 1 and 2. New York: Xlibris Publishing, 2004.

Fox, William F., Lt. Col. *U.S. Volunteers. Regimental Losses in the American Civil War 1861–1865*. Albany, NY: Albany Publishing Company, 1889.

Galloway, George Norton. "Ninety-fifth Pennsylvania Volunteers (Gosline's Pennsylvania Zouaves) in the Sixth Corps." A historical paper by G. Norton Galloway read at a reunion of the surviving members of the 95th Pennsylvania Volunteers, held at Germantown, PA, 1884.

Gibbs, James M. *History of the 187th Regiment, Pennsylvania Volunteer Infantry.* Harrisburg, PA: Central Printing and Publishing House, 1905.

Gracey, Samuel L. *Annals of the Sixth Pennsylvania Cavalry.* Reprint of 1868 original. New Introduction by Eric Wittenberg. N.p.: Vanberg Publishing, 2006.

Hagerty, Edward J. *Collis' Zouaves: The 114th Pennsylvania Volunteers in the Civil War.* Baton Rouge: Louisiana State University Press, 1997.

History of the Twenty Third Pennsylvania Volunteer Infantry: Birney's Zouaves, Three Months and Three Years Service Civil War, 1861–1865. Philadelphia, 1904.

Kirk, Charles H. *History of the Fifteenth Pennsylvania Volunteer Cavalry Known as the Anderson Cavalry in the Rebellion of 1861–1865.* Philadelphia, 1906.

Mackie, John. *Roster of the Grand Army Posts of Philadelphia.* N.p.: GAR Publication, 1892.

Maier, Larry B. *Rough and Regular: A History of the 119th Regiment of Pennsylvania Volunteer Infantry.* N.p.: Burd Street Press, 1997.

Medical and Surgical History of the War of the Rebellion 1861–1865, U.S. Army Surgeon General's Office. 6 vols. Washington, D.C., 1870.

Mills, Charles K., MD. "The Military History of the Falls of Schuylkill." Published in the *Weekly Forecast,* East Falls, 1913.

Mulholland, St. Clair A., Col. *Military Order of the Congress Medal of Honor Legion of the United States.* N.p., 1905.

———. *The Story of the 116th Regiment Pennsylvania Volunteers in the War for the Rebellion.* Reprint. Bronx, NY: Fordham University Press, 1996.

Nachtigall, Hermann. *Geschichte des 75sten Regiments, Pa. Vols. als Festgabe zum Andenken an die Errichtung und Einweihung des Denkmals zu Ehren ihrer im Bürgerkriege gefallenen Kameraden, von der Vereinigung der überlebenden Veteranen des 75sten Regiments, Pa.* Philadelphia: Druck von C.B. Kretschman, 1886.

Rawle, William Brooke, Captain. *History of the Third Pennsylvania Cavalry, Sixtieth Regiment Pennsylvania Volunteers, in the American Civil War, 1861–1865.* Philadelphia: Franklin Printing Co., 1905.

Smith, J.L. *History of the Corn Exchange Regiment—The 118th Pennsylvania Volunteers.* Philadelphia: Survivors' Association, 1881.

Sprogle, Howard O. *The Philadelphia Police. Past and Present.* Philadelphia, 1887.

Survivor's Association. *History of the 121st Regiment Pennsylvania Volunteers.* Philadelphia, 1893.

Sypher, J.R., Esq. *History of the Pennsylvania Reserve Corps: A Complete Record of the Organization.* Lancaster, PA: Elias Barr Co., 1865.

Vautier, John. *History of the 88th Pennsylvania Volunteers in the War for the Union, 1861–1865.* Philadelphia, 1894.

Veale, Moses. *"The 109th Regiment Penna. Veteran Volunteers." An address delivered at the unveiling of their monument on Culp's Hill, Gettysburg, PA, September 11, 1889.* Philadelphia: J. Beale, Printer, 1890.

Ward, George Washington. *History of the Second Pennsylvania Veteran Heavy Artillery (112th Regiment Pennsylvania Veteran Volunteers) 1861 to 1866.* Philadelphia: G.W. Ward, 1903.

Ward, Joseph R.C. *History of the One Hundred and Sixth Regiment Pennsylvania Volunteers, 2nd Brigade, 2nd Division, 2nd Corps, 1861–1865.* Philadelphia, 1883.

Wray, William J. *Birney's Zouaves Civil War: Life of the 23rd Pennsylvania Volunteers.* N.p.: Lisa Wray Productions, 2000.

PHILADELPHIA MILITARY

Bombaugh, Charles C. "Extracts from a Journal Kept during the Earlier Campaigns of the Army of the Potomac." *Maryland Historical Magazine* 5 (December 1910): 301.

Clark, William P. *Official History of the Militia and the National Guard of the State of Pennsylvania from the Earliest Period of Record to the Present Time.* 3 vols. Philadelphia, 1909–1912.

Coddington, Edwin B. "Pennsylvania Prepared for Invasion, 1863." *Pennsylvania History* 31 (April 1964): 157–75.

Easby-Smith, Anne. "Brevet Major General St. Clair A. Mulholland, Patriot and Catholic." *American Catholic Historical Society Records* 39 (December 1928): 347–55.

Everett, Edward G. "Pennsylvania Raises an Army, 1861." *Western Pennsylvania Historical Magazine* 39 (Summer 1956): 83–108.

First Troop Philadelphia City Cavalry. *By-Laws, Muster Roll, and Papers Selected from the Archives of the First Troop Philadelphia City Cavalry.* Philadelphia: James Smith Co., 1856.

———. *History of the First Troop Philadelphia City Cavalry; From Its Organization November 17th 1774 to Its Centennial Anniversary.* Philadelphia: Hallowell, 1875.

Hagerty, Edward Joseph. "The Blood of the Patriot: A Military and Social History of Collis's Zouaves, the 114th Regiment of Pennsylvania Volunteer Infantry in the Civil War." PhD diss., Temple University, 1993.

Hendler, Charles J., comp. *Official History of the Militia and National Guard of the State of Pennsylvania.* 4 vols. Philadelphia, 1936.

Howard-Smith, Logan, and J.F. Reynolds Scott. *The History of Battery A (Formerly Known as the Keystone Battery) and Troop A, NGP.* Philadelphia, 1912.

Kirk, Charles H. *History of the Fifteenth Pennsylvania Volunteer Cavalry*. Philadelphia: Society of the Fifteenth Pennsylvania Cavalry, 1906.

Kornweibel, Theodore, Jr. "Waiting for the War to Come: Union Camp Life in 1861–1862." *Niagara Frontier* 22 (Winter 1975): 87–97.

Lanard, Thomas S. *One Hundred Years with the State Fencibles; A History of the First Company State Fencibles, Infantry Corps State Fencibles, Infantry Battalion State Fencibles, and the Old Guard State Fencibles, 1813–1913*. Philadelphia, 1913.

Latta, James W. *History of the First Regiment Infantry National Guard of Pennsylvania (Gray Reserves) 1861–1911*. Philadelphia: Lippincott, 1912.

Medical and Surgical History of the War of the Rebellion 1861–1865, U.S. Army Surgeon General's Office. 6 vols. Washington, D.C.: Government Printing Office, 1870.

Mills, Charles K. *The Military History of the Falls of Schuylkill, The Weekly Forecast, East Falls*. N.p., 1913.

Rawle, William B. *History of the Third Pennsylvania Cavalry in the American Civil War, 1861–1865*. Philadelphia, 1905.

Smith, Wayne. "Pennsylvania and the American Civil War: Recent Trends and Interpretation." *Pennsylvania History* 51 (July 1984): 206–31.

Sturcke, Roger D., and Michael J. Winey. "1st Infantry Regiment (Gray Reserves), Reserve Brigade, Philadelphia Militia, 1861." *Military Collector and Historian* 34 (Summer 1982): 71.

Suran, Frank M., comp. *Guide to the Record Groups in the Pennsylvania State Archives*. Harrisburg: Pennsylvania Historical and Museum Commission, 1980.

Thompson, Barry E. "95th Pennsylvania Volunteer Infantry Regiment, 1861–1865 (Gosline's Zouaves)." *Military Collector and Historian* 20 (Fall 1968): 88–89.

Todd, Frederick P., and Harry C. Larter. "6th Pennsylvania Cavalry (Rush's Lancers), 1862." *Military Collector and Historian* 6 (Winter 1954): 102.

Winey, Michael J. "Landis' Philadelphia Battery of Light Artillery, 1863." *Military Collector and Historian* 26 (Winter 1974): 231–32.

Young, John Russell, ed. *Memorial History of the City of Philadelphia from Its First Settlement to the Year 1895. Vol. 1: Narrative and Critical History 1681–1895*. New York: New York History Company, 1895.

MANUSCRIPT COLLECTIONS OF THE HISTORICAL SOCIETY OF PENNSYLVANIA

Arnold, D.T. Letters (1862). Co. H, 90th PA Regiment (also 88th). Cartledge, Sgt. Cyrus. Civil War letters and discharge papers pertaining to Cartledge, Joseph Wallens, and William H. Miller. Co. E, 91st Pennsylvania Infantry. Doc Box 15.

Biddle, 1st Lt. James Cornell. Letters to wife, Gertrude G. Meredith, (1861–65). Cos. C & K, 27th PA Infantry. Collection no. 1881. Brown, Andrew. Letterbook (1862–64). Co. C, 91st Pennsylvania Infantry. Collection no. 82. Civil War: 23rd & 29th PA Infantry Regt.; Miscellaneous Papers: desertion, ordinance office correspondence, etc., Folder 5.

Cavada, Capt. Adolph F. Diary (1861–63). Co. C, 23rd PA Infantry. Collection no. 1995; call no. Am. 6956.

Collis, Col. Charles H.T. Letterbooks (1863–65). 114th PA Infantry Regt. Collection no. 1606; call no. Am. 04723 (3 vols.).

Drayton, Percival. Naval Letters, 1861–1865. New York Public Library.

Dreer Collection (ABC), filed under "Samuel S. Maker" correspondence.

Fox, Sgt. Isaac. Papers (1863–1869). Co. F, 114th PA Infantry Regt. Collection no. 1502.

Griffith, Richard. Diaries (1862–63). Companies D, & G, 23rd Infantry Regt. Collection no. 1542; Mrs. Irvin H. McKesson Papers.

Jones, William Thomas. Letters (typescript). Co. H, 23rd & 61st PA Infantry Regts. Collection no. 2023; call no. Am. 6697.

Kappler, Corp. Jacob C. Letters (in German). Co. D, 99th PA Infantry. Society Collection.

Manley, William H. Letters (Sept. 1861 to May, 1862). Co. E, 72nd PA Infantry Regt. Collection no. 1546; Box #9.

Margerum, Corp. Richard. Letters (1861–64). Co. H, 71st PA Infantry Regt. Society Collection.

McCarter, William. Reminiscences (1875). Co. A, 116th PA Infantry Regt. Collection no. 1307; call no. Am. 6952.

Smith, Corp. John L. Papers (1862–65); book of mimeographed/carbon-copied letters; miscellaneous, loose original letters; and diaries. Transferred from Co. K, 118th PA Infantry Regt. (the Corn Exchange Regt.) to Co. E, 91st PA Infantry Regt. Collection no. 610.

Stackhouse, William. Diaries (1863–65), 3 vols. Co. B, 119th PA Infantry Regt. Collection no. 1210; call no. Am. 15975.

Truefitt, Capt./Major Henry P., Jr. Letters/Papers. Co. G, 119th PA Infantry.

Voltaire, Louis. Papers. Co. I, 98th PA Infantry Regt. Society Miscellaneous Collection; Box 15-A.

Wallen, Augustus Burd. Letters (1862–65). 72nd & 183rd PA Infantry Regt.

WAR INDUSTRY

The Annual Reports of the Philadelphia Board of Trade and the Annual Reports of the Corn Exchange Association of Philadelphia. Philadelphia: Board of Trade, 1864.

Bacon, Benjamin W. *Sinews of War: How Technology, Industry, and Transportation Won the Civil War*. N.p.: Presidio Press, 1997.

Bruce, Robert V. *Lincoln and the Tools of War*. N.p.: Bobbs-Merrill Company, Inc., 1956.

Edwin T. Freedley's Philadelphia and Its Manufactures. Philadelphia, 1867.

Hess, Earl J. *Field Armies and Fortifications in the Civil War: The Eastern Campaigns, 1861–1864*. Chapel Hill: University of North Carolina Press, 2005.

The Industries of Philadelphia, as Shown by the Manufacturing Census of 1870. Philadelphia, 1877.

Lindstrom, Diane. *Economic Development in the Philadelphia Region, 1810–1850*. New York, 1978.

Lorin Blodget's Manufactures of Philadelphia. Census of Manufacturers 1860. Philadelphia, 1861.

McElroy's City Directory. Philadelphia, 1865.

Turner, George Edgar. *Victory Rode the Rails: The Strategic Place of the Railroads in the Civil War*. Indianapolis, IN: Bobbs-Merrill Company, Inc., 1953.

Weber, Thomas. *The Northern Railroads in the Civil War, 1861–1865*. New York: Columbia University Press, 1952.

Wheeler, Tom. *Mr. Lincoln's T-Mails: The Untold Story of How Abraham Lincoln Used the Telegraph to Win the Civil War*. New York: HarperCollins, 2006.

PHILADELPHIA NEWSPAPERS

Evening Bulletin, 1861–1865
Philadelphia Inquirer, 1861–1865
Philadelphia Sunday Transcript, 1861–1865
Public Ledger, 1861–1865

CEMETERIES

Annual Report of the Secretary of War, Volume 1: 229–38.

Brooks, Michael, and Anthony Waskie. *History and Guide to Laurel Hill Cemetery, 'Famous and Blameless.'* N.p.: Laurel Hill Cemetery Publication, 2000.

Keels, Thomas. *Philadelphia Graveyards and Cemeteries*. Charleston, SC: Arcadia Publishing, 2004.

PHILADELPHIA WOMEN IN THE CIVIL WAR

Bauer, Cricket. "Viva la Vivandieres: A Short History of Women in Pseudo-Military Costumes." *Military Images* (May–June 2000): 20–24.

Blockson, Charles. *African Americans in Pennsylvania: A History and Guide*. Baltimore, MD: Black Classic Press, 1994.

Burt, Nathaniel. *The Perennial Philadelphians: The Anatomy of an American Aristocracy*. Philadelphia: University of Pennsylvania Press, 1999.

Civil War Nurse. *The Diary and Letters of Hannah Ropes*. Introduction and commentary by John R. Brumgardt. Chattanooga: University of Tennessee Press, 1993.

Collis, Mrs. Septima. *A Woman's War Record: The Women of Collis' Zouaves*. N.p.: G.P. Putnam's Sons, n.d. Gettysburg, PA: Knickerbocker Press Reprint, Marinos Co. Publishing, 1998.

Conklin, Eileen F. *Women at Gettysburg 1863*. Gettysburg, PA: Thomas Publications, 1993.

Cromwell, Otelia. *Lucretia Mott*. Cambridge, MA: Harvard University Press, 1958.

Dubois, Muriel L. *To My Countrywomen: The Life of Sarah Josepha Hale*. Bedford, NH: Apprentice Shop Books, 2006.

DuBois, W.E.B. *The Philadelphia Negro*. Philadelphia, 1899.

Forten, Charlotte. *Life on the Sea Islands: The American Negro, His History and Literature, 1969*. New York: Arno Press, 1969.

Gallman, J. Matthew. *America's Joan of Arc: The Life of Anna Elizabeth Dickinson*. Oxford, UK: Oxford University Press, 2006.

———. *The North Fights the Civil War—The Home Front*. Chicago: Ivan E. Dee, 1994.

Gillespie, Elizabeth Duane. *A Book of Remembrance*. Philadelphia, 1901.

Gladstone, William. "Gettysburg Mystery Photo…more answers." *Military Images* (March–April 1982): 16–19.

Lane, Roger. *Roots of Violence in Black Philadelphia, 1860–1900*. Cambridge, MA: Harvard University Press, 1986.

McClure, Alexander K. *Old Time Notes of Pennsylvania*. Vol. 1. Philadelphia: Winston, 1905.

Melchiori, Marie V. "The Death of French Mary." *Military Images* (July–August 1983): 14–15.

New York Sunday World. "She Feared Not War." April 18, 1897.

Pittsburgh Dispatch. "Death of French Mary." May 15, 1901.

Rauscher, Frank. *Music on the March 1862–1865 with the Army of the Potomac.* Philadelphia: Press of William F. Fell & Co., 1892.

Saunders, John A. *100 Years After Emancipation: The Negro in Philadelphia History 1863–1963.* N.p.: self-published, 1963.

Waskie, Anthony. "Brief History of the Philadelphia Refreshment Saloons & Life of Anna Maria Ross, Civil War Volunteer Nurse." *Banner* (SUVCW magazine, 1997).

White, Charles. *Leon Gardiner Collection, 1822–1979* (Collection 0008B). Historical Society of Pennsylvania.

———. *Who's Who in Philadelphia: Biographical Sketches of Philadelphia's Leading Colored People.* Philadelphia: AME Book Concern, 1912.

Wills, Arthur. *Cecil's City: History of Blacks in Philadelphia, 1638–1979.* New York: Carleton Press, 1990.

Journals

Foner, Philip. "The Battle to End Discrimination vs. Negroes on Phila. Streetcars." Parts I & II. *Pennsylvania History* 40 (July 1973, October 1973).

Greenberg, Irwin, F. "Charles Ingersoll: The Aristocrat as Copperhead." *Pennsylvania Magazine of History and Biography* 93, no. 2 (April 1969).

Silcox, Harry, C. "Nineteenth Century Philadelphia Black Militant: Octavius Catto." *Pennsylvania History* 59 (January 1977).

Veit, Chuck. "The Innovative, Mysterious Alligator." *Naval History* (August 2010): 26–29.

Wainwright, Nicholas B. "The Loyal Opposition in Civil War Philadelphia." *Pennsylvania Magazine of History and Biography* 88, no. 3 (July 1964): 294–315.

Veterans' Organizations

Beath, Robert, B. *History of the Grand Army of the Republic.* New York: Bryan Taylor Publisher, 1888.

Devens, General Charles. "Twenty-fifth Anniversary Oration at the MOLLUS Reunion."

Mulholland, St. Claire A. *Military Order Congress Medal of Honor Legion of the United States.* Philadelphia: Town Printing Co., 1905.

Zell, Ellwood. "The Organization of the Loyal Legion." *United Service Magazine* (February 1889).

Index

A

armories 14, 23, 38, 91, 103, 104
arsenals 14, 101, 103

B

Baldwin, Matthias 13, 35, 36, 81, 84,
      90, 128
Baltimore Riot 35, 85
Biddle, Charles 41, 42
Birgfeld's Band 131, 134
Birney, General David B. 14, 64, 113,
      137, 149, 164, 177, 211
Bohlen, General Henry C. 14, 151,
      196
Boker, George Henry 80, 172
Brady, Mary A. 66
Buena Vista Guards 35

C

Cadwalader, General Charles 43, 150
Camp William Penn 12, 14, 30, 83,
      139, 140, 141, 143, 144, 145,
      170, 180, 186
Catto, Octavius V. 141, 142, 144, 169,
      170, 171, 172, 197

Central Democratic Club 40, 42
City Armory 104, 133, 141, 171
Civil War Memorials 208, 209, 210,
      211
Collis, General Charles H.T. 120, 150,
      175, 176, 217
consolidation 18, 86
Continental Hotel 22, 37, 46, 132
Cooke, Jay 93, 94, 95
Cooper Shop Refreshment Saloon 70,
      73, 77, 182
Copperhead 25, 39, 40
Corps d'Afrique 30
Crossman, Colonel George H. 90, 164
Curtin, Governor Andrew G. 37, 49,
      50, 86, 93, 98, 113, 114, 126,
      127, 131, 132, 185, 192, 211
Cuyler, Theodore 22, 221

D

Dahlgren, Admiral John A. 14, 156,
      157, 163, 211
Dahlgren, Colonel Ulric 157, 163
Daily Argus 25
Declaration of Independence 22, 45,
      47, 48, 51, 180

De Korpornay, Gabriel 31
Democratic Party 19, 25, 39, 41, 42, 80
Dickinson, Anna E. 186
Drayton, Commodore Percival 157
d'Utassy, Frederick George 31

E

election of 1860 19, 20, 45
engineers 87, 147, 152, 153
Episcopal Hospital 60

F

First City Troop 47, 105, 107, 124, 133, 134, 189
first fatal casualty 35
Fisher, Sidney George 44
Fishing Creek Confederacy 106, 122
Forney, John 20
Forten, Charlotte 185
forts
  Fort Dana 101
  Fort Delaware 31, 76, 106, 109, 123, 124, 129, 138, 152
  Fort Mifflin 73, 105, 106, 165
Frankford Arsenal 91, 102
free blacks 19, 29

G

Gerhard, Benjamin 80
German community 29, 107, 119
Gettysburg Campaign 102, 129, 136, 157, 167, 168, 207, 213
Grand Army of the Republic 9, 12, 14, 164, 199, 201, 203, 204, 207, 211
Great Central Sanitary Fair 55, 63, 88
Gregory, General Edgar M. 99

H

Hale, Sarah Josepha 178, 179
Harris, Mrs. John 66
Haupt, General Herman 87, 151
Hazlehurst, Isaac 22

Henry, Mayor 21, 22, 25, 26, 38, 39, 43, 131, 133, 167, 168, 188, 194
Home Guard 26, 37, 38, 78, 103, 104, 128, 132, 133, 168, 196
Humphreys, General Andrew A. 14, 30, 193
Husband, Mary Morris 164, 180, 181, 182
Hutter, Mrs. Elizabeth 67, 184

I

immigration 28, 29
Independence Hall 45, 46, 47, 48, 49, 50, 51, 129, 133, 150, 187, 188, 189, 191, 192, 194, 195, 196, 197, 202
Independence Square 21, 39, 40, 45, 51, 132, 191, 192, 199
industry 17, 18, 89, 91
Ingersoll, Charles 22, 41, 44
Ingersoll, Edward 22, 41, 44
Invalid Corps 61
Irish 17, 28, 29, 32, 36, 41, 107, 109, 119, 120, 121, 212

J

Jones, Miss Harriet "Hetty" 177, 178, 202, 211

K

Kemble, Fanny 42
Keystone Democratic Club 40
Koltes, Colonel John A. 14, 38, 196

L

Ladies' Aid Society 56, 66, 174
Lafayette Cemetery 166
Laurel Hill Cemetery 9, 12, 14, 125, 149, 150, 151, 152, 153, 157, 160, 163, 164, 168, 172, 173, 182, 185, 196, 197, 203, 206, 207
Lawnview Cemetery 183

Lebanon Cemetery 166, 171
Lee, Mrs. Mary 183, 184
Leisenring, George 33
Leland, Charles Godfrey 19
Lewis, William D. 22
Lex, Charles E. 22
Lincoln, Abraham 19, 20, 21, 22, 26,
        36, 40, 41, 42, 43, 44, 45, 46,
        47, 48, 49, 50, 51, 64, 80, 85,
        86, 87, 89, 106, 107, 111, 112,
        118, 122, 128, 129, 131, 137,
        145, 147, 148, 155, 167, 168,
        170, 173, 179, 184, 185, 186,
        188, 189, 194, 195, 197, 198,
        208
Lincoln Institution 67

M

marine corps 9, 145, 146, 158, 159,
        160, 161, 163, 204, 207
McCall, General George A. 115, 150
McCall, General Peter 41
McClellan, General George B. 14,
        40, 88, 125, 126, 127, 147, 208,
        211
McMichael, Morton 19, 173
McMullin's Rangers 29, 107, 109
Meade, General George G. 10, 12, 14,
        30, 64, 67, 115, 121, 134, 147,
        148, 149, 163, 164, 168, 181,
        185, 190, 192, 193, 194, 201,
        208, 211
Medal-of-Honor Legion 205
Meigs, Quartermaster General
        Montgomery C. 90
Memorial Day 164, 201, 202, 203
Meredith, William Morris 81
military hospitals
  Catherine Street 59
  Christian Street 58, 77
  Cooper Shop Soldiers' Home 60
  Episcopal 60
  Filbert Street 59, 77, 177, 178
  George Street 59
  Haddington 54, 58

  Hestonville 59
  Mower 11, 54, 56, 57
  Officers' 59
  Pennsylvania 35, 53, 54
  Race Street 59
  Satterlee 54, 55, 56, 57
  South Street 59
  St. Joseph's 59
  Turner's Lane 53, 59
  Union Volunteer Refreshment
        Saloon 60, 73
  Wood Street 59
Military Order of the Loyal Legion
        198
Mlotkowski, Captain Stanislaus 30
Monument Cemetery 166
monuments 165, 166, 182, 198, 203,
        208, 211
Morton, General James St. Clair 152
Mott, Lucretia 143, 144, 179, 180
Mount Moriah Cemetery 74, 166,
        208
Mulholland, General St. Clair A. 151,
        207
Musical Fund Hall 19

N

National Guards Hall 104
National Union Party 39
Naval Hospital and Home 161
navy yard 14, 21, 49, 60, 69, 72, 91,
        154, 155, 156, 157, 158, 160,
        183, 187

O

Owen, General Joshua T. 118

P

Palmetto Flag 25
parks 56, 98, 100, 105, 118, 119, 131,
        149, 166, 168, 172, 208, 211, 212
Patterson, General Francis E. 196
Patterson, General Robert 48, 78,
        149, 163, 196

Penn Relief Association 56, 67, 174
Pennsylvania Bucktails 42
Pennsylvania Railroad 50, 59, 84, 86, 87, 88, 126, 132
Pennsylvania Volunteers
  Cavalry
    2nd 29, 125
    5th 29, 30, 125
    6th 98, 125, 163, 207, 212
    8th 126, 207
    15th 30, 126
    19th 126
    213th 137
  Emergency Militia 78, 102, 128, 129, 133, 135, 136, 138, 145, 170
  Heavy Artillery 29, 122, 123, 124
  Infantry
    17th 108
    18th 107, 108, 120, 144
    19th 108, 119
    20th 108, 128, 133, 138
    21st 107, 108
    22nd 108, 143
    23rd 30, 78, 108, 113, 149
    24th 29, 107, 109, 143
    26th 111, 114
    27th 29, 30, 114, 133, 175, 176
    28th 31, 111, 114, 197
    29th 111, 114
    58th 98, 177, 196
    68th 117
    69th 29, 119
    71st 118, 119, 184
    72nd 78, 79, 119, 175, 183
    73rd 29, 119
    74th 29
    75th 29, 119, 151, 196
    82nd 119
    88th 61, 83, 119, 140
    90th 98, 119, 207
    91st 98, 99, 119
    95th 119
    98th 29, 105, 120
    99th 120
    106th 119
    109th 120, 163
    114th 30, 120, 121, 150, 175, 176, 177, 190
    115th 121, 163
    116th 29, 106, 121, 151, 207
    118th 121
    119th 121
    121st 121
    183rd 121, 122
    186th 122
    187th 122, 189
    188th 122
    192nd 136, 137, 138
    196th 138
    197th 138
    198th 137
    199th 137
    203rd 137
    214th 137, 189
    215th 138, 189
  Light Artillery 23, 123, 136
  Militia Pennsylvania Reserves 29, 93, 117, 121, 123, 137, 141, 148, 150, 202
Pennypacker, Galusha 151, 165, 208
Philadelphia 32
Philadelphia Brigade 29, 117, 118, 119
Philadelphia Ellets 152
Philadelphia ethnic populations 17, 29, 30, 107
Philadelphia National Cemetery 164, 211
Philadelphia, Wilmington and Baltimore Railroad 47, 69, 84
Philadelphia, Wilmington and Baltimore Railroad Depot 32, 34, 54, 58, 85, 86
Pleasonton, General Augustus J. 38, 125, 168
police 18, 20, 24, 25, 35, 43, 44, 58, 85, 122, 129, 133, 151, 167, 168, 193, 207

R

Reed, William B. 41, 42
regimental associations 203
Republican Party 19, 20, 167, 168, 170, 172, 206
Return of the Colors 191
Ross, Anna M. 60, 73, 76, 182, 183, 202, 211
Rush, Richard 41, 61, 125

S

Schimmelfennig, General Alexander 217
Schuylkill Arsenal 37, 90, 91, 100, 102
6th Massachusetts Regiment 32, 33, 85
Small, General William F. 24, 32, 33, 35, 85
Smith, Charles Ferguson 150, 163, 196
Soldiers' Relief Association 66, 68
Stewart, Commodore Charles 21, 156, 161, 164
Sully, General Alfred G. 152
Supervisory Committee for the Recruitment of Colored Troops 83, 140, 143

T

Tepe, Mary 175, 176, 177
training camps
  Camp Ballier 31
  Camp Cadwalader 98, 166, 190
  Camp Chase 99
  Camp Independence 196
  Camp Roxborough 145
  Civil War Plaza 98
transportation 13, 17, 18, 29, 50, 52, 54, 69, 70, 84, 86, 87, 96, 151, 167, 180, 184

U

Union League of Philadelphia 11, 137, 138, 171, 172, 173, 255

Union Volunteer Refreshment Committee 70, 72, 76, 99, 132, 143, 183, 184, 188
United States Christian Commission 65
United States Colored Troops 30, 141
United States Sanitary Commission 53, 62, 65, 66, 183
U.S. Army Laboratory 60
USS *Alligator* 155, 161
USS *New Ironsides* 160, 161

V

Vaux, Richard 41, 167
vivandiere 175, 176, 177
volunteer firemen 78, 119

W

Wagner, Colonel Louis 83, 140, 143, 144, 171
Washington Brigade 24, 32, 35, 53, 85, 114
Wharton, George 41
Wide Awakes 20
Wistar, Isaac 118
Women's Relief Corps 204
Woodlands Cemetery 57, 149, 156, 164, 206
Woodward, Judge George 22

Y

Young Men's Christian Association 36, 65

Z

Zeilin, Genereal Jacob 158, 159, 160, 163

About the Author

Professor Waskie was born in Bloomsburg, Pennsylvania, and pursued a languages/history major at Bloomsburg University. He studied abroad in Salzburg, Austria, pursued graduate study in Germany and received a scholarship to study Slavic at Charles University, Prague. He received MA and PhD degrees from New York University. He performed duty with the Army Reserves as a language specialist. He became a teacher of languages and history at Pennsbury School District in Bucks County. Waskie is a professor of languages at Temple University. He is a cofounder of the Civil War and Emancipation Studies at Temple.

As a Civil War historian, author and researcher specializing in Philadelphia and a historian of the life and career of General George G. Meade, Waskie seeks to promote the history of the city. He is a member of the Union League of Philadelphia. Waskie serves as president of the General Meade Society of Philadelphia and as a board member of a number of history-related institutions.

Visit us at

www.historypress.net